PATSY ADAM-S

There Was a Ship

The story of her years at sea

PENGUIN BOOKS

Penguin Books Australia Ltd
487 Maroondah Highway, PO Box 257,
Ringwood, Victoria 3134, Australia
Penguin Books Ltd
Harmondsworth, Middlesex, England
Viking Penguin. A Division of Penguin Books USA Inc.
375 Hudson Street, New York, New York 10014, USA
Penguin Books Canada Limited
10 Alcorn Avenue, Toronto, Ontario, Canada M4V 3B2
Penguin Books (N.Z.) Ltd
182–190 Wairau Road, Auckland 10, New Zealand

First published as two books by Rigby Australia: *Moonbird People* in 1965
and *There Was a Ship* in 1967

This edition published by Penguin Books Australia Ltd 1995

3 5 7 9 10 8 6 4

Typeset in 11½/13 pt Perpetua by Midland Typesetters, Maryborough

Printed in Australia by Australian Print Group, Maryborough

National Library of Australia
Cataloguing-in-Publication data

Adam-Smith, Patsy.
There was a ship.

ISBN 0 14 024656 8.

1. Voyages and travels. 2. Ocean travel. 3. Bass Strait (Tas. and Vic.).
4. Furneaux Islands (Tas.) – Social life and customs. I. Title.

994.67

Contents

1

There Was a Ship

The wave cry, the wind cry, the vast waters
Of the petrel and the porpoise. In the end is my beginning.
—T. S. ELIOT

From the time I first saw a trader ease her way out of the swell in Bass Strait, her masts and rigging festooned with birds, her deck awash as she wallowed, leaky, old, like the ship in Shakespeare's *Tempest*, and I heard her men talk of the sand shoals that shifted almost as they escaped them, of the mazes of reefs, of wrecks, of the people; from the time I smelt the oil oozing through the staves of the great wooden casks and listened to the folk-history of the islands, I was without reason. The islanders have a saying for it. 'The islands have got a holt on yer,' they say.

From the time I first heard of that place and its ships I knew I would go there. There was never any question that one day I would leave my treadmill of the Arts Society, repertory, music, ballet and domesticity, and step directly into a world which even the most reticent historian would describe as swashbuckling; live with the people who are descended from the oldest race known to modern man, and follow the bird that an eminent scientist believed was left behind when the moon fell from the face of the earth.

No one sailed to the Furneaux believing them to be the islands of romantic fiction. The men who told me about them never mentioned palm trees, romance and golden beaches, dancing, feasting and island belles. Instead they talked of adventure the like of which I had not known existed in the twentieth century, the like of which I'd never given up hope of being a part of. I would go to sea, I decided, and be a part of the danger these men spoke of that made my present life suddenly seem to be merely a marking of time until I should die.

My grandfather, James Adam-Smith, had been a bosun in Queen Victoria's Royal Navy, my father had been a gun-layer in the Royal Australian Navy in World War I. I had wakened all my childhood to the call, 'Heave Ho! Lash up and stow!' But for all that, the sea was unknown to me.

When I was a child my family lived in north-west Victoria in Sunset Country on the edge of the desert, a dry arid land where water had to be carted to us in iron wagons along the railway line. My father worked on the line so we received our tanker of water free; our few neighbours, scattered out of sight over the rim of the earth's curve, could afford no such thing in that time of Depression. As the great miasma of red dust sat lazily over our heads in the windless sky day after day, it seemed that more of their land was above them than below, and one by one these defeated families who had come to people the empty land 'walked off', leaving their debts and labours behind them in the waterless wastes where sand soon covered all evidence of their having been there.

Water of any sort was a novelty to us. Later, when my

sister and I were old enough for school, we moved further east and here, because the children had never seen the sea, the State School Mothers' Club organised a bus journey for us twelve scholars who attended the little bush school. We left after classes one Friday afternoon and the 1925 model truck that transported us on our long journey trundled south all through the night.

We huddled in blankets beside our mothers, too excited to sleep, chattering like a flock of parakeets about what we'd do when we got *there*. But when at last dawn came and we rattled over the end of the dirt road and topped the sandhills we were dumbfounded. None of us spoke. There was the sea, the glistening, glimmering sheet of silver reaching as far as the eye could see. It filled our eyes. We climbed stiffly down from the truck and stared at it. Some of us bent down and sifted sand through our fingers but we didn't take our eyes off *it*. At last, out of ear-shot of the grown-ups, Billy Wilson summed up our feelings.

'What a bloody lot of water,' he said.

As I grew up I didn't become any more intimate with the sea than I had been that day, and I still held it in the awe that we bush kids felt when it was left for Billy to speak up for us. And then, from scarcely knowing it, suddenly I knew nothing but the sea. Literally overnight I came from the wide sunburnt plains to the close confines of a ship. Water, water, everywhere, cried the ancient mariner, and like that aged song-singer it seemed I knew no other life.

After nursing for two and a half years in a military hospital in Queensland during World War II, a time of excitement, fun, horror, pain, love and purpose, I found myself in the 1950s, surely the most uninteresting, soul-destroying decade Australia has passed through.

I said to my partner of the time, what shall we do? One shouldn't moulder away. What shall we do? We should mark time until we die, he replied; that's what life is about. I was aged 19 and I came from a family who had not marked time for one day since we came to this land in 1842. I bided my time for nine years, waiting. And then I saw the *Willwatch* wallow in to the little port of Ulverstone on Tasmania's north-west coast. I ran down to the wharf, bewildered by the fluffy grey decoration all over her rigging.

'What is it?' I called, before they got the lines ashore.

'Mutton birds.'

'What?'

'Shearwaters.' The captain was young. 'They are the birds of St Peter, petrels, so named because they walk on water.' The little wooden vessel, unpainted, shabby, exquisite, lay low in the water. 'Some call them moonbirds.'

'Why?' He'd tied up now.

'Because a scientist once believed that the moon fell out of the pacific void and left them homeless. They come to land on the islands only to lay their eggs.'

'Where?' I'd clambered, unasked, over the side. (Looking back over thirty years one regrets the loss of that time when one unabashedly, without dignity, grabbed life by the hand and ran with it.)

'On the Furneaux islands,' he said.

'How can I get there?'

He was climbing over on to the wharf. There was a car waiting for him. 'You really do want to know?'

'Oh yes.' I was plain, matter-of-fact, 'I'm going to go there.'

We arranged to meet before he sailed next day, and I was on the wharf, waiting, when he came down.

He was George MacCarthy, master mariner, with a crew of three, and his waters were among the world's wildest. In the short time before he sailed that day, he told me all I needed to know about Bass Strait and her islands. Planes had begun to visit two of the one hundred and twenty odd islands and rocks in Bass Strait. 'And you won't learn anything from the air,' he said. 'You must go by ship.' There were no passenger ships. 'If you want to learn, you'll find a way.' He gave me the name of an owner-captain who sailed from Launceston. 'The best,' he said, 'but you'd have to work.'

'I was brought up in the bush,' I gave as my reference.

During the years that followed I never did thank him and now it is too late, he is dead. I heard him dying, listened to his voice, and could not stretch out a hand and say, you helped me to the best six years a woman could know.

Men came to help me wherever I walked. Russell Drysdale – 'Tas' to his friends – at that time at the peak of his career, sensed the social disapproval of my sudden departure from the secure, drear, 'respectable' world, and once he addressed me across a room where he was being fêted: 'Patsy,' he said, 'do you read Milton? My favourite Milton,' he announced to a silent room, 'is this: "I cannot praise a fugitive and cloistered virtue, unexercised and unbreathed, that never sallies out and sees her adversary, but slinks out of the race, where that immortal garland is to be run for, not without dust and heat".' Later, travelling among the islands in Bass Strait with Tas, I realised he himself could have written those words because he was a complete person.

It would be foolish to pretend that social disapprobation did not hurt. Of course it did. One does not slough off a lifetime of conditioning easily. When all the wheels within the wheels of social retribution began to turn, Tas Drysdale sent me the writings of Dean Inge, marking this passage with a small drawing: 'Public opinion is a vulgar, impertinent, anonymous tyrant who deliberately makes life unpleasant for anyone who is not content to be the average man.'

And, my oath, I wasn't content. I didn't know it, but that was the truth of the matter and I'm glad it was.

At first I did what Mac had told me not to do. I flew to the islands. I'd written – again with the arrogant certainty of the young – to Cyril Pearl, the editor of *Australia Magazine*, a new and splendid magazine, telling him that I was going to write about the most exciting place in the world, 'the last wild frontier'. I must have been persuasive. He sent me their leading photographer and air tickets, expenses and a cheque that to me spelt freedom.

I was going to sea, come what may, but I had not yet acquired the courage or the skill to discard discretion. I must for a time have 'a reason' for coming to the islands.

We were to stay there one week. The photographer stayed three days in what he called 'the end of the flaming earth'. I stayed years, sharing an obsession for the sea and for the islands with some very eminent people, a fact which did not impress those near to me as much as I had hoped when both sea and islands 'got a holt' on me, as the islanders, like a Greek chorus in the background, began to chant at me.

The forty-two islands of the Furneaux Group lie at the eastern entrance to Bass Strait, only three-quarters of an hour's flying time from Melbourne, a city of two million people, and an hour from Tasmania, yet they are relatively isolated, almost as much as when the settlement there was the first south of Sydney.

Looking down from the plane on my first trip thirty years ago I admired the postcard beauty of the sea-ways and the islands' heather-painted mountains surrounded by turquoise, amber, green, cream, and white water. Caught between the fierce riptides that scour through Bass Strait from the Indian Ocean to the west and from the Tasman and Pacific to the east, the seas around the Furneaux confuse and in turmoil build up sand shoals beneath the sea. The colour of the water varies according to the depth and mass of the sand.

A long cream band stretched as far as the eye could see through jade and white waters and was lost near an island with twin peaks. A little black, a mass of dark grey or ink blue would have lifted the delicate postcard quality to majesty. That first day there was nothing to tell a stranger to the sea that when the water down there is black and inky blue one does not admire its sinister beauty. If you have sailed those waters long enough, you have too much knowledge that brings too much fear of their danger, for they are known by seamen as among the most dangerous in the world. I was soon to join the band who knew this.

As we began our descent to the islands we saw a vast darkness on the water. Unlike the shadow of a cloud that passed earlier this patch did not move. It was not a rock; no water broke on its perimeter. Then, as we watched, the edges of the shape diffused and the whole black mass walked over the water, disintegrating as it went, each fragment a bird that then soared away and was lost to our sight.

Petrels. The birds of St Peter, so named because he too was said to have walked over the waves; shearwaters, moonbirds.

2

The *Sheerwater*

There was no easy way to see the Furneaux, as I found when I politely inquired of a sea captain if I could travel to the outer islands on his ship. 'Yes,' he said, 'I need a cook.' He was Les Jackson, Mac's friend. What he did not tell me was that in the first place a 96-tonne island trader cannot afford to carry a full-time cook – this position must be filled by someone able both to cook and either load cargo or take a 'trick' on the wheel. In the second place, the improved conditions gained by seamen since the days of *Two Years Before the Mast* hadn't percolated to the little traders.

In the galley of the *Sheerwater* was a very elegant slow-combustion stove, brand spanking new. It was more than a metre long by around half a metre wide and stood out from the wall to allow a water tank to be fitted behind it, so that in the three by two metre galley its presence was distinctly noticed but not necessarily felt, as it never warmed sufficiently to boil a kettle in much under two hours.

Because the galley was also a constantly-used alley-way with doorways at each end, the wind whistled past, through, in, and around this edifice.

'It's no good,' Pete, the boy, told me cheerfully. 'Look. Watch this.' He sat on it. 'See?'

The owner – captain was enamoured of it. He had bought it himself for this, his own ship. 'You have to follow the instructions with a thing like this.'

When I asked if anyone had managed to cook on it he looked at me almost sternly. 'I'll get it going full blast and cook you a batch of scones.'

He confidently set to work. As a young seaman he had also cooked for a crew, working to earn money to buy his first ship. He rescued the instruction book from a big airy gap behind the stove and read from it, tapping the relevant parts with an iron poker as he went. When he got to 'fuel may be either wood or coke' he said with certainty, 'Well, we've got that okay.' But I couldn't help wondering whether the manufacturers had in mind the sort of wood that found its way on to the *Sheerwater* – bits of sodden swamp gum that had been lying on the bank of a river, driftwood, tea-tree branches, old bits of decking, waterlogged flotsam, and odd pieces of scrub that the crew had dragged down from one of the islands.

'Now to get it going full blast.'

Pete was watching us, 'It'll make no difference,' he said. 'I'd still be able to sit on it. We call it Old Cold-Bum.'

The captain took no notice of him, just went on stoking the fire. After a while he announced that everything would be right now, so his scones went in the oven, light, feathery, and creamy white. They came out three hours later, still creamy white but no longer light and feathery. There was a slight firmness round the edges – inside was dough.

'It's the way she's set in,' the captain said, without suggesting doing anything at all to remedy the fault of the stove. So I learnt to add two or three hours to my cooking time of everything on top of the stove, and I threw away my oven recipes, and began using the oven as a store cupboard.

On the deck beside the stove there was a frying pan, alongside it was a saucepan in which a pup was fast asleep. The bottom of the pan was so dimpled from age and heat that not a tenth of its surface touched the hot plate, making it and Old Cold-Bum an ineffectual combination.

I lifted the pup from the saucepan. It sat on the floor and made a puddle, but that didn't matter as the boards were covered with debris, dirt, gear and old clothes, and hadn't been on view for many a day.

'Is this all the equipment?' I asked. 'A saucepan and a frying pan?'

The captain looked surprised. 'If you're not going to use the oven what other way can you cook except to fry and boil?' (He'd already taken the new baking dish that came with the stove down to his engine room to catch oil that was dripping from a pipe.)

I'd read about the spartan life lived on board ship and now I knew what it was like at first hand. Only one pan and one pot on board! Well, I'd have to buckle down and show that I was capable of adjusting to anything. I wanted to see every corner of these islands. One pot and one pan!

'Why!' I said aloud. 'I could do with just the pot if it came to a pinch. Boil in it first and fry in it afterwards.'

'Pity it wasn't the other way round,' the captain said. 'If you could do with just the pan I could use the pot in the dinghy as a bailer.'

I tipped the pup out of the pot where it was again curled up and hid pot and pan in the oven. Then I turned my attention to the provisions.

There were two spaces for storage: one a box built on the deck, the other a corner cupboard, and both were so small that one day when Pete was hotly denying to the police that we had game out of season he said, 'We've got no skeletons in our cupboards.' A policeman replied, 'A skeleton wouldn't fit in your cupboards' – and neither would it have done.

There was no need for me to look twice in the Lilliputian closets to see there was no food. I cried again, 'Is this all the food there is?'

'What!' the captain called back. 'Is there food there? We *are* in luck.'

He stood in the open doorway, grinning. I didn't want to tell him I'd never been in a ship before, that I didn't know what to expect.

There were enough eggs to make an omelette for breakfast as well as a few loaves of bread, a bag of potatoes, and a bag of onions. Was there some special place on a ship where food was stored? I looked slyly around. There were shelves up near whatever the ceiling of a ship is called. I could see tins of powdered milk and tins of bully-beef. I stood on the tiny table to investigate, not knowing that the table was hinged, and down I went, enamel pannikins, teapot, and all.

By the time I'd been down there long enough to study the deck and work out the number of blisters and aching muscles it was going to take me to get it clean, I realised no one was going to help me, so I stood up.

There was no food, the captain told me, because there was no refrigerator on board, and so meat, milk, butter, and vegetables wouldn't keep.

'Too much tinned stuff is no good to men who work hard as we do, often for twelve hours at a stretch and wet through to the skin. But you don't go hungry,' he said.

On board were the captain, Pete, two other men, and myself. The two men, Alec and Billy, were such a wild pair that the authorities had banned them from stepping over the ship's side at Flinders Island.

Billy had fired a .303 along a line of latrines on a construction camp on the island, and if they had been occupied six heads would have fallen. And there were other things, less funny and even more anti-social. But he never worried or even interested me, for he kept very much to himself and was always well mannered and considerate to me.

Alec was quick tongued and sharp, and his unpunished crimes were of the involved kind that result from a too amorous nature. This was surprising, because he looked like a grey-hound with a cold, was always broke, and had no decent clothes.

'What will I cook, Alec?' I said.

'Wallaby [that was the crew's nickname for Les Jackson, the captain, the man George MacCarthy had told me was the best in the Straits] will either catch it or scrounge it. You'll probably get fish for dinner; he's got the 'couta line over the stern. Sure to be goose for tea. He'll shoot a couple of Cape Barren geese. Other days you'll get perch, salmon, trumpeter, a dozen varieties of fish, a few wild ducks, and kangaroos if you like 'roo tail soup. And once the birdin' starts you'll have as many mutton birds as you like. Do you like mutton birds?'

I'd never tasted them.

'You'll like them, I reckon. And we have crayfish by the bagful, and sometimes quail and snipe . . . we live like kings in the *Sheerwater*.'

He wasn't joking. It was true.

Remembering Mrs Beaton's recipe for jugged hare, I waited to see what was caught before deciding whether to use the pot or the frying pan on this, my first day at sea.

The Furneaux were named after Captain Tobias Furneaux in 1773. He had seen the islands from the eastward and did not know that they lay at the entrance to a strait that divided

Tasmania from the rest of Australia. But eighty-year-old Guy Hamilton, a native of Glasgow, and his ship *Sydney Cove* were the true discoverers of the group. Renamed as a compliment to the new settlement at New South Wales, the *Sydney Cove* was one of the East India Company's more expendable vessels, old and unseaworthy. She was a suitable ship to risk taking a 'speculation' cargo, the first vessel to attempt to open trade with the colony. (Until then ships had been employed transporting convicts and stores under Government contract.) The cargo the company thought would be most welcome in the new settlement was rum and whisky, 7000 gallons of which they loaded on her.

Sailing out from the Hooghly, India, on 10 November 1796, Hamilton took his ship down to the Roaring Forties, south of Van Diemen's Land. He did not know this was an island. His charts consisted of Tasman's 1642 rough map of the south coast of Van Diemen's Land, and an equally rough chart of the Furneaux group of islands, drawn by Furneaux.

From the beginning misfortune dogged the old man. Gale after gale struck the ship. Early in the voyage she sprang a leak. In the extreme cold of the Forties, Lascars died at the pumps. The second mate, Mr Leishman, up aloft trying to save the tops'l in the gale, was lost overboard.

As the ship rounded Van Diemen's Land and headed north, gales of hurricane force blew from the east, making the east coast of what is now Tasmania a dead lee shore. In distress, the ship wallowed, leaking, water pouring in at the rate of fifteen to twenty centimetres an hour. In the dark of night the gale drove her through Banks Strait (the ship's company were unaware of its existence, they being the first recorded travellers to pass this way), a rocky, even now uninhabited, inhospitable shore.

But the ship was sinking and had to be beached quickly. As day dawned on 8 February 1797 Hamilton headed for a small sandy beach on what he named Preservation Island. There, when his crew were safely ashore, he ordered the cargo of rum to be salvaged and placed on a near-by island, which he named Rum Island.

But the saga that had begun three months before was not yet ended. Three weeks later the long boat was launched and eighteen men set off in her to take news of the wreck to Sydney. Steering north across Bass Strait they became the first white men to visit the State of Victoria when their boat was driven ashore and wrecked on the Ninety Mile Beach. The mate, Hugh Thompson, led and drove them 480 kilometres, an average of sixteen kilometres a day, across rivers and past attacking blacks. Nine men fell in this time. A month later Thompson, speared and in great pain, stayed behind to look after the sick carpenter and ordered Clarke the purser to push on with the remaining two men, who could barely stagger. These men reached Sydney on 16 May 1797, seventy-eight days after leaving the wreck, the only survivors of that terrible journey.

The saga of the 'speculation cargo' was not yet over. Before it was done another ship was lost; the stage was set for the birth of a whole new race of people; two of the greatest navigators in Australian history made important discoveries; and the first Australian settlement south of Sydney was set up.

On 11 June 1797 the little ships *Francis* and *Eliza* reached the wreck to rescue the crew and salvage the cargo. The *Eliza*, a small-decked boat of ten tonnes, took off some of the crew and cargo, sailed from Preservation Island, and was never seen again.

On board the *Francis* on her second trip to Preservation in February 1798 was Matthew Flinders, then second lieutenant of HMS. *Reliance*. He was sent 'to make what observations he could among those islands relative to anchorages, etc.'

At the same time, Flinders's surgeon friend George Bass was on his famous whaleboat voyage into what was later to be known as Bass Strait.

On his whaleboat voyage of 3 December 1797 Bass had six men to row and six weeks' provisions. He followed the coast down to Cape Everard (Point Hicks) and then made a dash down south into the strait – though of course unaware as yet that there was a passage between mainland Australia and Van Diemen's Land. His purpose was to locate the wreck of the *Sydney Cove* and search for rice, which would enable his party to continue their voyage for a longer period than the original six weeks planned. All night the men rowed southwards, intending to reach the Van Diemen's Land coast and follow it eastwards to the island. It was a wild and dirty night. Bass and his men had been out thirty nights and days, exposed to the weather and sea wrack, when the boat sprang a leak. He knew they could not risk too great a struggle with the elements. Besides this, from the time they lost sight of the promontory on the mainland they did not know where they were, and bearings could not be taken. So next day he turned his small ship about and headed north. After rowing for twenty-four hours he came in sight of land once more. It was during this voyage that Bass became convinced that because of the set of the tides and the appearance of the land, this area could not be a great bay but must be an open seaway between New South Wales and Van Diemen's Land.

In the meantime, Flinders at the Furneaux Islands was also becoming interested in tides, and when the two friends met again in Sydney and compared notes they resolved to prove their theory about the division of Van Diemen's Land from the mainland. Setting out in the *Norfolk*, a ship of under 30 tonnes, from Port Jackson on 7 October of that year, 1798, they went through the passage into the Indian Ocean, thence southwards, circumnavigated Van Diemen's Land, and returned to Sydney.

Since the time of Flinders, who first charted these waters, there has been little added to guide mariners over them. With a copy of Flinders's own narratives of his voyages around the islands, I set off on my first trip through Hamilton Roads, named after Hamilton of the East India Company; Armstrong Passage, commemorating the Captain of the lost *Eliza*; Preservation and Rum Islands; and Clarke Island, named for the supercargo of *Sydney Cove*, the man who eventually brought news of the wreck to the nine-year-old settlement at Sydney. I was aboard the *Sheerwater*, bound for isolated, uninhabited Passage Island, from whose unfenced wilderness we were to attempt to take thirty head of wild cattle.

Before we sailed, Captain Jackson called out across the wharf to a fisherman.

'Hey, Jim! Like to come for a run?'

Jim appeared on the deck of his fishing boat. 'I wouldn't mind, Wallaby,' he drawled. 'But I'm ready for off. Got my tucker on and all. Just waiting for the mist to clear. Should be gone by this arvo.'

'That's fine. You've got plenty of time on your hands. Hop aboard. Let that for'ard line go as you come.'

So Booby-trap Jim came aboard.

Jim was one of the four Robinsons, all named Jim, who lived on Flinders Island. To prevent confusion they had distinguishing prefixes to their names. There was Big River Jim, Five-mile Jim, Booby-trap Jim, and 'old' Tuck. The first two were named after the localities in which they lived; no one, not even 'old' Tuck himself, knew where his name came from. As for our Jim, why, everyone knew where Booby-trap got his name.

He'd had Tinkettle Island on lease from the Government and used to run sheep on it. No one lived on the island, but there was a shack on it where he could camp overnight if he was caught by weather or needed to stay to finish a job. In this hut he left a plentiful supply of provisions. But word of these leaked out and as often as he stocked up the larder marauding fishermen would come and raid it.

This, not suprisingly, angered Jim, so he rigged up his gun inside the hut so that when the door was opened it would fire . . . a booby-trap. It worked. The first trespasser to break in collected a shot in the legs, and Jim was hauled to court on a charge of what he called 'attempted all-sorts'. But the only penalty he incurred was a name that would stick for life, Booby-trap Jim.

He was tall and strong and doing well with his fishing boat. As the morning wore on and afternoon began he told us about it. His was top boat in the fleet now, and he was very proud of this. By tonight he'd be sailing into the crayfishing grounds to the east of Flinders Island, and by tomorrow he'd be filling up with big 'thin-shellers', the crayfish immediately after they have shed their old shell on the rocks. The season for crayfish opens each year just after this and the spawning have taken place. ('By tomorrow I'll have the well half full,' Jim told us. But the captain had other plans. By tomorrow Jim would be down Armstrong Passage rounding up wild bulls on a wild horse, and it would be a week before he saw his beloved boat again.)

'You ought to have a good old talk to Patsy in the galley,' the captain had told Jim when he came aboard. 'She's come to the islands to learn all about us. Wants to know everything. Everything! Just think of that! Tell her about crayfishing.'

Booby-trap Jim needed no second asking. He told me about how he made his pots out of melaleuca, a strong springy scrub that grows on the islands; about the regulations that forbid boats to carry more than thirty cray pots in State-controlled waters; about the wars between fishermen and patrol boats and police. 'Things get a bit willing at times,' he said.

'Some men [not Jim. No! Never!] they bring in spawny she's [females with eggs], jinks [undersized crays], everything they haul up in their pots. The cops get on to them; you'll see tar and feathers fly then.'

The morning passed with stories galore, interspersed with

cups of tea and plates of pancakes. Then lunch, then afternoon tea.

'Say, Wallaby,' Booby-trap Jim drawled at last. 'When are you going to get into some work?'

'Soon.'

'Where are you going, anyway?'

'Round the corner.'

Boob-trap was getting suspicious. 'I want to be back well before dark so I can get out.'

'That's right, Jim.'

Then for the first time that day Booby-trap Jim caught sight of Bill Holloway, the owner of Passage Island. The truth dawned on him.

'Hey, wait a minute!' he bellowed, racing out on deck and realising where the ship was heading. 'You couldn't do this to me,' he said to the captain.

'What? Do what?' said the captain.

'Shanghai me ... take me to Passage ... '

'Oh, that. That's nothing. It could happen to anyone.'

Jim wasn't the best of travelling companions after that. He was morose, taciturn, aggressive, glowering. But the boys assured me that I'd see his worth when we got to Passage. It took a long time to get there, though in actual distance it wasn't far. The channel between Clarke and Cape Barren Islands, criss-crossed with sand shoals, is rarely used by ships. The lessee of the island hadn't been there for two years and the direction he suggested led us into a maze of shoals that had swept in since his last visit. The ship bumped hard, rode over one, and bumped another before Captain Jackson got the ship turned round and headed towards another channel. His reputation for skill in navigating shoal water won him his nick-name, Wallaby (jumping the shoals).

It was rough going all the way. No one made jokes any more. The boys told me of the wrecks that had been there. There was nothing left of them now except odd place names –

Rum Island, where the 7000 gallons of rum were unloaded from the *Sydney Cove*; Piano Point and Key Island, where pianos were washed up from another wreck; and Armstrong Passage, which we were now trying to navigate. When we anchored just before dusk that night the boys went ashore with a gun and brought back a young wild pig. Even that came from a wreck, they told me, its forefathers having swum ashore from the *City of Foochow*, a barge wrecked here in 1877. We ate it, anchored off Passage Island, the next day. The anchorage was bad, the wind was bad, and there was no sign of the cattle.

The men went ashore and rounded up the horses, great raw-boned animals as high as church steeples. These men could ride well but Booby-trap Jim outdid them all. He was a joy to watch, and what he didn't know about rounding up cattle wasn't worth knowing.

The bulls were so unused to seeing men that they charged every time they saw a man on foot. But they knew the horses, and the men were reasonably safe once they were in the saddle.

It took most of the day to round them up and get them to the stockyards, leading on to the steep rocks at the water's edge.

The *Sheerwater* was brought as near the shore as they dared. Great anchors were taken out to hold her off shore and strong cables were holding her on to the rocks on shore so she couldn't ride up on the reefs round about her.

After lunch I went ashore in the dinghy, hauling myself along one of the shorelines. I was scarcely on shore when a rumble of hooves started me running for safety behind the stockade. Along came Pete, way up in the air on top of a roan horse, looking like a gargoyle on a cathedral, and after him came the cattle.

'Ride into the race!' the men yelled, wanting Pete to lead the cattle towards the race. But Pete wasn't having any of that. As the moving mountain he was astride ranged up near the stockyard he jumped, landed on top of the rails, and stood there. Many of the cattle charged down into the race before they could ease up, but those that were in the rear steadied, and in front of them was Pete, high up it was true, but not so high that they thought him an impossible target. They pawed the ground, threw up their heads, and bellowed. One tried to climb the rails. Pete was straddling the narrow opening above them.

'Jump, Pete or they'll rip your . . . ' Alex saw me cowering behind the stockade. 'They'll . . . you'll be emasculated.'

Pete sprang, and with both feet on the top rail he ran along to the crush at the head of the race and jumped down into it, shielded from the mad bulls behind him by the thick gate. Harry, a new man, rode round in front and tripped open the gate leading from the crush. Pete charged out into the open bellowing as loudly as any of the bulls imprisoned behind him.

There were so many near accidents as the afternoon wore on that they became commonplace. I was just beginning to realise how very isolated was the land outside my own back door.

The bulls in the race were jamming up crazily, some trying to climb up the rails. They were in beautiful condition and would bring top market prices. The men began loading immediately. First the gate leading from the race into the crush was hauled up, and then as soon as a bull rushed in it was dropped down again, leaving the animal penned tightly with a gate in front and another behind him. From the top of the rails Booby-trap Jim lassoed the beast round the horns. There were two ropes leading from the lasso, one attached to a line running ashore from the winch on the ship, and the other held by a man on shore to guide the animal in the water.

When all was ready the outer gate was tripped and the enraged bull sprang out. Immediately in front of the gate the rocks sloped downward sharply and, as the bull sprang, his front feet hit air, his back legs buckled under him, and he slid down the rocks on his bottom, looking like a cartoon of a bull on a skating rink. Many of the animals got such a surprise they cut off their bellowing in the middle of a note and were down in the water before they could regain their sound.

From there on the ship began its work, Pete operating the winch by direction from the boys on shore. The new hand held the long rope ashore, pulling each bull's head round as the drift of the tide dragged it across to the reef.

'Hang on to it!' the captain yelled from the ship. 'Hang on to it!'

The bull was so fighting mad once it got over the shock of skating on the rocks that it went plunging through the water, looking as if it was walking on the top of the sea.

Captain Jackson was in the dinghy beside the *Sheerwater*. As the winch hauled the bull close to the ship a sling was lowered, the captain leaning over the boat to guide it beneath the bull's forelegs and around its belly. Then he gave the signal to hoist away and the derrick lifted the bull into the air, then lowered it to the hold of the ship. The first bull took this part calmly. Up in the air it swept, encircled by the belly band. Up and over the bulwarks it glided, its great brown eyes gazing unconcernedly down at the rigging and the deck beneath, unconscious of its ludicrous dangling legs and becorseted belly.

But not all the bulls went aboard as calmly as this. Some plunged wildly around in the air, kicked, reared, and bellowed. Some tried to walk on air, their feet methodically going out in front feeling for a surface to tread. Others stepped upwards as though they were climbing an invisible staircase.

One fell out of the sling. It was high above the deck, just about to be lowered, when it reared, leapt, twisted, and suddenly clawed right out of the sling, plummeting down to the hold below.

The loading went on until dark. Those ashore were kept busy forcing the beasts into the race from the enclosure, scampering along the top rail, prodding them forward with a big stick, and letting out loud cowboy yells.

Captain Jackson, working in oilskins and thigh boots in the dinghy, didn't stay dry. Tossed into the water twice during the afternoon, he called it 'Coming off second best to the bulls'. Alec swore that once he signalled to the winchman to hoist away only to find it was Wallaby in the sling, not the bull.

Before I went back on the ship I had a ride on one of the mountainous horses. I climbed to the top of the rails to get on to its back. The boys thought this was because of its great height – I didn't tell them I'd never got on a horse any other way. When we were children we always mounted the horse from the nearest fence post, and it was childhood experience that made me choose the horse they had taken the saddle from. 'Real tough,' the boys said when they saw me astride the cathedral with only a bag over its back. I didn't tell them I couldn't manage a saddle. We bush girls rode astride in our ordinary dresses with nothing but a bran bag between us and the horse.

Here was my chance to show everybody what I could do. My ignorance of the sea and ships had been immediately seized upon by the crew, who made me feel both incompetent and freakish, so that all I wanted was to demonstrate to them one field in which I had considerable prowess in the style they could appreciate.

I got on the horse, walked the monster out of the enclosure, and was about to dig my heels in when suddenly it lit out without my encouragement. It had seen the wide open spaces before it and was heading for home. All I could do was to go with it. When it decided it had gone far enough and was on its own stamping ground it stopped and permitted me to dismount, remove the bridle, and walk all the way back to the yards.

The following day when we were riding out a storm, rolling

badly in the fierce riptide that sweeps through the islands, a bull went berserk and later it had to be destroyed. It had not been in the hold, as the last few animals were left corralled on deck. The bull that fell from the sling had been hauled out of the hold, destroyed and hoisted overboard the previous day. Now this one first turned on its fellows, then charged the bulwark, and finally slipped and fell on the sea-wet deck. Two of the boys who had been imprisoned in the fo'c'sle head by the charging beast now rushed out. 'It's had it,' they called.

I saw the owner get the axe from the wheelhouse so I went into the galley and shut the doors. In a while there was a dull thud, a choked bellow and a moan, and after a while a splash as they put the dead beast over the side.

Next morning Wallaby dropped the pick (oh, yes, I was picking up the jargon fast) in the bay on the nor'-west corner of Clarke Island. The Cooper family were there to attend to their stock, and as their children were due home that day from boarding school for the holidays Captain Jackson thought they might like the opportunity of getting back to Flinders.

'Go ashore and offer them a lift home,' he said to Pete, as though we were offering his suburban neighbours a lift out from town.

The motor dinghy was lowered, and Pete went over the side to get the engine started. After a few minutes he called out, 'Hey, Pat, you got a hanky?' I hadn't noticed Pete make play with a handkerchief before. I took one out to him and as I handed it down I said, 'You got a cold, Pete?'

'Very funny,' he said. 'When do we laugh?'

Pete had a small piece of machinery in his hand and he wiped it carefully with my white hanky.

'Maggie,' he replied tersely to my inquiry.

So began the long line of my handkerchiefs sacrificed on the altar of the magneto of the dinghy. Left uncovered on the deck, the motor of the dinghy was usually encrusted with salt rime and the maggie would be wet and wouldn't work. This day not even my hanky would dry it, so Pete brought it up and put it on the ledge of the stove's fire-box.

'I had a hanky once,' he said, as he waited for the maggie to dry. He used so many of mine I could soon say the same.

I went ashore with the crew and after tying the dinghy up to the rocks we climbed the cliff and set off to look for the house in the scrub nearby. Mrs Cooper was putting bread down to rise when we knocked at the door. She didn't answer at once. We knocked again, and I called out, woman fashion, 'Yoo-hoo, anyone home?'

We got under way as soon as we were all safely on board. There was a strong wind blowing in-shore and the anchor had been dragging, so we were glad to steam out into open water.

3

Roistering Buccaneers

As we rolled in the cross currents sweeping between the islands Mrs Cooper pointed out the sites where 'the roistering buccaneers' had settled before Melbourne or Hobart were founded. In later years I travelled to all these places but never again did I experience the excitement that I felt that day, sailing for the first time in a small ship – as small as those of most of the early adventures, in waters unmarked and treacherous as in their day, past shores and islands as isolated and lonely today as they were a century and a half ago.

In the wake of the *Sydney Cove* had come desperadoes, lured to the islands by hopes of what the wreck would yield and by reports brought to Sydney by Flinders.

Bass, on his way back to the coast of the Australian mainland in the whaleboat, met seven men who had been trying to reach the Furneaux. When he returned to Sydney he told Governor Hunter that on passing a small island he saw 'a smoke'. At first he thought it might have been natives, but when he rowed closer in to the rocky shore, he found seven white men in tattered clothing, convicts, part of a group of fourteen who had seized a boat in October 1797 on the Hawkesbury River, stolen what stores they could and escaped through Port Jackson heads. Maybe it was the rum that attracted them, or perhaps it was the hope that the *Sydney Cove* could be refloated and sailed to safety that persuaded them to sail southwards instead of to the north, where escaping convicts had usually headed until that time.

They did not reach the wreck. Instead, seven of the men treacherously abandoned the others on desolate, barren, Glennie Island and sailed away. On 3 January 1798 Bass chanced on the seven abandoned men. His nine metre boat could hold no more without endangering all, and he was short of food for his return trip.

He picked up five of the convicts and landed them on the mainland so that they could try to make their way northwards by land as the *Sydney Cove* men had done. He gave them a musket, ammunition, a pocket compass, fish hooks and lines, and shared his food and clothing with them. The two 'who were decrepit' he decided to take all the way to Sydney. At parting 'tears were shed on both sides' and Bass's heavily laden boat moved away. Three days later Bass touched on the coast and saw the five castaways once more, the last seen of them.

The wreck became the Mecca of escaping convicts, deserting seamen, and any man who needed to reject society for private reasons. As well, there were the sealers. When Matthew Flinders took back a report on the vast numbers of seals and sea-lions in the straits, the whalers raced southwards to reap the harvest. These men settled ashore on Kent Bay, Cape Barren Island, opposite Mrs Cooper's Clarke Island home. Amaso Delano, a forebear of Franklin D. Roosevelt, was there, and Ebor Bunker, the Yankee skipper from Nantucket; but the man I always thought of when we sailed these waters was Charles Bishop with his brig the *Nautilus*.

On his arrival in Port Jackson in 1798 he had heard the report of seals down south: Flinders had just returned after visiting the wreck of the *Sydney Cove*. In October of that year, when Bass and Flinders set sail southwards in the *Norfolk* to circumnavigate Van Diemen's Land, Bishop accompanied them in the *Nautilus*. He missed few opportunities.

He had already recorded that he intended to proceed 'with a strong crew of 25 men and 2 whale boats to kill and dry skins for China and boil out seal oil for this market, to secure the ship in a good harbour and then divide the People in Separate Parties to the Different Islands under the command of myself and officers, keeping a few of the crew boiling oil.'

He parted company with Bass and Flinders at the Furneaux and anchored at Kent Bay, where he set up his boiling-down works on shore. He planted a garden, again the first in the region. (Bligh had planted several varieties of foodstuff on Bruny Island off the Tasmanian south coast, but did not stay to cultivate or reap and eat them as did Bishop.)

Within a few months the crew of the *Nautilus* had gathered 5000 seal skins and 350 gallons of oil. When provisions ran short Bishop sailed up to Sydney for supplies.

Early in 1799 his men reaped a further 7500 skins and 300 gallons of oil.

Bishop then gathered his men from the rocks and islands and sailed off with this rich cargo, sold it in Port Jackson and, after a few more Pacific sorties, he sailed for Canton with George Bass as companion. There he sold his cargo and his ship, the redoubtable old *Nautilus*, and set off for England to his employer-financier after an absence of six years.

Such voyages did not help to make these men genteel.

Isolated for six years from the influence of family, women, and social contact with their own kind, and living all the time among brutality – the twenty-five men on the *Nautilus*, to have won 12,500 seals, must have killed an average of 500 each, all by hand – the sealers became notorious for their callousness. By 1804 the straits sealers were whooping it up to such a degree that Governor King yearned for faster, better-armed cutters to chase the 'American pirates' whom he believed beat up or kidnapped the sealing gangs in Bass Strait. Amasa Delano was reported to have flogged an English captain unconscious for 'inciting ill-will', but by the time King's cutter arrived to intercept Delano 'the piratical fellow' had sailed away, taking with him thirteen British convict sealers.

As early as 1800 there were two hundred sealers operating in and around Bass Strait. Trade was profitable. A single sealskin was fetching eighteen to twenty-five shillings on the Sydney market. The *Sydney Gazette* tells us that between 9 March 1803 and 28 May 1804 the schooner *Endeavour* got nine thousand five hundred and fourteen seal skins from Bass Strait. From March to September 1803, the schooner *Surprise* got fifteen thousand eight hundred and forty skins, and in September 1803 another unnamed vessel brought eleven thousand skins to Sydney.

The sealers went at their task, slaughtering without regard for their own livelihood, carrying away what they could, leaving the rest to rot on the rocks. In a paper read to the Royal Society of Tasmania on 10 October 1871, C. Gould told of a case where no fewer than three hundred cubs had been left to die on a seal bank because their mothers had been slaughtered and it would not have been worthwhile killing the cubs for their skins.

This would have been the case referred to in the *Hobart Town Gazette* in 1826, when one Scott, '... an inhabitant of the Straits who has cohabited with a blackwoman by whom he has three children', made a similar report.

In 1815 the *Hobart Town Gazette* was calling for closed seasons. With the world market glutted, the price of skins had fallen to five shillings.

The big schooners stayed only while the seals were plentiful and called less frequently as they saw the indiscriminate slaughter ruining the industry. But they left behind isolated bands and individual sealers, who were to become notorious as 'rude, wife-snatchers, wreckers, free-booters, slave drivers, murderers, rum swillers, sea wolves and sea rats'. Of the early islanders this may have been true. It was said of them that, debauched by drink, they would pour rum into a hole in the earth floor of their huts so they could drink when they could no longer stand – the type of exaggerated legendary tale that nevertheless may have some grain of truth in it. As for 'wife-snatching', the twelve men who founded the race known as Cape Barren Islanders can all be named, indeed their names are almost the sum of surnames on Cape Barren. Of the nine Tasmanian and four Australian women and one Maori woman they took with them, many of the names have been remembered by the islanders and those whose names are not remembered can be identified. The wreck of the *Sydney Cove*, which was responsible for so many strange and historical events, was also indirectly responsible for the preservation of the last strains of the Tasmanian Aboriginal race.

When Europeans first arrived in Van Diemen's Land they found a race of people already in occupation. These people, numbering only about two thousand in 1800, were gone by 1876.

Charles Darwin said, 'I do not know a more striking instance of a comparative rate of increase of a civilized over a savage people.'

By 1835 George Augustus Robinson had gathered two hundred and three people together – all that was left of the Tasmanians. 'They came,' a journalist wrote, 'the sad remnant of a bygone race, the surviving mourners of a nation's dead. They tread upon their nation's tomb.'

There were two men to every woman; three women to every child; no babes in arms. The forced marches and malnutrition through lack of their natural foods had sounded the last knell of death for this ancient people. But the tragedy had to be played out to the final curtain. From Hobart they were sent first to Swan Island, then to Guncarriage (or Vansittart), and finally to Flinders Island, where they pined and died at Wybalena – 'black man's home'.

It is a sad little cemetery at Wybalena. The first tombstone I cleared of wild growth had the inscription:

> Elizabeth, the much loved wife of Joseph Milligan, and daughter of W.E. Lawrence M.L.C. Van Diemen's Land. Departed this life 31st July, 1844, ten days after her confinement and in the Nineteenth year of her age.

With a piece of decayed iron railing I dragged away the spiky box-thorn from the grave of 'Margaret Monaghan and her two children' and read on the stone erected by 'her loving husband Private Patrick Monaghan, King's own Light Infantry (may the Lord rest their souls in peace)', that she had come with the infants on HM Brig *Tamar* to join her husband who was garrisoned at the Aboriginal settlement. On 23 December 1840 the brig anchored off, and they were to go ashore by longboat, but as they were lowering away a gust of wind caught the young wife's crinoline, tangling it in the rigging, and before the boat could be righted it capsized.

And there are the graves that are graves no more, roughly marked with stones, the places where the exiled Aborigines had been buried. Now there are no bodies. The skeletons were disinterred a century ago and sold to museums in Britain and on the Continent.

It is interesting to note that the Australian Aborigines are believed to have arrived in their present home thirty thousand years ago, and that seventeen thousand years ago parts of Bass

Strait could have been dry land. Scientists believe that the deluge spoken of in the Book of Genesis, which forms part of the folklore of most ancient peoples, was due to a world-wide rise in sea level, which flooded coastal lands six thousand years ago, rather than to rainfall.

Seventeen thousand years ago the sea began to rise, and it went on rising until six thousand years ago, having risen in this time an average of a hundred metres. As Bass Strait at its deepest is around a hundred metres, the trek by the retreating primitives could perhaps have taken them on foot over Bass Strait. One of the objections raised to the theory that they were castaways or navigators on boats or rafts from the Pacific is their disinterest in sea-craft of any kind.

4

The Sea Can't Sink a Good Ship

The laughter and camaraderie that went with the grim battle against wind and sea were hard to resist. I had never been in a ship before and everything was strange and new. There have always been women travelling on boats around the islands, but island women were used to the style of transport, having grown up with the stormy dangerous waters as a fence around their island homes.

After that first trip by a commercial airline to the islands I never travelled that way again. When I needed to get on or off the islands I got a lift from one of the single-engined planes or in one of the island traders, usually the *Sheerwater* because she was worked hardest and turned fastest, spending little time in port.

Captain Les Jackson, owner of the *Sheerwater*, the *Prion* and the *Margaret Twaits*, and Jack-of-all-trades, was brought up on Prime Seals Island (marked on charts as The Sisters, as Furneaux named it in 1773, but known to locals as Prime Seals because the best seals were caught in that area), and was travelling on inter-island boats before he could walk. He was earning money from the three trades that island boys must learn – fishing, trapping, and mutton-birding – before he reached his teens. He studied first by correspondence and later the Jacksons brought over a governess to teach their three daughters and Les. He learned to play the violin, piano, and 'cello, but never had an ear for music. Aboard the *Sheerwater* he sang constantly, making up the words as he went along, but in such a tuneless voice that it was a painful ordeal for the listener.

Later he was sent as a boarder to Australia's oldest independent school, Launceston Grammar. For an island-bred boy whose parents had impressed independence and self-sufficiency on him, the dull discipline of school life came as a challenge. 'I don't think he purposely tries to lead us a dance,' one of his reports said, 'but he does.'

By the time he left school he had decided in traditional island style to be his own master. He did work for others but only to further his ambitions. He went shearing to learn how it was done, as he wanted to run sheep later in life. He worked on ships as a deck hand to 'get his time in', to sit for a master's ticket: he even cooked on ships to get the higher pay of a cook. He bred and trained kangaroo dogs for sale. There were good training grounds on Prime Seals and he sold thousands of wallaby skins he had collected there. For a while he was rouseabout on a station.

All this time he was saving as few high-spirited boys can. He bought a property on Flinders Island and another on the mainland of Australia, but not yet ready to settle, he went to sea again. By the time he had his master's ticket, he also had enough money saved to buy his first ship, the ninety-six-tonne *Sheerwater*.

Les Jackson was good to travel with. Interested in everything himself, he took it for granted that everyone else was also, and he would talk and answer questions by the hour. He and his wife (whose brothers were small-ships' captains), knew the straits and shipping well.

One evening I carried my kit-bag on board the ship at Launceston, bound for Whitemark, 'capital' of Flinders Island. On board were three unlikely lads 'fresh from Her Majesty's guest house', as Pete insisted on telling the friends who had driven me to the wharf. (I hadn't wanted this. I could think of nothing I wanted less.) 'The clink,' says Pete, 'the cooler.' My friends were to go on to the theatre, an opening night. Rene was in a long frock, Henry and Ray in dinner jackets. Captain Jackson, Wallaby, was watching and listening to all this, grinning from ear to ear, leaning out the wheelhouse door.

Pete thought he was cutting quite a figure. He volunteered all sorts of information, including the story of an islander who disappeared on the waterfront. 'They still haven't found him when we get back to Launceston, so they come and ask us to see if he's on the bottom. Well, we go backwards and forwards up along the wharf with our propeller going great guns stirring up the mud from the bottom. Up popped empty jam tins, up popped a bottle, then up popped old Judah.'

When it was time to go, I went aboard and my friends waved goodbye. I had a suspicion that they would be the last send-off party to come down to a wharf to see me off – and it was. 'What a lot of golly-wogs!' Pete dismissed them. 'Did you cop those ties? Stupid! Don't know nothing, never seen nothing neither. A dead weight on the world them sort are. The rest of us are carrying them on our backs.'

The three boys who were ex-guests of Her Majesty were nice enough once they realised I was going to sail with the ship. They looked very young and boyish, but one of them told me that he was twenty-eight. Pete told me that this one had been in gaol for a total period of six years spread over the past twelve years. He was a strange boy. He could quote all sorts of unexpected things, such as bits of Sanskrit verse, the last verse of 'Auld Lang Syne', and he could rattle off a letter from Boswell to Johnson to the effect that no man was such a fool as to exchange a prison sentence for a life at sea. 'I agree with him,' he said. 'A man gets better food, lodging, and company in gaol, better books to read, and more leisure. And he's not so closely confined. Give me gaol any time. A man's got a lot more freedom there than he has on a ship!'

But in between these fluent bursts he would speak disjointedly, like a retarded child, and he could put a German Luger together in the time it took me to peel the potatoes for lunch. I know because he did it on the table beside my dish. Then he brought out dozens of parts of other pistols and guns and started to assemble them. With the ship's saw, he tediously cut parts of one gun to fit parts of another, and hammered them into shape with an iron marlin spike. He had strong, beautiful white teeth, and he bit and twisted wire with them. When I admired this strength, he took the top off a sauce bottle to demonstrate the useful purposes the habit could be turned to. I must have applauded too much for he then took the drinking glass I had bought the previous day for myself, chewed it to pieces, and spat the pieces out into his hand like uncut diamonds.

'Does he shoot people?' I asked Pete, as soon as I could escape from the galley without raising suspicion.

'No! Don't be a nong! What would he want to shoot people for? He just likes guns.'

Life was simple for Pete.

That night the sea was rough, and the *Sheerwater* was 'cutting a dido' as Pete said. I stood out on deck near the galley door watching the black night all around. The navigation lights on either side of the ship should not, by law, be seen from astern, but the spume sweeping past them reflected the green glow on the starboard side and a pinky red on the port.

When my eyes became accustomed to the dark, I could see a figure on the top of the fo'c'sle, crouched over a white handkerchief he had spread on the deck. It was the gun boy with parts of his pistols. Unable to sleep, he had come out on the cool deck and gone on working, unseeing, but feeling with his sensitive, skilled fingers in the dark.

'Will the pistol boy get caught again?'

'Of course,' Pete said. 'They all will. They always do.' Pete declared we gave them a free ride over 'just so's we'll get their passage money back plus the copper's as well.' And so we did.

The police were resigned to escort duty. They sat up all night on the crossing from Flinders Island to Launceston, talked with the boy on the wheel, shared cocoa in the galley, and told us all the scandal we'd missed out on since our last trip. Their charges were completely free and usually took a turn at the wheel themselves or played cards in the galley with us. When we reached Launceston the island cop suddenly became very officious, buttoned up his tunic and reached for his cap in the debris of the galley or the cabins. Sometimes he waved handcuffs and shouted at the boy who now became the prisoner. A police van awaited them on the wharf. The boys always waved and called messages to us, but the police merely slipped us a quick wink when they could.

One day when we berthed, the tide was out and the ship therefore was very low in the water, so low that our deck was well below the wharf. The only way to get off the ship was to climb the rigging and jump for it. Pete went first. 'Jeez!' he commented as usual. I went next.

We were sawing about a bit. Some of the rigging was loose, some broken, and all of it swayed with the surge of the changing tide. I climbed until I was opposite, a little above the wharf, but we were two metres out at the nearest, four metres when she rolled. I tried to appear nonchalant but I needn't have bothered. Pete's face, like a water spout on a medieval cathedral, leered at me from the wharf. To spite that face any army in flight would have rallied. I jumped without waiting to see if we were on an inward or outward roll. As I landed there was a cry like a sea bird from the stays – 'Ahtchk'. It was the constable, cap and all. He'd followed me up the rigging, watched me launch into space, and now knew it was his turn. Behind him his prisoner, a boy who'd worked his way over with us only a month previously, was climbing.

'What's the matter? Got the tom-tits?' said the *enfant terrible* on the wharf, grinning his gargoyle face into gullies. 'Come on. You can only die once.' But the policeman couldn't move. The boy he was taking in was now behind him; he'd climbed so that his arms were now round his captor's hips. 'You'll be jake. Just get your leg around the other side.' But that was the trouble. Once up the rigging you had to turn around before you could make the jump to the wharf. And this the policeman could not do. By now a few people were about, the agent and a consignee or two and the driver of the police van. And all the while the *Sheerwater* yawed into the piles beneath the wharf and out again, and the man in blue hung on like a limpet as though he were using the whole of his body as suction.

Wallaby had already got ashore by making a leap from the bulwarks on to the transoms and clambered up the barnacles on the piles. He now stood on the wharf. 'When I say go, let go and jump,' he said quietly. His eyes flickered to the boy who was the prisoner and back to the constable. The ship was on the way in, the rigging trembled. 'OK. Ready now. Jump!' Wallaby stretched his arms as if to catch the man, the boy on the rigging wrenched the man's hands free and pushed, and the constable dropped to the wharf. On the next inward surge his prisoner followed him. 'See you later,' the boy said. We nodded, and the van drove off.

I boarded the *Sheerwater* at Whitemark once to travel up to beautiful Killiecrankie Bay on the north of Flinders Island and as usual was immediately put to work in the galley while the crew continued to unload cargo. These small ships were always non-union ships and the crew loaded and unloaded their own vessels.

I began the task I always did first of all on a *Sheerwater* voyage – cleaning the galley. I scraped the floor clean, lifted the dirty clothes up with a stick, and dropped them over the side. 'Hey! That's me loading shirt.' 'Struth break it down! That's me strides. Nothing wrong with them that a few nails skew-wise won't fix.' 'There's nothing safe when a woman's about. Where's me hat?' The crews of the *Prion* and the *Margaret Twaits* came across the pier to have a look. 'Old Dutch Cleanser!' they shouted.

I scrubbed and scrubbed. There was no bucket on board, only a tin dish in which they washed themselves (I presumed this, I never actually saw them wash) and I peeled the vegetables too. I now used this for scrubbing the floor and table.

On the freshly scrubbed floor I spread newspapers and put clean sacks outside each door for the crew to wipe their feet. Pete came in for a drink of water and ignored the sacks, but when I told him that he ought to wipe his feet he dragged the soles of his boots one after the other up the legs of his trousers.

On deck the crew had nearly finished unloading the cargo – boxes of groceries, crates of beer, bags of vegetables, and coils of fencing wire. But instead of going higher in the water as the load came out of her, the ship was sinking. I looked up in alarm – first as the top of the wharf, then as the barnacle-covered piles came into view through the galley port-hole. I hurried out on to the deck.

There, a marvellous sight met my eyes. There was no water

for us to sink in. The sea had disappeared and in its place was an acre of dull sand on which our ship was sitting, with the other ships resting likewise opposite us.

We were just settling down when I came out on deck. High above I could see the crew loosening the lines that tied the ship to the wharf, and I knew why. We were slowly rolling sideways. Suddenly I felt my feet starting to slide and I clutched the door frame. The door swung shut and missed my fingers by a whisker. I heard a crash inside the deckhouse, but I couldn't go in to see what it was. I thought the ship was going to roll right over, but I couldn't get off it because I couldn't walk up the hill of the sloping deck. Some coils of wire that had been stacked on deck began to slide towards me, and for a while I played a desperate sort of skipping game with them as they slid by under my feet. I was near the end of this game, the last of the wire just coming my way, when the crew vaulted down on deck.

'What happened?' I gasped.

'We're always on the bottom here when the tide goes out. There's around a three metre rise and fall.'

I was frightened that when the tide came in the ship mightn't right itself but be washed over by the water. I wanted to get safely on to the wharf. Instead, Captain Jackson said I should go down on the sea bed and 'have a look at her bottom'. Once I saw how small wooden ships were constructed to withstand all the odd things that happen in the shallow water area they trade in I would feel safer, he said.

'She won't know what you're talking about,' Pete said. 'I didn't when you showed me and I'm not even a woman.'

With Alec on one side of me, the captain on the other and the kid jigging round the lot of us like a monkey on a string, I learnt that wooden coastal tramps are very different from the large vessels that trade in deep waters.

'Yes,' Pete said. 'They're smaller.'

To get to the little, out-of-the-way places where they have

to take goods these small ships must be built to withstand the stresses and strains of their timbers when they lie on the bottom when the tide goes out.

'And when they hit the bottom too,' Alec said.

'You mean ... sink?' I said the unmentionable word.

'No, get into shallow water ports or shallow bays. There's a saying that the little wooden ship that hasn't scraped the bottom hasn't been worked properly.'

We walked around the *Sheerwater*. She wasn't pointed on the bottom of her keel as is a steel ship; she was rounded. I'd gone down to the sea-bed to humour this ribald group, but now I was fascinated.

My first lesson had begun. Half jokingly, then with increasing enthusiasm as they sensed my interest, they began to describe her build. The keel that had once been a single tall tree and was now shaped to be her backbone; the stem rising up from that, shielding and joining her side planks like a breastbone; the planks, strakes as the seamen call them, from the garboard strake up to the sheer strake on the gunwale, and underneath them the ribs, the keelson, the sister keelsons, butts, and stringers.

My impression of a ship being built on the principle of a hollowed-out log was wiped out in that first trip underneath the *Sheerwater*. A wooden ship is built on the principle of a bread basket; it must 'work' in the water for the same reason that a tall building must 'sway' in the wind, so that the strain will not cause it to snap. When big seas throw their weight at little ships the size of the *Sheerwater*, all the force of thousands of kilometres of water crashing at once on the wooden vessel doesn't break it. The harder the sea attacks, the more the ship works, groaning and moaning as her timbers take up the stress and strain.

'It's a reassuring sound once you know why it does it,' Wallaby said. 'The sea can't sink a good ship. Only the land can do that.'

The ship's home port was Launceston, on Tasmania's north coast. This was my first blue-water voyage, my initiation, and I was elated as we set off. But Pete could deflate anyone.

'You got false teeth?' he asked. 'You want to take them out and put them in your pocket. They're the first thing to go over the side when you're perking.'

I hadn't thought of sea-sickness. Panicky, I thought I should have bought some sea-sickness tablets I'd seen advertised.

'Do you no good,' Alec assured me. 'If yer gonna go green you'll go green, tablets or not.'

I needn't have worried. I wasn't sick. And that wasn't wise. I should have been, for they expected it of me. I was certainly a 'rum 'un' now, as Tasmanians would say.

They took it in turns to watch me. As we got out of the lee of the island and started to cross the strait the wind and sea began their work on the little ship. She began to dip her bows down deep and come up with water streaming off her, a fore and aft roll, as Pete informed me while taking his turn at the watch.

'Wait till she does a corkscrew,' he jeered.

They put a new boy on the wheel for a trial and she corkscrewed then because he had her yawing about. Alec had relieved Pete by now. 'Bet this sets you off,' he said as the ship twisted and rolled and twisted again.

'Do you *want* me to be sick?' I asked him.

He told me that he personally didn't, but Wallaby Jackson bet he and Pete ten shillings that I wouldn't be sick, and he and Pete, though not wishing me harm, didn't want to miss out on ten bob.

'We won't,' he said. 'She'll deck and deck it like she's doing now for as long as this kid's got the wheel. You oughta see him. Gives her no rest, winds the wheel madly one way then the other. He's sweating and swearing like a trooper. Go out and have a look. It might turn you up.'

The boy was certainly working hard at it. He dragged the

big wheel round until the ship was broadside on to the sea, then dragged it back again with the ship slowly, sluggishly following till her bows were into it.

'Did you ever see anything like that galoot?' Pete yelped. 'Nearly rolled me out of me bunk. A bloke oughta step up and snotter him.'

A snotter, I had learnt while they were unloading, was the rope used to secure bundles of cargo for loading or unloading. Slowly, the ship heeled over again and I leaned against a bulwark.

'Haw,' Pete pounced. 'You feelin' crook? How about a greasy big pork chop, eh?'

He followed me into the galley where he sat cross-legged on the bread box and began to mend his pants, his only pants. There was a rent from below the knee to the thigh on the front of the leg and a small tear which he described as 'skew-wise' across the seat. He had a sail needle and thread and with tremendous concentration drew the two sides of the rent together with inch-long stitches. The stitch was known as 'homeward bounder' he told me. He finished it off with a few half-hitches and cut the twine with the bread knife.

To see the rip on the seat he had to stand up. First he tried squinting down the middle of his back and nearly twisted his head off; then he stuck his bottom out – but still he couldn't see it. So he lifted his seat up in the air with both hands.

'Ah,' he said with satisfaction. He could now see it. 'You little bottler!'

But he couldn't hold it and sew as well. So he had to do it blind, with his hands round the back of him. From where I was standing it looked like a game of sticking the tail on the donkey. The denim of the trousers was very tough, and with one hand holding the sides of the rip together he had only one hand free to sew with. Unable to pierce the material, he jabbed harder and harder, and then, exasperated, he held the needle out at arm's length and stabbed.

He roared like a bull, howled like a dingo, and went up in the air like a sky rocket. Then he sat down on the bread box. But the needle was still embedded in him. He sprang up again, howling and roaring even louder. After a while he settled down.

'That stirred the possums in me, didn't it?' he said. 'I sure cut a dido.'

You mightn't be able to work out the exact literal translation of Pete's words, but you were never left in doubt as to his meaning.

The ship was 'cutting a dido' now; the new boy was still on the wheel. I was holding a big kettle of boiling water on top of the stove, not knowing what else to do with it. If I let it go it would rocket on to the floor; if I stood it on the floor it would tip over. I thought of taking it out on the deck and emptying it over the side, but I was afraid I might fall over with it.

'You silly or something?' Pete said when he saw what I was doing. 'Tie it on.'

He got a piece of hay band and tied the kettle backwards on to the flue and forwards on to the handle of the fire-box door.

I took another look at the boy. He was desperately wrestling with the wheel. As soon as the ship swung her bow a little to port (I knew already my left from my starboard) he wrenched the wheel around to starboard. It was a big wheel and he put his whole weight on to it, dragging it round as far as it would go, his head disappearing out of sight beneath the window as he lay over the spokes, pushing. By the time he righted himself and could see out again the ship had answered the wheel and was spinning majestically around, the horizon scudding past his eyes like a Fitzpatrick travelogue, until he was heading back the way we had come. Then he'd have to haul her back again, laying over the wheel, dragging it around, inch by unwilling inch, and the whole process would be reversed, for as soon as the ship began to turn, off she'd go in the opposite direction, spinning like a top.

'Well,' Pete said in great glee. 'Up till now Wallaby reckoned I was the world's worst helmsman. After this I'm not any longer.'

The captain came out and laconically said at this rate it would be a long time before we got anywhere – considering the ship's name was being written in the water behind us.

'You take her for a while, Pete,' he told the disgusted boy. 'Give the boy a breather.'

The boy went straight to the fo'c'sle to lie down. We didn't see him till late in the afternoon – Alec said he was a great reader of wild westerns. When he came into the galley again he left the door open, and we heard the sound of something bumping on the deck. Alec went out to see what it was, then came back and said to him, 'Did you notice any cargo adrift when you crossed the deck?'

'Yep. But it didn't worry me. I stepped over it.'

He didn't go back near the wheel, and when Pete was relieved hours later he said, 'That's the longest breather I've ever heard of.'

Wallaby (don't call him Captain Jackson or he'll 'do the lolly' Pete had at last impressed on me, after trying since I first came on board) said he was going to finish him up when we got to Launceston. Not for laziness – 'there's ways of getting work out of the laziest man.' But, 'if a person can't see what's needing to be done on a ship that person shouldn't be at sea.'

As he went out I looked for something to do.

Quarters on board the coasters were austere. Even to someone like me, who had nothing to compare them with, their rigid severity was a surprise. For instance Les Jackson, ship's master and financially comfortable, slept on bare boards and covered himself with a quilt affair made of crocheted silk stockings. He said it saved him buying an alarm clock.

'The boards are so uncomfortable I can't sleep for long without waking. Then I get up, go for a walk round the ship, check the anchor if we're anchored, or the lines if we're tied up, or the compass if we're under way, and make sure the helmsman is awake. Then I turn in again and sleep till the boards wake me again and so on through the night.'

'And no blankets?'

'That saves putting the alarm clock in the kerosene tin. If the hard boards don't wake me promptly the cold air does. By the time I've taken a turn or two round the deck in the cold night air the bunk seems warm and cosy when I return to it.'

I asked what the boys who slept in the fo'c'sle had.

'Cyclone wire gates,' Alec bawled.

This was another of Wallaby's innovations.

'I used to have rubber mattresses there for the crew,' he said. 'But they weren't any good so I had to throw them overboard.'

'What was wrong with them?'

'They made the crew unwilling to get up in the morning. Made them too … um …'

'Comfortable?'

'No, just weary, lazy, unhealthy. You can't tell me staying in bed so long can be healthy. I threw them over the side.'

So now they spread newspapers over the wire mesh and were only too happy to get out of a morning.

The permanent crew (if a man stayed in the *Sheerwater* a month he was considered permanent) made their bunks a little more comfortable with old mattresses they had 'picked up', but the majority of the crew just did one or two trips sleeping on the wire, and were never seen again.

Ships as small as the *Sheerwater*, though they sail 'on articles' as do the biggest ships in the world, nevertheless have a meagre manning scale. There is no need to carry a qualified engineer – the master is the only man on board required to have a certificate or experience. To qualify for this economical manning scale small ships can register as auxiliary ketches, assuring the authorities that in the event of their motors breaking down the ship could be sailed under canvas. But they don't have to prove this to the authorities, and just as well. As for deckhands and crew, they could pick up anyone at all. The only qualification needed was to be able to stand it.

5

On the Wheel

Alec and the man-who-shot-at-lavatories disappeared one day, shortly after we tied up at Whitemark, so the ship sailed without them. 'They'll get into strife if they're caught on the island,' Pete protested.

'They asked for it.' And off we sailed, the captain, the boy, and I.

Huddled round Flinders Island are the other forty-one islands of the Furneaux Group. Some are as small as a suburban backyard, others are thousands of acres in area. Some are flat, others mountainous. Few are inhabited now, but most have known some settlement in the past. This day we went to Chappell Island, which stuck out of the sea like a pyramid.

Matthew Flinders named this island for Ann Chappell, whom he later married.

'Come here,' Les the captain ordered as we came closer to the island. Pete was up on the fo'c'sle belting something with the back of the axe, so I knew that it was me being called.

'Take the wheel while I go and help Pete.' As he stepped down from the wheelhouse he said over his shoulder, 'Steady as she goes, heading for the small beach.' I took hold of the great wheel and strained my eyes ahead at the island that only a few minutes ago was so far away, yet now seemed so close I thought I was about to wreck the ship on it.

Beach? There was no beach! There was not even water. I could see no more than the topmost peak of the island. I now realised the limitations of my stature – I was so short I couldn't see the horizon. So I stood on the bench behind the wheel. Ah, yes, the beach. The size of a pocket handkerchief, but the only beach in sight, and the ship's head was swinging away from it. I turned the wheel slowly as you would steer a car and the ship came round slowly. It was uncomfortable leaning down from the bench and I was afraid the men would see me, so I picked out a point of the mountain immediately above the beach to steer to and hopped down again. Whenever the mast veered off this point of mountain I'd bring her back again. Gently does it. I wasn't going to sweat at it like that boy.

Closer and closer the mountain came. Les didn't call to give me any instructions so I stood on the bench to see him. He was with Pete, and they were both banging away at the anchor chain with their backs to the shore. It must be okay, I thought, so I got back down again and gave the wheel a spoke one way to keep it on course for the mountain peak.

The motors had been chuff-chuffing away steadily. Surely they were going faster now? Faster and faster? Where I had thought sea travel was leisurely a day ago we now seemed to be skiing along, flying. The mountain was coming closer. I stood up on the bench again. Les was swinging an axe over his head, bringing the back of it down on whatever was holding the anchor. Pete was hanging over the side, only the southern portion of him visible, and yelling something about the anchor. I decided to yell too.

'Les?'

'Yep?'

'Er ... we're ... um ... getting ..., do I just keep heading in towards the beach?'

'Yep.' He banged away a bit more and I got down from the bench. The metallic clunk sounded every now and then as his axe hit the anchor chain.

I clambered back up on to the bench. The island was close, Les was casually disappearing down into the fo'c'sle, and the boy was dismantling something on the windlass that raised and lowered the anchor. They didn't appear to notice where we were!

I got down and steered for a while longer.

When the mountain towered above the ship I got back up. I wished I was at home with my mother making cakes for a church stall. Les was wielding a big king spanner now, Pete was banging away with the axe. Les got the spanner on a bolt and stood on it to lever it round.

'Les?'

'Yep?' He was standing on the spanner.

'We're getting close ...'

'Close to what?'

'Close to where you said to go.'

He gave the spanner another bounce along. 'Let's know when we get there.' I climbed down and waited.

The motor chuffed faster than ever, the mountain rushed forward to meet us. Should I clamber back up on the bench and tell them about my not being able to swim?

'Pat!'

I sprang up. 'Yes?'

It was Les. He was still facing the wheelhouse and I swear he hadn't once looked round at the island.

'Where are we now?'

'There.'

'Good.' He told me to turn a small wheel on the wall in front of me to the left. I spun it. The motor slowed, the ship slowed. It was in neutral.

'Let her go!'

Me? I jumped back on to the bench. Me? No, Pete with the anchor. Pete gave the chain a kick and the anchor rattled down. I climbed down.

'Now, again!'

Me? I climbed up again. Yes, me.

'Again to your left.' I spun the little wheel again, the motor stuttered, and the ship began to charge backwards. Oh, God! There was a loud bang. Pete had hit the windlass with the back of the axe again. I wanted badly to go and lay the table for dinner, anything.

'That's enough.'

Me? Yes, me. I wished I had never been born.

'Enough what?'

Pete straightened up and stared, and I knew by the grimace on his face he was saying, 'Jeez!'

'Put her in neutral.'

'Natural,' called Pete.

I spun the little wheel, we steadied, slowed, stopped.

It was months before I realised that though Les couldn't see Chappell Island he knew exactly our position by the position of the other islands around us. In fact, some of the courses the ships here take to avoid reefs and shoals are marked simply by keeping a particular mountain peak or point of land in line with your mast over the stern. Even a tree or a rock becomes a landmark for a course to steer.

I was now alone on the ship. Les and Pete had taken some timber ashore in the dinghy. A sea breeze was blowing and the ship was moving. The anchor must have slipped. (I couldn't think of the seafaring term for it, but decided that was what had happened.) The ship was swinging round. She had been pointed bow first at the island when we anchored and was now pointed towards the open sea. Like a girl guide I wet my finger and held it up to test the direction of the wind. As I thought: coming over the bow. Not knowing what this proved, I looked over the side. Little ripples skipped off the waves that raced back from the bow. We were under way all right. My hair prickled and raised from my scalp. What should I do? I didn't know how to stop her so perhaps I should steer her somewhere? But where? Towards the open sea or head for the land? What if I found myself out in the wide Pacific? I could bump into anything. Perhaps Les would set out in pursuit in the dinghy. I went back aft through the galley to scream for help and as I opened the door I nearly knocked him over. There, tied to the stern, was the dinghy, with the kid in it grinning. 'Sneaked up on yer, eh?' he said.

And just where we'd left it, no farther and no nearer to us, was the beach of Chappell Island. I was 'rum' enough now without asking for an explanation. I had three cups of tea instead. When I came out of the galley the bow was pointing in towards the island. Casually, I asked why it had pointed out to sea half an hour ago and was now pointing shorewards, and was told that a ship on anchor is always bow into the wind and today the wind was 'all over the place'.

Keeping the boy's dismissal in mind always, I looked for work when I had not been given any. In this way it could never be said of me that I shouldn't be at sea because I didn't know what to do. Nursing the many injuries and minor ailments that cropped up gave me fairly constant employment, but not much satisfaction.

Pete cut his arm deeply and I bandaged it carefully, using one narrow bandage first, then a wider one to secure it firmly.

The finished job looked quite professional, and when Les came up for a cup of tea later and I told him how proud I was of it, he went off to inspect it.

He came back a minute later. 'Too late,' he said, 'Pete's had to take the bandage off.'

'Why?'

'To wipe the maggie dry. It got wet.' As though it were the most natural thing in the world.

Wallaby bought what he called a first-aid kit – a dozen bandages and a bottle of antiseptic lotion.

For open wounds I found absolute cleanliness followed by fresh air better than any ointments or salves. I'd wash and swab cuts, gashes, and tears, putting plenty of salt in the water if there were no antiseptic left, even salt on the wounds if they were not too deep or too open. This 'stirred the possums' in them, but kept them clean, and my Grandmother Adams used to swear by it. I'd leave a bandage on for the minimum of time, just long enough for the bleeding to stop and to keep dirt out till the flesh had a chance to bring along reinforcements; then I'd remove the bandage and let my Granny Smith's fresh air and sunshine cure do the rest.

Apart from the cuts there were a tremendous number of skin eruptions aboard the *Sheerwater* – pimples, boils, and carbuncles. These usually responded to a bread poultice.

I had only one failure, and that was such a dismal affair that it not only ravaged the crew but me too, and left scars on the back of my neck that will be there till the day I die. The incurable were salt-water boils, and I'd like to state here and now that though we all went to doctors at different places and times, they couldn't help us either. Mine recurred for three years and were the most foul and painful things.

Alec brought them to the *Sheerwater* from another ship he had been in. At first he thought they were ordinary boils, which didn't appear to be serious; just eruptions on his forearms. Then they came up like small boils on his neck and hands. I washed and sterilised and poulticed until his skin was like putty. Pete got them, then the others, and finally me. A salt-water boil doesn't have a head like a true boil has. The whole eruption sluffs open and oozes foulness. The more I washed and softened them the worse they became, bursting open completely. I still don't know what would cure them – although some fishermen swear by oil of turpentine – but I do know that constant washing not only spreads them but stops them from healing. They are very contagious, but only to people in contact with salt water.

Mine stayed on the back of my neck for three years until I realised that they always flared up and became unbearable immediately after I washed my hair. So I didn't shampoo it for four weeks and they almost dried up. Within a year they had dried away. When I complained to May Jackson, Les's mother, of my boils she said, 'Of course you'll get boils. I've had them all my life. Whenever a woman does a man's work she gets boils.'

Nothing could alarm these patients. It was I who had all the alarms. There was, for example, the night Les was sitting at the table taking the top off a powdered-milk can.

'They put a sharp seal on these tins,' he said, conversationally.

I agreed, and continued serving the tea at the stove. A while later I set his tea on the table before him, and then sat down quickly. He had cut a slice off the top of his thumb with the milk tin, and there was a pool of blood on the table that would have filled a soup plate.

'I told you it was sharp,' he said.

These boys needed no encouragement from me to get well. Les gave them all they needed. 'If you're too sick to work you'd better hop ashore.' This had immediate results.

Try as I might to be matter-of-fact, there were things at sea that I had never expected. Perhaps no one else could have done so either.

Whoever walled in the spare corner on the deck of the *Sheerwater* and called it a toilet never intended it to be used as a place where 'readin', figurin', or thinkin'' could be done.

One day, to my surprise, I came on it by chance. The men, I knew, took it in turns to see that I stayed in the galley while the rest disappeared on deck, but no one made any suggestions about me. After experimenting one night at anchor when all the crew were in at tea I found that with the door shut there wasn't room in this floating privy to get your slacks down. It was never a place to relax in.

The first day I sat in it, a fountain of icy cold sea-water smacked up on me from below with such force I was almost lifted up into the air, and this was likely to happen every time we were rolling in a big sea. At times like this the outlet became an inlet. All very hygienic, very French.

In the *Prion* another woman and I were offered a bucket on a rope. My friend lowered it over the side later in the day and I had to grab her by the legs to save her going in after it when the sea caught it.

6

The Moonbirds

I'd not heard of mutton birds until I saw them festooning the masts and rigging of the old *Willwatch*, but you couldn't remain ignorant of them on the Furneaux.

Puffinus tenuirostris, known to the Tasmanian Aborigines as *yolla*, to ornithologists as the Short-tailed Shearwater, to some as the moonbird and to gourmets as mutton bird, is the most closely-studied bird in Australian waters.

I first met Dr Dominic Louis Serventy when the *Sheerwater* gave him a lift to outlying islands. He was then Chief Officer of the Wildlife Survey Department of the Commonwealth Scientific and Industrial Research Organisation, and set up a banding programme in the early 1950s. To observe the habits of the mutton birds, Serventy voluntarily put up with many hardships. To reach the Babel Island and Cat Island sanctuaries he had to be taken through the Pot Boil, a maelstrom of black swirling water through which many men have refused to sail. Usually he was taken out in the police boat *Aralla*, but he often travelled on the *Sheerwater*. Because mutton birds are active only at night, he spent many nights out on the rookery observing them.

Some of us were with Dom when he received one of the bands back, a rare one, taken from the leg of a dead mutton bird found tangled in a fisherman's net near St Lawrence Island in the Bering Sea on the edge of the Arctic Circle. It had been returned as requested on the band, 'Notify Fauna Board, Hobart, Tasmania, Australia'. By means of this band, Dom received the confirmation he had sought for twelve years on the migrating habits of this particular bird. The finding of the band in the Bering Sea area, the third found in that region, was an end product of his long years of voluntary hardship studying the birds.

For this, and other reports, Serventy had slept among the grass tussocks with the sky for a roof, on lonely, uninhabited Bass Strait islands, walked hundreds of kilometres over rock peaks, and pushed through scrub where venomous two-metre tiger snakes lay curled in such large numbers that he once saw thirty killed in one day.

He had carried his gear and his food on his shoulders up cliff faces where fishing boats had put him ashore, and sailed twice a year through the dreaded tidal swirl called the Pot Boil, east of Bass Strait, where few seamen care to go.

The band found on the bird's leg was one of the 20,000 that Serventy had carefully fixed to the legs of mutton birds, hoping that at least one would be returned and so help in solving one of the puzzles surrounding these mysterious creatures.

For a century and a half men of the southern hemisphere had been arguing about where the mutton bird spent the southern winter months. Each September, so regularly that even the timing itself was a mystery, mutton birds have come to the islands south of the southern coast of Australia, and just as regularly each April disappeared, not to be seen again until the following September.

That so many birds – their numbers are estimated at many millions – could vanish for six months seemed impossible. When Matthew Flinders sailed through the Bass Strait islands in 1798, he noted that more than a hundred and fifty-one million birds passed over his ship in 1½ hours – and that was only one flock. He wrote:

> They were 50 to 80 yards in depth and 300 yards or more in breadth. The birds were not scattered but flying as compactly as free movement of their wings seemed to allow. During a full one and a half hours this stream of petrels continued to pass without interruption at the swiftness of a pigeon.

He estimated the number of birds to have been 151,500,000 needing 75,750,000 burrows to lodge them. Allowing a square yard to each burrow, he reckoned on their covering more than 18½ square miles.

In the northern hemisphere explorers had noted the same species of bird in the Arctic Ocean, and it was here it was given its scientific name of *Puffinus tenuirostris* by the Dutch ornithologist Conrad Jacob Temminck in 1835, although it had been described and noted by many earlier voyagers.

Captain Cook recorded the birds during his third voyage in 1778 as being in latitude 70° north, in the Arctic Ocean between Asia and America. Earlier still, in 1755, Krashininnokov, a Russian, recorded a mutton bird in the waters of the Kurile Islands, north of Japan.

In June and July of each year fishermen in these waters have frequently reported great groups of the birds feeding on the surface of the sea. But for many years the breeding grounds of these birds were a mystery.

It was taken for granted that there could be no connection between the northern hemisphere group and those of the Bass Strait islands, because if they were in fact the same birds, they could have taken only five to six weeks to fly more than 8000 kilometres from the time they were last seen in the islands south of Australia in April, and the time they were first seen north of Japan and the Aleutian Islands in June.

It was also at this time recognised by ornithologists that migratory birds usually choose the cooler of the two regions between which they migrate to breed. The temperature of the surface waters around the islands in Bass Strait from November to April was much higher (14 to 17° centigrade) than could be found at any time of the year in the north Pacific, where it dropped to 6°C. So, for many years, scientists were studying two groups of birds, the northerners who disappeared at breeding time, and the southerners who appeared at breeding time.

There were many odd things noticed by the scientists in Australia about this bird. It spent all its days at sea, coming to land only at night to scratch a burrow in the ground, like a rabbit, in which to lay its single large egg. The sexes couldn't be distinguished, and the bird's calendar was so regular that not only did the flocks appear on the breeding grounds exactly in the first week of September each year, but the female laid its single egg always between 20 November and 27 November. And when the bird tried to become airborne from the waves it appeared to walk over the water.

Dr Serventy, the world authority on the mutton bird, says, 'Probably no bird has brought people who come in contact with it so much under its spell as this one has, nor has any bird been written about so much.' I also fell under its spell and accompanied Dr Serventy's party to uninhabited islands banding birds.

Many unusual and interesting articles have been written on the mutton bird. Professor F. Wood Jones of Melbourne advanced the unusual theory that they were refugees from the moon. Writing in 1933, Professor Jones said:

> It is best not to mince matters but to declare boldly and in the face of all opposition that the moon came out of the Pacific; it could well fit into the Pacific void. And, when the moon went from the earth, what happened? Did she carry to a cold death a whole realm of earth life? Did she leave homeless some creatures that had made their home on her terrestrial surface?
>
> In the whole array of living things there is only one order that is homeless and is alien on any land; only one group that lives upon no continental mass, but owns the moon void as its playground and its scattered and mostly newly made islands as its only home.
>
> Every island of the moon void – that is, the Pacific – has its petrel and no petrel ever comes to land on any continent.
>
> Truly the birds of St Peter are birds of the moon. Of all birds they are birds of the Pacific void and have moon time for all their activities. There is perhaps as much mystery lurking in the story of the petrels as in that of the tides.

For a hundred years birds have been slaughtered here at the rate of half a million annually, yet apparently they never diminish in number.

In 1947 the Tasmanian Fauna Board and the CSIRO combined to solve these mysteries, detailing Dr Serventy to set up a field station on a small island in Bass Strait.

In order that they could be traced, Serventy decided to band every bird on the three rookeries on his island. A local policeman, Sergeant George Fisher, had already banded a few birds in an attempt to study their habits, and to honour him Serventy had the name of the island changed from Little Island to Fisher Island. On tiny Fisher Island, Serventy mapped and pinpointed every mutton-bird burrow. Over the years every bird has been banded, the metal strips bent around the bird's left leg with a pair of long-nosed pliers, and left loose enough to slip up and down. Each band carries a serial number and the request to contact the Fauna Board. The serial number allotted to each bird is entered in a detailed card index system. With this record Serventy's study began.

He became a sort of ornithological private eye. He knew where every bird and its mate lived on the island, when they went to bed, when they argued, when they were unfaithful, when they left home, and when their young were born.

Silas Mansell, a Cape Barren Islander, caught and held birds while Serventy fastened bands on legs. 'Doc, do these birds dilly-dally? Or are they faithful to each other year in year out.'

'I'll keep my eyes open and let you know,' Serventy told him.

It took a few years, but he eventually found the answer. 'Mostly they're faithful and mate year after year with the same partner. But sometimes they do dilly-dally.'

He produced leg band No. 12458, which had been placed on its wearer on 30 November 1951. The following year, Serventy's records showed it had been checked in at Fisher Island, still with the same mate of the previous year. In 1953 there was no record of it, but on 6 April 1954 just as dusk fell No. 12458 swooped in to land on Little Green Island, not quite a kilometre from Fisher Island. Serventy was there to capture it and make a note of its arrival. His records showed that its mate of 1951 and 1952 was occupying the same burrow on Fisher, but was breeding with another partner. 'So you see, Silas it happens in all walks of life.'

To compensate for that particular matrimonial split twenty-three other bands were recovered at their usual burrows, one bird, 10706, returning faithfully with the same mate for ten years.

The islanders had, of course, observed the bird's behaviour and habits for a century. They knew the timing of the remarkable pre-egglaying exodus. The birds come to the Furneaux group of islands in September, to scratch out their nests, and if possible occupy the same burrow each year. Then suddenly, during the first week in November, they desert the islands and every burrow is empty. It stays that way till the end part of the month when they all come ashore at dusk in a big cloud, swooping down to their burrows. The following day they lay their eggs.

The older islanders told Serventy that the one- and two-year-old birds didn't return to the breeding islands. After five years of banding, Serventy proved them right.

When the mutton-bird fledgling leaves its burrow it sets off on a first remarkable flight, not making a landfall until three or four years later. When it reaches the age of five it comes in with the mature breeding birds. Females begin to breed at from five to seven years; males from seven to eight years. For a bird of this size, its period of immaturity is very long.

While he was waiting for results of the banding on Fisher Island (which had ben set aside for research purposes), Serventy began banding birds on the near-by commercial islands, Big Dog, Little Dog, Chappell and Green Islands, and out at Babel Island, farthest east of all the islands in the strait.

These observations enabled him to make a rough estimate of the inroads the industry was making on the birds, and also to provide additional data to that being collected on Fisher, which was the home of only a hundred and twenty pairs of birds.

Between 1947 and 1956 he banded 16,870 fledglings on the commercial islands. Of these 9229 birds survived the hunters. As only fledglings are permitted to be harvested these birds will not be available to birders again, so there is little chance of their being exterminated as they were on Norfolk Island, where they were called 'the flying sheep'.

Serventy banded more than 20,000 birds both on commercial rookeries and in sanctuaries such as Fisher and Cat Island (near Babel Island). Most seasons he banded 2000 birds, usually 240 a day. On one day on Cat Island when I was with him he did a record number of 400.

Theoretically, there is only a small number of bands likely to be recovered but, remembering that in some other species of birds it has oddly enough been surprisingly high, Serventy is optimistic.

He wrote articles describing his banding programme and had them translated into various languages, including Japanese. These he sent to commercial fishermen's magazines in the hope that fishermen would return any bands they found.

Several Japanese did so. The first, No. 22208, was banded on Babel Island on 13 March 1955, and 75 days later, on 27 May, was found off Tanoura, Shikoku Island, 8,050 kilometres away. This proved conclusively that the northern and the southern hemisphere groups, originally thought to be two separate species, were one and the same.

The bird found by an Eskimo at St Lawrence Island in the Bering Sea was proved to have covered 8850 kilometres from the Bass Strait islands in less than a month. (That was the bird's first flight. It had been banded as a fledgling in the burrow in 1957.)

It also confirmed the main migration route plotted on the basis of museum specimens and of sight records of a Russian woman scientist, Madame Sudilovskaya, who had reported the bird as far north as Wrangel Island. As for the rule that migrating birds breed in the cooler of the two regions they inhabit, *Puffinus tenuirostris* is the exception.

As the bird spends most of its life on the wing, coming in to land only because of its breeding obligations, it develops a great power of flight. It has been known to wander 1000 kilometres and more away from the breeding islands for food.

To accommodate its moult to its migration the bird moults

head and body in the southern hemisphere, then waits until the long flight is over and it is safely in the northern hemisphere before moulting its wings and tail. At this time, the Eskimos report, the waters of the icy north are covered with its sooty brown feathers.

On the long migratory flight, which roughly resembles a figure eight, the birds are assisted all the way by the strength and direction of prevailing winds, except on the last leg of their flight back to the east coast of Australia. Then the south-east trade winds, which blow all the year round across the Pacific, batter them badly. Some years the birds suffer tremendous mortality at this spot on their circuit and thousands of their bodies are washed on to the beaches of New South Wales.

Banded birds that have been washed up on New South Wales beaches are usually only one-year-olds, the same age as those that became enmeshed in the Japanese fishing nets.

Because of their webbed feet and long wing span (over a metre) the birds cannot rise directly from the land, but must climb a rock or a cliff face to get the lift of a breeze under their wings.

To climb the steep rock face they beat the air furiously with their wings (my camera shutter set at a speed of 1/500th of a second couldn't 'stop' them) and scramble upwards, helped on the smooth rock by their webbed feet and beak. As often as they fall down they start upwards again, in silent determination to become airborne. They are clumsy on land, waddling along with their wings close to their bodies and their heads down, yet when they become airborne they are masters of flight. On their return to the islands to feed the young at night, they come in packed as close as flight permits, yet never collide.

When the ship went on the slip for her annual overhaul and the crew signed off, I sometimes stayed with Cape Barren

Islanders and here I learnt of 'the bird', as they called it.

The islanders' dependence on mutton birds dates back to the 1840s. When the seals were exterminated the islanders fell on hard times. There was no livelihood there for them any more. It was then they turned their attention to the strange grey bird that came to the islands out of the sea every September. They had watched it come in its myriad thousands at dusk and watched it scratch out a burrow. They knew that it laid its single egg there on roughly the same date every year, 28 November – and it was then that they collected the eggs and had a great feast, so the old people told me.

Observing that the bird ate plankton, krill, and small anchovies, they thought it might have the same oil content as whales, these also being the staple diet of the whale, so they trapped some birds and threw them in their old iron try-pots to boil down for oil.

Taking advantage of the birds' inability to take off from the ground, the islanders built fences of bark leading to pits they had dug. They drove the birds down between these fences until they had the pits full and then they smothered the birds with bark, merely for their feathers which were sold for mattresses and pillows.

Pounds and pounds of feathers are still sold every year. I couldn't think what the faint oily smell in my expensive sleeping bag was until I got my first smell of the birdin'. It was padded with mutton-bird feathers. The old islanders had a method of getting rid of the smell. They used to starve the birds to death in the pits and in this way no odour would be left on the feathers. This is, of course, now forbidden.

The next step was to taste the bird. At first they tried the adult birds and these they likened to old mutton, hence the name mutton bird. Then they tried the young bird. It tasted like neither fish nor fowl – its flavour was unique.

The birding developed into an industry that for many years provided the islanders' total income. The whole season is high excitement, the getting away to the 'birdin' islands' conjuring up the vision of adventure. One year I was on Cape Barren when the people were preparing to leave for the birdin'.

Jim Robinson's boat was loading at the wharf, taking on birders, a dog, a kitten, shoes in dishes, frying pans, kettles, pots, a child's toy motor car, bags of bedding, bundles of wood. Dray loads had been coming in since the early morning.

As they waited they chewed the tops out of yacca gum – one of the oldest known forms of vegetation, known as black-boy in other communities; they sucked the red sweet juice of the pig-face, *Mysembryanthemum*; and they ate she-oak apples and potato vines. I find the taste of most of these unpleasant except for yacca gum tops, which are both palatable and nutritious, and have the flavour of sweet corn. (A scientific expedition to the straits in 1912 brought gifts of toothbrushes and paste to the island children, but they found that eight out of twenty-five children had perfect teeth compared with one in five hundred at Port Melbourne, and this was credited to the wild plants the islanders ate.)

Dray loads of goods were still arriving, kettles and pots and pans clanking loosely among crates of fowls and tins of powdered milk. Many of the families had been camping around in the scrub near the beach for days waiting for the ship to come in, and these women were now sitting, staring out to sea from the hillside.

The tide had now gone out, and because the bottom here was rocky the ship could not rest on it but had to be anchored off-shore. Beatrice Everett suggested I might like to come to lunch at her home.

We sat on the floor of her dray, and the old horse plodded off up the sandy road, past the cemetery and in through the scrub that in places met over our heads. The cart jolted and bumped and several times I grabbed Beatrice Everett's arm to save myself from being thrown out as the road rumbled by.

Garland Grove, a comfortable house, had three bedrooms,

a porcelain bath and a hand basin. There were flowers everywhere. Her sister Minnie met us at the door when we arrived. Minnie was born completely deaf and consequently couldn't speak, but it was easy to communicate with her by sign language and laughter.

On the way back to the wharf I decided to travel on hands and knees in the dray. I was very tender. Minnie was with us this time as she was going to Babel Island too. Dalton Everett, the son of the family, was staying at home with his wife to look after the sheep on their property at Garland Grove. Minnie gave me a rug to sit on in the dray, but it wasn't much consolation – I was still sore for days afterwards.

7

Cat Island

I threw myself into everything that was part of the sea and the islands.

Travelling with Dominic Serventy and his bird-banding brigade was always a delight. There was the time we went to Cat Island, off Babel Island, to band gannets. Trooper Lew Bailey of the Tasmanian police took us out on the police boat *Aralla*, with Silas Mansell from Cape Barren Island as 'local knowledge', through the Vansittart Shoals.

'The wind and tide's got her!' was Lew's well-known cry when going through the Pot Boil. He was a good-enough sailor but never really at ease on the water. 'The department would hang, draw and quarter a man if he lost the *Aralla*,' he said. We went first to Babel Island to band shearwaters and waved goodbye to Lew from the top of Big Gulch. 'The wind and tide's got her!' Tas Drysdale shouted as the pretty little vessel began to head and tail it southwards in a rough sea.

It was March, summertime, warm and still on Babel. By midday each day we were weary, with sweat running down the back of our shirts, and hungry. Dom never cared for meals at midday in the field. Tas did care for meals, but if he couldn't eat he would at least have fun.

'Look at that medieval cathedral,' he'd call. 'Oh, Cromwell!' And he'd grab a long stick and off he'd charge. 'Down with the monasteries!' Whack, whack, whack! he'd belt an old fallen-down mutton-birder's shed. 'Come on Dom! After those monks!' Dominic would belt off down the valleys and over the rises, stick in hand, thwacking tussocks as he went. Then, 'Patsy! Remember your forebears in Connemara and County Galway. After Ludlow!' It was my turn. Over the rookeries I'd charge, belaying the perpetrators of ancient crimes as I triumphed over bush and grass clump. 'Beware the furious O'Flahertys!'

The three of us would rampage across the lonely island, until suddenly Dom said, 'Banding,' and off we would go, arms down burrows, hauling birds out for Dom to clip alloy bands on legs, shoving birds back down burrows, while Dom entered the numbers of the leg-bands in his field note-book. Hour after hour after hot hour.

When Dom was satisfied with his work, we put up a smoke and within a few hours the *Robert John* would sail in, pick us up from the rocks in Big Gulch and dump us on the tricky, rock-encircled Cat Island. It is a flat, featureless, tussock-covered islet, so named because a cat was loosed there many years ago. To observe the elegant gannets one must conceal oneself in the spiky tussocks that stick through trouser and shirt.

The gannetry on Cat Island is estimated to be built on a bed of guano five metres deep, evidence of the long period that the birds have been nesting there. The guano gives the whole nesting area a dazzling white appearance, providing camouflage for the fluffy white chicks as well as the sleek, white-plumaged nesting adults. When a party of ornithologists visited Cat Island in 1912 they found a teeming population of adult birds, newly hatched chicks, 'prospectors' (as the young male birds without a mate are called), and young females. They reported: 'One acre of ground was covered with the gannets' volcano shaped nest-mounds on which they lay their eggs and hatch their young. The birds all sat with their beaks pointing in one direction. It was a moving and beautiful sight.' They estimated that at least 10,000 birds were on the island.

When we arrived in 1959 there were two dozen. It is thought that in the past cray fishermen baited their pots with the bodies of these lovely birds until their numbers were so diminished there were not enough birds to warrant raiding the gannetry. And it was unlikely a colony could revive with so few birds left. It was said that 2500 birds were hatched in 1912. The year we banded on Cat only thirteen birds were hatched.

The nests of seaweed are seventy-four centimetres apart, just far enough for a bird to evade the razor-sharp beak of its neighbour. The newly-hatched chick is a remarkably ugly bag of bones, but it quickly sprouts fluffy white down and from here on is an enchantingly attractive creature. It becomes a speckled brown for camouflage as it begins to adventure into the brown tussock grass surrounding the rookery and eventually it achieves the snowy white adult plumage, its wings black-tipped, head and neck a beautiful golden amber, eyes, almost white, encircled with bright blue rings.

Long before it reaches this elegance, the young bird becomes anxious to become airborne. As even the adult bird finds this difficult the ungainly young hop and flop ludicrously over the ground, trying to catch an air current beneath their wings. For three days I watched one young bird struggling to become airborne, beating its wings vigorously and flapping about and falling over. Finally, in desperation, it struggled to a rock on the water's edge, flopped into the sea and swam off in the direction its elders had taken when they flew away.

Once up, the bird is skilled and graceful, and the sight of our gannets tumbling into the sea 'like snowflakes melting into the waves', as Tas said, thrilled us. 'Quick! Quick!' we'd call to one another when the birds sighted a shoal of fish and began diving, their wings folded in tightly to their bodies, streamlined, as they plummeted down.

The beak has a serrated inner edge, the barbs facing inwards to gaff fish. The parents brought most of their catch back to Cat to feed their young and in its anxiety to get at the food the chick dipped its beak so far into the beak of the parent bird it sometimes disappeared up to the neck as it tugged at a fish.

Banding was a tricky business. The bird is as big as a small goose, twice as fast, and has a razor-sharp beak. Unless it is held firmly it can inflict a painful wound, as each of us soon found out. It took two to band each bird, one to hold it while the other placed the band on its leg.

Dominic decided to band adult mutton birds here. The bird catcher did not come to the rookery this night, only Dominic, Tas and me. As these birds only come in to land after dusk we stumbled about the rookeries, falling over, shouting, laughing, roaring when a bird took umbrage and nipped us, yelling for one another to hold the torch still and stop flashing it round the sky like a search light as he – or she – fell over. And then, suddenly, we were four, not three. Tas shone the torch on the face of a man he had never seen before. 'I thought someone was getting killed over here,' Johnny Lipscombe the fisherman told us. 'I anchored off-shore and saw flashing lights and heard shouting and yelling . . . struth! It gave a man quite a turn.'

Johnny Lipscombe had had bad luck. Three weeks before

we came out to Babel I'd seen him unload his whole catch of crayfish into the sea at Lady Barron. Eager, anxious, teetering on the brink of financial disaster as are many other fishermen, he had brought in too many crays on his first catch and they had died through lack of space. Poor Johnny. The instalments on a boat are heavy and the demands must be met promptly. He could have only one more chance – this was it.

After we had been at Cat Island a few days Johnny came ashore one night with a bag of scale fish for us. He had caught no crays. When he left us to row back out to his boat anchored in the bay I told the field party of his bad luck. Tas Drysdale said nothing, but later in the night he began carving into a cuttlefish. He had done several of these during the day. Now he sculptured a fearsome face, elongated, tiki-like, hair flowing down the side of the pumice material, carved in maritime symbols and things of the sea. Two of us were to go out to Johnny's boat in the morning and go with him to pull his pots during the day.

'Take this and give it to him,' Tas said. 'Tell him he must throw it into the water, into the sea, where he casts his pots.'

I should have liked to keep it. I looked at it a long time. It was so beautiful a thing to appease a cruel, wanton, capricious god. But I took it out to Johnny in the morning and he cast it into the sea when he shot his pots. That evening, when we went back out near the continental shelf, where the flags of the marker buoys bent down in the gale that was coming up, we all had to lend a hand when Johnny hauled in: each pot was so laden and the crayfish were so big.

When dawn came a jubilant Johnny sailed back into our bay and came ashore to help us carry our gear. He had come to return us to Lady Barron, through the Vansittart Shoals and the black Pot Boil, jubilant in the rolling heaving sea.

8

In the Manner of a Grand Actor

For most of the time I was in the *Sheerwater* Honest Tom was also a semi-permanent floating resident. Tom's real name was Thomas Langley Esquire. He was local postmaster, storekeeper, baker, taxi proprietor, town councillor, churchwarden, agent, fish buyer, mutton-bird dealer, hardware merchant, grocer, and tailor at Lady Barron on Flinders Island. He threw himself so wholly into each one of these undertakings that, in the manner of a grand actor, he would lose himself completely in the part.

I had seen him only once before he came aboard the *Sheerwater*. It was at the local Council Chambers. He was dressed in slick, city fashion then – narrow-lapelled coat, bob-tailed tie, and highly polished shoes. That day he was a councillor representing his ward.

When he came aboard I realised he had shed that role. He was now the bird buyer.

'Honest Tom, they call me,' he introduced himself affably. 'Honest Tom, the Birder's friend.'

He wore sandshoes without laces, 'So I can kick them off easily if the boat sinks.' And an old coat and overalls, 'In case anyone throws anything at me.' The *Sheerwater* was, this day, taking the birders and their gear to the small islands in Franklin Sound where they are legally permitted to bird. In all, five islands are released by the Government Fauna Board to be birded. One of these, Babel Island, is by itself out to the east of Flinders Island; the other four are Big Dog, Little Dog, Green and Chappell Islands.

Honest Tom was shipping empty barrels and bags of salt to Big Dog Island, where he leased stands of birding areas from the Government. On each he had built sheds and living huts to which he sent teams of workers. From the word go, Honest Tom and these teams had but one thought in their minds – how best to 'diddle' one another.

Tom's side of the bargain was to supply the teams with barrels and salt, provisions for eight weeks, and transport to and from the islands. In return they agreed to bird his stand and sell the processed birds to him at a certain fixed price. It all seemed clear and reasonable.

The fun began when we were still tied up at Lady Barron wharf. Some of his island families had come there ready for transport to Big Dog Island. We were just about to sail when a whole family, a complete team for one stand, stepped back on to the wharf.

'Sorry, Tom, old man,' the father said. 'We can't come.'

'Why?'

'No clothes.'

'Who hasn't no – I mean any clothes?' Tom was still a few jumps behind.

'Me and the missus. Not a stitch to stretch between us.'

'Well, what's that you're wearing?'

This was the opening the birder had been waiting for. He pounced, 'Cut it out, old man. These are the Sunday clothes of the missus and me.' He turned to a knot of others on the wharf. 'Did you hear him? He wants us to bird for him in our Sunday clothes now!' He turned back to Tom. 'Well, that's the limit that is. I have been birdin' man and boy for sixty years and me father before me and his father and so forth, but I never heard better than that. You'll have to do a lot better old man if you want to get a team.' Facing the other teams on deck now, 'Hear what he said? Honest Tom the birder's friend. Ha ha!'

The men on deck began to mutter. One of them lifted his suitcase up on to the bulwarks.

'Where are you going?' Honest Tom asked. 'Now hold on a minute.' Desperately. He could see his whole army vamoosing even before the season began.

'What do you need?'

The first birder who had spoken swiftly whipped a tatty piece of paper out of his pocket and gave it to Tom.

Tom read it. Half-way through he said, 'Two pair of ladies bloomers? Hey! cut it out!'

'Well,' the birder replied earnestly, 'one pair would wear out before birdin' was over, like as how she's sittin' down pluckin' most of the day.' That seemed to finish Honest Tom. He told Les he'd be back in a jiffy, and went off in the direction of his drapery shop. He returned with a bundle of clothes.

The next round went to Tom.

At Big Dog Island he was approached by a private lessee of one of the stands who offered to sell Tom his birds without any outlay on Tom's part for the same price as he, Tom, was offering his birders from his own stand.

Tom naturally accepted and just as naturally didn't want nearly so many birds from his own stand, so he didn't put out the usual number of barrels. It was a while before his team realised what was happening, because getting ashore at the birdin' islands is chaos. Apart from men, wives, and families, there were hens, roosters, and chickens, bedding rolls and mattresses, a baby's bath with pumpkins in it, kerosene tins with wire handles and full of bath towels, sugar bags bulging with clothing, cats hidden under overcoats so the Health Department, who forbade cats on birdin' stands, wouldn't see them, and toys and Easter eggs because they would be there over Easter. The ship was about to move on round the island when the head of the team realised he had not been given enough barrels, or salt. He guessed what had happened. Tom was ashore and was trying to get back on board before the storm burst, but he was only half-way down the beach when the man, his wife, his brothers, and two women came running after him.

We were all out on deck to watch. Tom was running along at a smart canter, but when he heard the team in pursuit he broke it down to a fast but dignified walk, with his eyes on the ship's boat waiting for him out near the breakers. He rolled his trouser legs up while he was still on the move and headed into the water to walk diagonally to the boat. But the team followed him into the water and half-way out they caught up with him. He kept walking. The men were on either side of him, their arms waving like windmills. The women weren't able to keep up the pace and were floundering along in his wake until one of them managed to grab the tail of his coat and then skied along behind him. Tom kept bravely on, his snowy, prematurely grey head erect, his chin up.

Then, as suddenly as they had come, the birders turned and retreated. When he got to the ship's side we wanted to know what he had said to pacify them. He had told them he would be back, he was only going to the ship to find out why Wallaby hadn't put more of his barrels ashore. 'Alas,' he said in his charming voice, waving goodbye to the birders as the ship moved on, 'business so often prevents a gentleman from keeping his word.' On shore the birders were running up and down, shaking their fists and screaming. 'Bye, bye, old chap,' Tom called. 'Cheerio, my dear,' to a lady, who made a very rude gesture.

Tom had come from a mainland city where he managed a chain of grocery stores. 'I intended to make my fortune in five years on the islands and then retire to Queensland's Gold Coast for the rest of my life.' That was probably the most honest thing he ever said, for most people think these islands are treasure troves. The first settlers to the islands went there with the idea of loot, and it's an idea that has persisted subconsciously ever since.

Why did he stay?

'These islands get a hold on you. Once they get into your blood you can never stay away. Besides, I don't know if I could do without the excitement.' Tom was definitely an islander now. The islanders abused him to his face and stuck up for him behind his back, a thing they'd never do for an outsider.

'Honest Tom!' they'd snort. 'That'll be the day!' But let anyone else say it in that tone of voice and they'd throw down their hats in the time-honoured manner of islanders wanting a fight.

The Cape Barren Islanders loved his wife, Barbara. 'That Honest Tom!' they'd say, 'he's a rogue. But his wife's a white woman!' Tom revelled in the prefix 'Honest' before his name. Barbara naturally didn't like it. If Barbara had seen her Tom chased down the beach by outraged islanders as often as we did in the two months of the season, she would have been surprised.

One year a new bird buyer came on the scene. He was a gigantic man with a stomach protruding so far in front of him that Pete said if he fell over, he'd rock backwards and forwards for twenty minutes before he could regain his feet.

'Just call me Jack,' he boomed as he came down to the ship to make arrangements to ship his barrels. 'A trustworthy old name for a trustworthy man,' he said heartily.

From then on he was naturally known as Trustworthy Jack.

Honest Tom and Trustworthy Jack took to each other at their first meeting. The one was small, neat, and immaculate, the other was gross and untidy, but they were both shrewd business men. They quickly summed each other up. They knew it was going to be war – whether it was to be a friendly war or a bitter and exhausting battle was up to them. They chose the former. It was ding-dong, hammer and tongs, no-holds-barred war, but by their standards friendly; by ours very funny.

The first thing Trustworthy Jack did when he came on board the *Sheerwater* was go down into the hold and paint over the initials on Tom's barrels and replace them with his own. Not all the barrels, of course; just enough for it not to look suspicious.

When Honest Tom went down there he recognised the signs immediately. 'I grew out of that ten years ago,' he said disgustedly to us as he came up. His remedy was simple. He went to Trustworthy Jack's office (Jack was very posh, he kept his books in a corner of a cool store). Tom asked could he put a phone call through. 'Sure,' said the affable Jack and waited to listen. Honest Tom phoned the police at Whitemark. He told them he was short of barrels. 'They just might have been pinched,' he said. 'Then again they might be lying on the wharf somewhere; I'm pretty careless you know. Just thought I'd let you know. If they don't turn up by lunch time I'll give you another tinkle and you can get on the trail.'

So poor, fat Trustworthy Jack had to go down into our hold again and remove his own paint and repaint Tom's initials. But he didn't have the same colour paint as Tom had used. There was only one thing he could do. He had to borrow the paint from Honest Tom.

Almost daily they pulled some trick on each other. On shore, the birders told us, they spent more time trying to outsmart each other than they did trying to buy birds.

I staggered into the midst of one of their wars one day and was wounded so severely I could hardly walk for days after. Tom and Jack were both on shore on Big Dog Island, and Les had told them he'd send word when he was ready to leave. Like many odd jobs that no one else wanted, it fell to me to go.

'Which direction are they in?' I asked.

'Towards Riddle's.' When I tramped to Riddle's they hadn't had a visit from either all morning, but they had seen Honest Tom walk off towards Dave Rhodes's. I headed towards Dave Rhodes's, through the scrub and over the burrow-riddled rookeries. Some of the rookeries were covered with low scrub, others with tussocks. But no matter how carefully you walked you couldn't avoid the burrows. Flinders had estimated that the birds burrow one in every square metre, but in places it would be double that density. As the morning wore on and I trekked after the two buyers, who were busy somewhere trying to outwit each other, I stumbled into and out of burrows so often it seemed I was walking knee-deep in the ground. Sometimes both my legs would disappear at the one time down separate burrows.

When I got to Rhodes's shed Dave told me both the buyers had been there. 'It was an accident,' he said. 'They came creeping out of the scrub in opposite directions and nearly collided.' He told me they each had the same idea. 'Each wants the other to get to a shed first so that he can come in after him and offer a little more.' Consequently they were now dodging around the hills and valleys and patches of scrub on the island, doubling back when they were hidden from view, making bold, decoying sallies when they were in sight. I floundered after them. I knew where all the sheds were from the seaward side, but on land I was bushed. I'd come stumbling down a rookery and have to walk right round the front of the shabby buildings before I knew where I was. Once I stepped on a man who was lying stretched out flat among the tussocks with his arm down a burrow. I don't know who got the biggest fright, but I know who was most abused.

It was while I was up on this rookery suffering the righteous abuse of this birder that I saw the ship sailing off round the island. I didn't know it, but the two buyers were back on board and Les was now looking for me. I began to run after it. By the time I reached the beach it had gone round the corner. I cut across the island, thinking to get to one of the bays before it, but the bay, like the huts, was unfamiliar from land and I missed it, and the ship sailed on again. I reached the stand of the Willises, a white birdin' family, and they said Les had sent word in to tell me to keep coming.

I was too nervous to stop for the cup of tea Mrs Willis offered me, and stumbled onwards, dot and carry, with one leg always down a burrow. I was soon sorry I hadn't accepted the offer of tea, because most of the time birders are too busy to worry about the social niceties, and if you happen along at the time when they are not having tea, then it is not offered.

Once I got close enough to the ship to see Les, watching through his telescope my graceless descent across a rookery, but when he pointed at a beach and signalled me to go there, I lost my way again. I climbed to the top of Big Knob, the highest point on the island, and from there I couldn't see the ship at all.

Eventually they picked me up in front of the Willises, the next stand to Riddle's, where I had first gone ashore.

I was much too weary and sore to mind their ribbing. My hands were painful with gravel rash where they'd taken the brunt of the many falls I'd had in the sandy-soiled rookeries, and my legs were aching. I cursed the two who had been responsible, and swore I'd never go chasing them again.

9

The Beautiful Evil

Babel Island is beautiful. The islanders say it is evil. They say 'it goes out after you'. But still they say it is beautiful, and they love it.

Separated from the northern end of Flinders Island by only a narrow sand spit, it is nevertheless the most isolated and hardest to visit of all the islands in the group. To get to it you must leave Lady Barron and go out through the treacherous Vansittart Shoals and the dreaded Pot Boil.

On my first trip to Babel I travelled in the *Margaret Twaits*, one of Les Jackson's three ships. At that time the *Sheerwater* had a male cook who helped with the heavy loading. The captain of the *Margaret Twaits* had not been to Babel Island before so, as the chart advised, he brought 'local knowledge' with him. I didn't know where this 'local knowledge' was and nearly sat on it before it materialised.

Honest Tom the birder's friend and some health inspectors were on board. The birders were sitting on deck, 'Corner Coves', after The Corner, their settlement on Cape Barren Island, Pete now called them; 'Shady Characters' black Leedham Maynard said. My friend Beatrice Everett wasn't among them. Her gear was on board and she had been too until a few minutes before the ship sailed.

As the lines were being let go she clambered back on to the wharf, taking deaf Minnie her sister with her. 'I couldn't bear it,' she said. 'I'm scared, afraid.'

I thought it must have been her first time to go out to Babel, but no, she said she was first taken out there as a baby more than sixty years ago and had been going regularly ever since. 'But I'm always the same,' she said. 'I'm always scared, I'll try to get out some other way.'

You couldn't go out by road and in those days tiny planes had not begun to land on the beach as they sometimes do now. I thought Babel wouldn't see her that year, but she said confidently, 'Would you watch that they put my gear off at Little Gulch for me. Otherwise it might go ashore anywhere at all on the island and I'll have to hump it all the way round to my stand.'

She gave me a list of the things belonging to her that were in the hold and I wrote them on the back of my notebook; I have it still. It reads: One bedding roll with blue patch on outside; one kerosene can with vegetables; one iron kettle; an iron camp oven; one port tied with brown shoe lace; oval boiler; Tilley light; big tea chest with tenting over top; cardboard Fluid Magnesia box.

None of the others chided her for being so afraid, and I soon saw why; they were all just as afraid as she was and couldn't be sure how they would react once we got under way.

When we got to the Pot Boil they took one look over the side and buried their faces in their laps. I looked over the side then. I was standing up in the wheelhouse, so I couldn't put my head in my lap. I shut my eyes instead.

We were sailing through a black maelstrom; inky black with oily smooth circles within circles of suction. There was not a sea bird near. Not a thing moved on that surface except us. There was no wave, no ripple, no foam, nothing but the smooth, silent, black circles.

It was still early in the morning and in the dull light I saw a pile of bags and old coats in a corner of the wheelhouse. I went to sit on it but it seemed unsteady so I just stood and looked out at the Pot Boil.

There was no motion in the ship here. It just slid along the top of the oily surface. It was sinister.

'It gives me the creeps,' Honest Tom said.

He was one of the few men ever to escape from the Pot Boil. He was in a small boat he owned named the *Lady Margaret*. At that time he was buying fish, as 'Honest Tom the fisherman's friend'. There were three others with him: two men to work the boat, and a parson. The parson wished to give a service on Babel Island and Tom offered him a lift, but in the middle of the Pot Boil their motor cut out. They weren't very worried at first because it was a small fault that could be easily remedied. But as they tinkered with the engine they drifted to the edge of the Pot Boil. The maelstrom is caused by riptides sweeping through between the islands and meeting above an uneven, shallow sea floor. At the edge where the *Lady Margaret* drifted were shoals, over which the sea broke heavily, and as they drifted on to them the sea broke over the boat and flooded their engine. There was nothing they could do now but swim for it. Tom is a very strong swimmer and he set out for the shore. The others hit the sand shoals and waded to safety.

The islanders tell and retell this story. 'Not even the Pot Boil could catch Honest Tom,' they say.

But Honest Tom no longer trusted it. He mumbled execrations at it all the while we slid over it.

Then we went straight out of it without an interval into the Vansittart Shoals. Stretching for miles east of Flinders and Vansittart Islands, these shoals are of hard-packed sands. They are uncharted because they are constantly moving – a hopeless puzzle to any but the locals who know them.

First one crazy sea hit the ship and rolled it one way, then a second rolled it the other way.

'She's always like this,' Tom said gloomily. 'Rough.'

There was a sound like a fire siren on deck. Then another, and another, until it sounded like Sydney the night the war ended. It was the islanders. Quiet as we passed over the Pot Boil, they now let go of their control. 'And they're always like this too,' Tom added.

The fear came on them so suddenly it was like a fit. They were not conscious of anything but their fear. Two young lovers who had been spooning near the rail stretched out on deck and plastered themselves together, he as terrified as she. The old ladies were the noisiest, but the old men looked the most frightened. Some young chaps tried to appear nonchalant, but their eyes looked like those of frightened horses. Even the children joined in the caterwauling, it was so contagious. I nearly accompanied them. But I didn't expect Honest Tom suddenly to throw back his head and howl like a dog.

For a while we couldn't understand what he was saying, he was capering round and thumping his chest so furiously. Then he calmed down. 'My teeth,' he lisped. 'I've just remembered I left my false teeth at home.' With the possibility of weeks of tough food ahead of him at Babel his despair was profound.

The pile of bags and coats I had been going to sit on began to stir, and in the rosy light of dawn I saw a hand come out, an arm, a body, and then a head with a high-crowned hat jammed firmly down on the ears. The owner of all this rubbed his whiskers, stood up, righted a few bottles that were sticking out of his pockets, and very formally said good morning.

Bill Barrett was a member of a white family that had lived on the islands almost as long as the islanders. He and his brother owned Long Island, but Bill spent most of his time in the small boats. Now with his local knowledge he was to pilot the *Margaret Twaits* through the Vansittart Shoals; he'd been alseep here in the corner since the previous night, yet he knew the moment the ship entered the shoals and woke himself up as promptly as if an alarm had rung.

He stood right up on the bow of the ship and signalled with his hands, a little to starboard, a little to port. The spray came over and drenched him, but he didn't move. He looked like a mahogany figurehead on our bow.

Near the point that those with 'local knowledge' use to turn towards Babel is the wreck of the *Farsund*. Any resemblance of self-control among the islanders was lost when she came into view. As the gale had driven her on to the shoals in 1912, the swirling sands quickly filled her holds, giving her ballast to stand upright, and as the years went by she became fast in the sand beneath and within her, as upright as when she had sailed the seven seas. Her three masts and yard-arms were still intact in the days when first I was at sea. Later only two masts remained.

If the *Farsund* were not there on the shoals, the danger might be vague, unreal, and you might be able to feel that nothing could happen to you – but not with that thousand tonne ship wrecked where your eighty-two tonne tramp is attempting to pass. You knew all right. All around you the sea is wild as the waters roll in and hit the mountains of sand. As the sun came up it lent colour to the scene and showed the shallow patches pale green and milky yellow where the loose sand swirled. The deep patches were blue, the shoals capped with white waves where the sea broke on sand only a short distance beneath the surface.

Whenever a wave slapped the ship the islanders screamed.

'How I wish they'd shut up!' one of the crew said.

They affected everyone; even old Bill Barrett up on the bow looked round at them prostrate on the deck every once in a while, then resumed his signalling – a litle more to starboard, now to port, more, more, more, farther yet, right, steady. And when the ship turned you could see the shoals there below the water near the wake the ship left behind. It's probably these hateful shoals that make Babel look so beautiful, because all the time you're in the shoals you can see her twin peaks ahead and you know there are no shoals like these around her, and you think you've never seen anything quite so beautiful as that blue island.

The smaller peak the birders call High Hill; the larger, Shark Mouth. Under High Hill is Big Gulch, where Les's sister Phyl, who once cooked for him in the *Sheerwater*, had a house built on the cliff top. She came here to start a small shop, which she kept during the birding and where she housed the health inspectors, the bird buyers, and now, generously, me.

I'd found relics of her in the *Sheerwater*. Jelly moulds, now battered out of shape and used for patching woodwork; cake-tins, now belted in between timbers to stop them from creaking, and odd packets of mouldy jellies, junket tablets, and other delicacies I knew no one but she would have used. The nearest I ever got to a compliment in that ship was when Les looked at my scrubbed floors and said, 'It's nearly as clean as Phyl used to get it.' I was anxious to meet her. She was a beautiful girl, the only true ash blonde I've ever seen. Her personality was so charming that no one had thought to add that she had been crippled since childhood and could neither walk nor stand upright. Using her arms for leverage she swung deftly from place to place, gaining support from the backs of chairs and door frames. She was rarely still. She baked bread, cleaned the house, made the beds, played cards savagely and for keeps, and bullied the birders. Just as the others had, I forgot her disability.

Leedham Maynard was staying at her house. She chaffed and teased him and laid all sorts of booby traps for him. In return he silently adored her and showed off whenever she was looking. One day I got the benefit of this. He was birding part way up High Hill, threading birds on a wooden spit through the soft part of the beak. Usually a man carries at the most from forty to fifty of these birds at the one time. They weigh up to a kilogram each so this is quite a weight on the man's shoulders as he picks his way over the uneven, burrow-riddled ground.

I was sitting down on the rocks in Big Gulch watching Leedham up the hill. I had on a big hat I'd taken from behind the door in Phyl's house, and for a change I'd put a skirt on. From the distance my skirt and the old hat must have reminded him of Phyl. He decided that only the best was good enough for her. Other men might bring one spitload of birds down – he would bring two. With one balanced on each shoulder he walked erect down the slope, his blue-black face and chest glistening in the bright sunlight, his black hair shining, a smile on his handsome face.

But it hadn't been done for my benefit. This was the man whose battered body was fished out of the Tamar River a few years later. The coroner had no option but to proclaim the cause of death unknown.

Beatrice Everett arrived out in the *Alicia*. We saw the little fishing boat coming miles away and watched as it battled through the seas. One minute it was high in the air, the next we could see only its mast as it dropped into a trough. Yet sitting up on deck, smiling happily, were Beatrice and Minnie. 'I always feel better in a little ship,' Beatrice said when they were ferried ashore.

But not everyone felt the same as Beatrice. Jim, the boat owner, told us he'd had to lock two girls below decks because they attempted to throw themselves over the side in fear when they were going through the Vansittart Shoals.

The *Margaret Twaits* had gone now, and the *Alicia* left as soon as she got the birders ashore. One day, as Phyl and I talked over the breakfast washing up, a knot of islanders came to the door. After a lot of preamble they helped a fourteen-year-old boy forward. He was hopping on one foot. The other foot was slit up the middle and hanging open.

'I cut it with an axe,' he said apologetically.

While Phyl got some clean cloth I cut the sandshoe and sock off. The lad's name was Claude Mansell and he was a charming little boy, well mannered, but so uncomplaining that in the end I had to say, 'Cry, kid, for God's sake cry!' I was sponging his foot and it must have been extremely painful. The foot was very dirty, for washing facilities on the island are poor and the soil is singularly filthy. I wanted to get as much of the dirt from it as I could, but it was bleeding so much that I could hardly see the skin.

The islanders had left us alone with him and gone back to their huts; before they went they dropped the remark that there had been two cases of tetanus on the island in the past two years. 'One bloke died.' Then they pointed at Phyl and she held up one hand with a finger missing. 'Two years ago,' she said. 'I got out on a fishing boat as soon as I could, but the doctor had to take my finger to save my life.'

We were between the Devil and the deep blue sea . . . whether to bind the boy's foot tightly to prevent the loss of blood or keep it open and cleanse it to prevent tetanus.

The cut was between the big toe and the next, and gaping open. I flushed it with water and for the split second before the blood gushed again I could see the dirt the axe had dragged up into the cut. I thought the boy would die if we didn't get him off the island.

'Yes,' said Phyl in her matter-of-fact way. 'We'll have to get him off.' She left me and was gone a long time. When she came back we had lunch, mutton birds, and I stayed with the boy while she went out again. We had his foot propped up high, but still the blood flowed out. Everything Phyl gave me to wrap round it was dripping with red blood now.

When she returned she said, 'The ship's here, we'll take him down.'

'Ship? What ship?' There had been no ship near the island, there was no boat on the island and no radio to send for help. Where has a ship come from so opportunely?

'We signalled for it,' she said. 'It's just coming up now. We put up a smoke.'

I went out into the sunlight and there it was up on the hill, a sulky coil of smoke spiralling upwards from the green wood fire, and across to the east was another one. The lighting of two fires is to prevent confusion. One smoke may be someone burning rubbish, two on separate hillocks are always a call for help. And help had come. The *Margaret Twaits* had seen the smoke on the horizon and returned, and the *Robert John*, the fishing boat, had come in from the craying grounds. It was decided to send the boy in the *Margaret Twaits*, as it was quicker and roomier. Bill and Ted aboard the *Robert John* would send a message over their radio warning the doctor on Flinders Island of our dash with the injured boy. The *Margaret Twaits*'s boat was brought into Big Gulch and Claude and I were lowered down a steep wooden whim. Leedham was at the bottom to catch us up as we slid by and put us over the rocks into the boat with the boy still in my arms.

The captain gave Claude his bunk. The cabin was so spotless that I felt like wiping my shoes on the legs of my slacks like Pete did before I entered. He brought me two clean sheets for the boy's foot, gave him chocolate and a cup of tea, and then got the ship under way.

Claude was quiet and good. He had lost much blood and was very weak, but he smiled and said 'Thank you' every time I did anything for him. He was such a nice lad and so brave I thought I would offer to nurse him in the bush hospital when we got him safely in.

The sea was fairly calm, but once when the ship rolled his foot fell off the support we had made for it, and blood spurted out through the sheet we had wrapped round it. The captain got out two more sheets and then another two. The foot was bound tightly, but still it bled. The captain decided it didn't look too good. 'We must get him in quicker. We won't be able to go via the outer channel,' he said. That channel was the one we had come out through, and by now he would have known it reasonably well. 'I'm going to have a go at the inner channel.'

We had been steaming a couple of hours when I left the boy and went out on deck. We were in the midst of the shoals. They were the way the seamen like to see them best of all, with heavy seas breaking over them showing them up as clearly as white painted fences down either side of the ship. Then suddenly a fence appeared across in front of us, a wall of broken water. We had steamed into a trap. 'Hardaport!' the captain bellowed. 'Get her round!' He and the helmsman both swung their weight on to the wheel and together they began to spin her. The ship bumped once, then twice as they strained silently, desperately, at the wheel. Then we were in deep water again, heading back the way we had come, to stand out the long way round to Lady Barron.

It was dark when we tied up at the wharf. I was weary and a bit sick from the smell and the sight of blood and the vomit of the sick boy on my head, my arms and hands – wherever the rolling of the ship had sent it as I tended him. Claude was whisked off to Whitemark hospital while I was cleaning myself up. I phoned later and asked after him, but there was no need of my help. He wasn't there. They had stitched his foot up and let him go.

'Where will he sleep?' I asked the captain.

'In the scrub, on the ground.'

10

The Corner

The *Margaret Twaits* sailed off, back to the voyage our 'smoke' had interrupted. I was now 'on the beach' as the men say, waiting for a ship to turn up. And one did. Tuck Robinson appeared and called out to me: 'Well! Are ya comin' or ain't ya?' Tuck was in a hurry to get to the island for a funeral. I climbed onto *Tassie*, his pride and joy, the small craft he used as a mail boat to Cape Barren Island.

Charlie Saville took our line at The Corner. 'So you've come to visit us at last,' he said.

'You knew this man,' Charlie Saville said. 'You knew what George was like in life better than I did.' Charlie didn't mince words. He was there to read the burial service and to tell of another life that he believed in. His eulogy of the dead man was as simple as the procession to the grave on Cape Barren Island.

Charlie's wife Una, a triple-certificated nursing sister, had laid out the corpse. Charlie had shrouded it and made up the coffin. When the time came for the body to be buried the island men took the coffin out to the cart and, with all the islanders walking alongside, the horse began to trundle down the track from the two-roomed house to the road.

The small wooden church at The Corner was open. Una was playing the organ, dressed now for the funeral.

Now the day is over,
Night is drawing nigh;
Shadows of the evening
Steal across the sky.

The coffin rested on four chairs from Una's kitchen.

When Charlie had finished, the men carried the coffin back to the cart and the walk to the cemetery began. One of the Everetts stood in the cart to drive the horse; Ucky Mansell the grave-digger walked in front. Ucky was very short, under five feet, and getting old, so he couldn't walk as fast even as the old horse. Instead of him leading the animal it seemed that the horse was pushing Ucky along. Once it leaned over Ucky's shoulder and nuzzled him. The old man pushed the horse's head back, but the walk in the deep sand made Ucky weary, and before the pine trees at the cemetery were reached he let the horse rest its head over his shoulder and plodded soberly onwards.

Walking with the cart were the whole island population, stretched out on either side in the bush because the track was so narrow. A couple of little boys, playing around throwing pebbles at one another, were quickly grabbed by their mothers. 'You behave yourself or you'll be taken off the island,' they berated the children. 'They'll take you away,' as though to be taken away from the island was the ultimate in punishment.

At the cemetery the grave, two metres deep, was ready. Some of the graves cannot be dug so deep as the soil is too hard. Charlie Saville spoke again, 'He that believeth in me, saith the Lord, though he be dead shall live.' Near by were the graves of babies and little children and sailors. 'Sleep my beloved. Sleep and take thy rest' over the grave of 'To the sacred memory of Adam Newitt, accidentally drowned 13th October 1895 aged 49 years.' Not far away his captain lay beneath another stone. 'In remembrance of Captain James Mulligan who was drowned in the wreck of the Ketch *GVH* October 13th 1895 aged 40 years. Also Oscar Ackland, native of Sweden. Rest in Peace.'

All the soil had now been shovelled into the grave, and the women and children came up with wreaths and bunches of flowers. Some of the posies were of wildflowers, untamed, beautiful things, too fragile to bear being torn up and bound, and they wilted and died. Everyone knew this man, most were related to him; some of the children had never known his surname. The only man called mister on Cape Barren was Charlie Saville. The duties connected with his position as teacher on the island were many: Special Police Constable number 200, minister of religion, undertaker, radio operator, diesel engineer with a 4½ h.p. motor that gave light to the church hall, the school, and the school house; librarian, Poll Officer, and shoe mender. He had to kill sheep, milk a cow, and grow vegetables. A bush lawyer by necessity rather than by choice, he must also fill out social service forms and stock and crop returns. A good boatman, he ferried passengers out to coasters unable to come in to the wharf. The islanders tell the story of the day a cow fell off the wharf and Charlie dived in after it. 'Boots and all,' they say. As captain of the island footbeall team, he encouraged the 'white' teams on Flinders

Island to challenge the Cape Barreners. 'That's right, Charlie. You go through the lot of them!' the islanders called, forgetting his surname in the excitement. Una, his wife, taught sewing in the school, played the organ in church, nursed the sick.

There was a knock on the door in the middle of the night. It was one of the Maynards. The father was ill. Could Mrs Saville come at once. It was midnight. The old man had been in bed for days. Why had they not come for her before? I asked.

'You'd never make a bush nurse,' Una told me as we set off on the cart behind young Maynard, jolting through the bush, the little bag of equipment clasped in Una's arms. When we left the road the bush sprang in on us, and we were constantly ducking to escape low branches and twigs. The cart rumbled and jerked and lurched.

The house was indistinguishable from the bush. I never saw it in daylight, but at night it seemed that we stepped straight through the foliage of dense undergrowth into it. The cart driver, holding back some greenery, told us to go in and called to the inmates, 'She's here.'

Nothing but a troupe of midgets could have stumped through that door without bending in two, it was so low. Inside, by the dim glow from a near-dead fire, Una went to work. The old man was on a bed on the floor. He was not dangerously ill. There were several people in the room; you could sense rather than hear them, and I was standing upright. There was a cough near my ear as though from someone suspended from the ceiling. I screamed and leapt aside.

'There's someone in a bunk on the wall,' Una calmed me, going on with her work. All around the wall it seemed there were people levitated, unsupported. I was glad to be back on the cart, jolting along in the mysterious glow of the false dawn.

11

The Sea Forever Waits

I had by now found out that the *Sheerwater* was not the *Queen Mary* of the merchant fleet and that I could scarcely have got myself a berth in a tougher ship. In fact I've often been asked how she managed to get a crew at all with the rough conditions on board.

The answer was simple. There was always something of interest happening, and it was the happiest ship afloat, with laughter never far away. All other ships, when they were forced to shelter in bad weather, were full of the most miserable, bad-tempered men. No seaman worth his salt likes going on the anchor.

But the *Sheerwater* got as much fun out of going on the anchor as going into port. At one time, near the end of the birdin', we were on anchor at Babel for many days. The seas were too rough to work in and the winds too strong to go home in, so for two weeks, in company with seven fishing boats, we were sheltered in a bay on Flinders Island called The Cellar.

At night the lights of the fishing boats were a little city around us and we'd stand on deck and argue about which was which, the *Black Witch*, the *Robert John*, the *Fair Venture*, the *Eden Star*, or the *Gazelle* which we called the *Guzzle*. In time you came to recognise a ship at night by the position of her lights, or sometimes her peculiarities; during the day, even from a great distance, by the height of her mast or the position of her deck house and, when the whole ship was scarcely visible, by what my grandmothers called 'feeling'.

To fill in a day, when it was too bad to get into the beaches to load, we went for a trip in the *Fair Venture* when they were 'shooting' their cray pots.

The little ship dipped and dived in a way the bigger *Sheerwater* never did. Talk about a bushman's holiday! We rolled and pitched and got wet through and had a scratch meal just as if we were back in the *Sheerwater*.

During the day Ray Friend, the skipper-owner, had received a message over his radio intended for Peter Pickett, a young fisherman on a boat that had no radio, so we bobbed off to look for him.

But when we came abeam to his boat it was too rough and tricky to move close alongside. First she would be up high on a hill of water, and next either one of us would wallow in a valley out of sight. Ray bellowed the message out, but the wind blew the words away. So he lined us up along the side of the *Fair Venture*, and as we ran by the other boat we all yielded in unison, 'Hello, Daddy!'

Peter Pickett pointed to himself unbelievingly, like a little boy singled out by Santa Claus, and then he shouted, 'Yahoo!'

It was his first child.

Four years later – I knew it was four years because the

newspaper said Peter had left a wife and four tiny children – he was in a storm at sea and didn't come home. Now, said the Melbourne dailies, his fellow fisherman, Ray Friend, was sailing up and down the fishing ports of eastern Australia collecting donations from the fishermen for the destitute family he had left behind. A newspaper launched an appeal that raised several thousands of pounds. The family was better off financially than they had ever been, better probably than they would ever have been had the father not been drowned. All that money! But nothing would compensate for never seeing again the blue eyes and the yellow hair of the boy who said so joyously and unbelievingly, 'Me?' when we called out 'Hello, Daddy,' such a short time ago.

Truly ships have changed down the ages, and men change too. But the sea never changes. It is always waiting.

Bill and Ted, the men from the *Robert John*, called by the *Sheerwater* one morning and cruised slowly about while they repeated the weather report from Melbourne radio – these ships' radios were great things all right, Les said. Then round us once again while they talked about mutton birds and asked how to cook them, because they had caught some, no mention of licence needed; then round us once again while I was hustled over the side to go on board and cook the birds for them. 'But I'm in my slippers,' I wailed, clutching at straws. I didn't want to cook on a fourteen-metre boat.

'So long as you can cook birds you can come barefoot,' they said.

Oh, yes. I could cook the birds. By now I must have prepared a thousand. I tasted bird in every bite I ate and even in my tea. The old islanders had told me that in time the smell of the oily bird came through your skin and I believed it now. I was scared that my prowess as a cooker of mutton birds was going to gain me such notoriety that I'd be bundled off to every ship that had filched a few illegal birds.

But I needn't have worried. The men of the *Robert John* didn't want me to cook birds. They wanted someone to talk music to.

'We heard you liked music,' was their only explanation or apology. The boys in the *Sheerwater* had done the rest by bragging about the meals I turned out.

As soon as we were out of earshot of the mosquito fleet they produced their musical instruments, and from nine in the morning till six in the evening they gave the fish and the seabirds a concert. They had borrowed an old violin from a family on Flinders Island although neither of them played it well. It happened that this was the only instrument other than a piano that I did play. So my name went down on the programme.

They had brass and woodwind, and the beautifully harmonised voices I had heard before when they sang their theme song about 'web-footed friends' at Whitemark Hotel. When Ted Ryan was in port he played in a band at his home town of Queenscliff as well as appearing in the big eisteddfod. He was good enough to be up among the best.

Bill Withers was less highbrow, but he had tremendous appreciation. And together they sang. In the morning, way out on the troubled blue water, with the land a heather-coloured smudge above the curve of the ocean, they sang as they shot the pots. Then they played band music. I forgot all about cooking and when lunch-time came I felt embarrassed. But soon I was laughing. In their spotless galley we sat down to delicious baked mutton bird, done to perfection. They'd had them in the oven slowly cooking even as they chuffed round the *Sheerwater* that morning.

They were great poultry men. The ship's mast ran up through the middle of the table, and up its length were threaded the wishbones of the many and varied birds they had eaten – wild duck, swan, teal, Cape Barren goose, quail, and snipe were among them.

After the meal, while they waited for the usual four hours

to elapse before going back to pull the pots, they stood on deck and Ted played the trumpet. There was only a thirty-centimetre-high rail round the deck of the *Robert John*, so I sat on deck for safety, but Ted stood, his feet apart in the middle of the rolling deck, blowing golden notes into the sea air. He played for an hour. A flock of Cape Barren geese went by, honking as they flew, and he turned the shiny silver piece of music towards them and echoed their primitive cry. As though magnetised they wheeled and followed their leader in low over the ship, two by two in their marital pairs. For a brief span they were there with us – then they were gone.

The music was shattered near sundown when the barracouta lines, which had been trailing over the stern all day, suddenly began to jerk. Bill put a 'beckett' on the wheel, so the ship would turn in a tight circle, and grabbed a 'jig'. After a while I took one too, a gaily coloured piece of wood with a big hook fastened to it attached by a trace to a short wooden pole which is held in the hand. When they see this piece of nonsense flashing through the water the 'couta go mad and snap at it.

Most of the time the three of us were pulling in together. 'Couta is a fierce fish, quite often over a metre long, and it swims in a pack. Its teeth are razor sharp and vicious. When the fish struck, you flipped it out of the water, bashed it down heavily on the deck, belted its head in with a piece of iron left there for the purpose, tore the hook out of its mouth, and tossed the line back into the water for another try.

Before the run was ended the deck was covered with the huge iridescent cannibals. In a box set aside were three pike, each a metre long, which I had caught. I had never fished before and I haven't fished since. I rest on the laurels earned in that brief Indian summer.

For tea we shared a wild duck and a snipe. When the men went out to get the boat ready to return me, I stood on the table and added the wishbones to the mast. The bones were all odd shapes; some, particularly the swan's, weren't like a wishbone at all but more like a tiny horse collar.

It had been arranged that they were to put me ashore at the far side of the island where they were setting their pots and I was to walk across to Big Gulch and be picked up there. Darkness fell early those nights at the end of April, and I climbed over the side of the boat into a black world. Over my shoulder I carried my three pike on a stick, in my other hand I clutched a sack full of small crayfish.

'Real *Sheerwater* touch,' Ted Ryan said as he bade me farewell. Bill pushed off and, standing in the stern of the boat, began sculling towards the dark shore. I was rather proud to be going back with such a larder on my shoulder.

The water was black, and the sky and the land ahead were black, but as Bill propelled the oar round and round in the sea phosphorus began to congregate, and then it spread and bright green lights along our wake illuminated our pathway from the *Robert John*, running up the oar and along the planks of the boat.

Bill spoke. 'Might be a bit tricky getting you ashore. Only rocks here and there's a fair swell running. Reckon you'll get your slippers wet.' I got all of me wet.

Trustworthy Jack, the opposition buyer to Honest Tom, was waiting for me on the rocks with a torch and a lot of enthusiasm and weight. He aimed both at the boat as it came near, intending, he said later, 'to hang onto it'. His great bulk fell with a roar on to one side of the tiny boat and over it went with its two occupants. Now all was dark again.

It happened so quickly it must only have been minutes to the time I was being pushed up the rocks by the fisherman and left floundering, wet, like a seal. In the darkness I could hear Bill grunting as he righted the boat. 'Pull her farther up out of the sea,' he shouted to Trustworthy Jack, who by now was ready to throw chivalry to the winds and head for home. 'Oh, all right,' he said ungraciously. 'Give me both your hands.'

'I can't,' I said, thereby making a small legend for myself because it was told thereafter that I wouldn't let go of my fish even to save myself from drowning. It sounded so good that I never said I was just so flabbergasted I couldn't tell my legs from my arms. I'd never been under the sea, head and all, in my life before, and I can't swim. I didn't have time to be frightened, but I was certainly surprised.

Bill Withers the fisherman had not only grabbed me and pulled me to the surface, but had pushed me up on to the slippery rocks, fish and all, righted the boat, and was starting to scull back out by the time I had my wind again.

'Watch out, Patsy,' he called. 'Babel's after you. She'll come again. She always does. Just hang on to your fish and you'll be jake!'

At that time Gracie Fields's recording of 'Pedro the Fisherman' was all the rage, and as he went he shouted, 'Goodbye Pedro, we'll see you again.'

We never would meet again, but none of us knew it that night. Back aboard the *Robert John* Ted was playing his trumpet. At first the bird buyer and I couldn't pick up the tune; then, as he sculled, Bill's clear true voice sang back the words:

Fare thee well for I must leave thee
Do not let this parting grieve thee
But remember that the best of friends must part . . .

Standing on the rocks Trustworthy Jack let go with a voice that matched his figure, shapeless and immense:

Adieu, adieu, kind friends, adieu, yes adieu.
I can no longer stay with yer, stay with yer her her
I'll hang my heart on a weeping willow tree . . .

Bill, getting farther and farther away and discernible only by the green phosphorus swirling round his oar, went on:

And may the world go well with thee, hee, hee, hee.

The trumpet made rude noises, the two men laughed, and we on shore went on our way, through the rookery where the birds that had come in to feed their young were busily scurrying round the burrows.

One night we had what Les called 'a real slap-up party'. He never carried liquor on board. He said accidents happen easily enough at sea without artificially producing them. Anyway, he'd never have been able to hide it from the crew.

'A needle in a haystack would be child's play to a seaman if the needle had one drop of grog on the point of it,' Alec once told me proudly, when I found him with an empty flask which the day before had been full of brandy. It was one my mother had given me 'for emergencies' and I'd hidden it behind old Cold-Bum and told no one about it.

But when Les announced that he was going to have a 'real slap-up party' we were surprised. The man-who-shot-at-lavatories and Alec were sent to bed. Pete went ashore to carry on his courting. He was full of quotations that night, coming out with 'Lightning never strikes in the same place twice', 'Forewarned is forearmed', and, the one that really charmed us, 'A faint heart never won a fair lady.'

Les put him ashore from the motor boat and then went round some of the fishing boats to gather a boatload of fishermen.

Tom and I were reading in the galley when they climbed over the side and suddenly filled our living space, dressed in their fishing togs, most with hats on, and each clutching his big pannikin in one weather-scarred hand – in the other a bottle.

My first thought was for my white board floor. But it was too late to spread anything over it now. I don't know where the dirt comes from at sea but no house ever needed the work to keep it clean that a small ship does.

I caused the only uneasiness of the evening by producing

crayfish for supper. But after a small hush these cray fishermen, who often have to eat crays three times a day for weeks on end, partied on again. Kindly Jack Busk picked one up and handled it and chewed it a bit to ease my embarrassment, but I imagine that it's the only time crayfish have been so scorned at a beer party.

The rest of the evening was very happy. The fishermen told jokes against themselves and their boats; Wallaby recited; Pete was picked up and told us with all the frills of his night out, with much emphasis on the fact that he 'stirred the possums' in her for keeping him waiting half an hour in Bull Head Scrub; Tom jumped up on the bread box and began to sing a song, 'Now all you folk have been to sea, I know of course you have'. At this point he decided to add a little dance step and hopped up in the air on one leg, hitting his head on a deck beam, and we didn't hear any more from him for some time, in fact, not until he fell over the side of the ship later on. The fishermen had been taken back to their boats on a shuttle service and as Pete, who had been kept on deck to work, brought the boat past the *Gazelle* on his last trip the skipper called out to say that they had left their pannikins on board. So as they came alongside the *Sheerwater* Pete called out, and Honest Tom ambled happily out and tried to pass the pannikins over the after railings. 'Lean down farther with them,' Pete complained. Honest Tom leaned, and over he went, pannikins and all, right on top of Les, both of them crashing to the bottom of the boat. As always, Tom fell on his feet, or rather this time on his back, but as his back came down on poor squashed Les he must have been very comfortable in comparison to the captain.

There were lights in one of the huts on shore and as there was no clock on the ship (you begin work at daylight and you end at dusk, why would you need a clock, was Wallaby's contention) we thought it might be because they would soon be starting the day's work.

'I don't care what time it is,' Honest Tom said, enjoying what he claimed was the most carefree night he'd had in his life. 'It's too early for the party to end.' They roared off to deliver the pannikins, then set out for a cruise round the bay, careering round the anchored ships and yahooing at the top of their voices.

I was nearly asleep when they returned, but I heard Honest Tom say that it was the best party he had ever been to. 'And the good thing is that it will be too rough to do anything but sleep tomorrow,' he said. 'That's certain.'

There was only one thing you could be sure of at sea and that was that you could be certain of nothing at all.

By seven that morning we were steaming down through the Vansittart Shoals 'rolling our insides out' and all feeling as near to death as the child battling for life in our deck house.

The men had scarcely turned in when I saw the alarm fire on the beach, immediately in front of the house that had been lit up.

I called to Les, 'There's a fire on the beach.'

'Don't be silly!' He was crisp.

Honest Tom mumbled sleepily, and his bunk creaked as he turned and called, 'Pat, don't make a nuisance of yourself, there's a dear girl.'

'But there's a smoke going up!'

Soon Les was cooeeing out from the motor boat in the water alongside the ship.

'Get my bunk ready for a child,' he called.

'What?'

'She's got meningitis.'

'Who says?'

'Mum says.'

May Jackson's word was good enough for anyone, and I got the bunk ready. They brought a little island girl on board in a litter made from two sticks of melaleuca covered with bags, and laid her, still on the litter, on Les's bunk.

Her mother sat beside her, and her father squatted on the floor. In the dawn light coming through the tiny porthole in the captain's cabin, I thought I saw food round the child's mouth.

'What have you been giving her to eat?' I asked.

'Nothing,' said the mother. 'That is coming from inside her. For hours it's been coming.'

I bent low over the child and saw that it was froth welling through her clenched teeth and bubbling out through her drawn-back lips. As often as I wiped her with my wet face-washer it gurgled out again and joined the sweat running down from her little forehead; her pulse was so faint that for a long time I couldn't find it. Even so close to death she seemed to efface herself.

Her mother was crying all the time, silently. 'She's going to die,' was all she said; I brought her cups of tea, but she couldn't drink. 'Is she going to die, Pat?'

'No,' I said, but I thought she would.

We had a rough trip and soon the mother was prostrate, throwing up everywhere. After a long while she curled up on the bottom of the bunk and closed her eyes. Sea-sickness is such a terrible thing that one can quite easily forget everything in the world but one's own suffering; I know this through watching others. The father sat mopping the little girl's face all the way. 'She's my little girl. She's my little girl.'

It was stifling in the cabin, with the strange smell coming from the child. I went out on deck for a breather and there was Tom, hanging over the ship's side, a glass in one hand and his head in the other.

Word had been sent ahead over fishermen's radio that the child was being brought in and when the *Sheerwater* berthed the police and a doctor were waiting on the wharf at Lady Barron. The little girl was whisked away and we heard she had been flown across the strait to Launceston.

We heard no more until some weeks later when we were ready to sail from Launceston. A taxi pulled up on the wharf, a smartly dressed woman and a man in a blue suit beckoned us over, and there was the child sitting between them – her parents.

When we told Honest Tom all he said was, 'She recovered a lot quicker than I did then.'

I was on shore when I heard that Bill and Ted were dead, and the *Robert John* was lost. A lighthouse keeper at the entrance to Port Phillip Bay, Melbourne, had seen the mast and part of a boat sinking three-quarters of a kilometre off shore. The straits were so wild that day that no other boats were out, they were all sheltering. He said, 'No one could have survived in that sea. I only hope that it was a boat that broke loose from its moorings and was unmanned.'

But it was Bill and Ted. They had left the shelter of the islands in Bass Strait and sailed for home against their better judgment as seamen. The Governor-General was visiting their home port, Queenscliff, the following day, and they wanted to be home to play in the band to welcome him.

When the day came the band was silent, mourning, and His Excellency, Sir William Slim, mourned with them. 'Your whole town is in sorrowing bereavement,' he said. 'My wife and I offer you our deepest sympathy and grieve with you for these two fishermen, your friends.'

My friends said, 'They must've been important men to have merited all that mourning. A whole town of it!' But how could you explain that Bill and Ted weren't important at all in the way importance is usually judged in our community; they were just loved a lot, that was all. Or maybe that is everything.

'Fare thee well for I must leave thee,' they sang that last night at Babel as I stood drenched on the rocks beside Trustworthy Jack.

'But remember that the best of friends must part.'

I remembered the mast of the *Robert John* decorated with the wishbones of wildfowl. But mostly I remembered their music coming over the water, the geese flying low and honking in reply to them, and their songs.

When next we went back to Babel the weather was again bad. The fishermen said it was good until we arrived. We lay at The Cellar again for days, racing in and taking barrels off whenever there was a break, then battling out to safety and shelter when it became impossible to work.

The birdin' ended and the birders were anxious to get off. But Les wished to make the one trip do for the lot, the cargo and the passengers.

At last there came a day when the birders could wait no longer: a little deputation went out to the *Sheerwater* with the last dinghy load of the day. Standing up, hanging on to the side of the ship as the boat bounced and rocked, they put their case to Les who was standing on the deck.

'Got to get back to get food for the women and kids, old man,' they said.

'But . . .' Pete interrupted.

'Got two babies on the island. Got no tinned milk for them. Got to get back old man; no tinned milk.'

'But . . .' Pete was stuttering.

'Hold it,' Les ordered him.

'We can't wait any longer. D'ye think you can make it tomorrow, old man?'

'No,' Les told them honestly. 'But the day after if the weather comes good.'

'Too late, old man, those babies are crying out for food.'

And away back to shore they bobbed, their worried faces drawn and anxious in the light of the lantern they carried.

'But Wallaby . . .'

Les turned to Pete. 'I know . . .' We had brought a cargo of food out and it could hardly have been touched; also there was powdered milk at the store shed at Big Gulch; lastly, what difference could another day make?

'I'll tell you. They're going. Nothing we could do or say would stop them. It's an urge like the bird gets when he has to go to sea.

'These lot are thirsty, dangerously thirsty. They might even try to swim for it. They've done that before when the pull is too great for them to resist. Don't worry. They'll make it somehow.'

But he was worried. After tea he stood out on the little afterdeck for a long while. A fishing boat came by and the boys called out to the fishermen asking to borrow a pack of cards. Not knowing there was a woman on board, they threw a pack over, and when the boys and I were playing Five Hundred there was a silent second when two of us got cards hand embossed with more erotic imagination than art. Later we heard another motor come by and reverse.

It was the *Eden Star*, a beautiful little purse seiner. The owner Bill Warne and his son Neville were aboard her.

'There's been trouble on shore, Wallaby,' old Bill called out.

'What sort of trouble?'

'They're short of food. There's a baby nearly dead it's so long since it's had condensed milk, they say. They want me to take them over and drop them on the north end of Flinders in the morning.'

'You ought to take Pat to help with the women.'

'Right.' So the islanders were going to get off by dint of Bill's big heart, and I was going to be swapped over like a bag of potatoes. Les came in and went to his bunk, and we went on playing cards, with part of the skill being unobtrusively to prevent my getting the obscene Queen of Hearts and the amazingly agile Jack of Diamonds.

The morning dawned clear and sunny, with a living gale blowing. Riding at anchor, we were charging forward the length of the cable, then rearing backwards like a circus pony.

I made a blancmange and mixed a red jelly and put the two

to set on top of the wheelhouse in the open, ready for tea. I had found that containers can safely be left on a rolling ship if stood on a cloth soaked with water. Then I climbed down to the waiting dinghy and journeyed forth in leaps and bounds to the *Eden Star* and a mixed bag of a day.

The few who were 'really hard pressed for tucker' were sitting down on the beach with their backs to the water, and the women didn't want to come. Sure, they'd kicked up a shindy about it and henpecked the men into getting transport off, but now with the sea foaming white between them and the *Eden Star* a couple of hundred yards offshore they'd changed their minds.

So had the men, but they weren't going to show it. They bullied the women and were the big brave bosses when the seamen were near, but when they thought they were alone they surreptitiously helped the women move their gear farther back towards the scrub.

This could have continued until they disappeared into the bush if Big Neville Warne hadn't gone on shore and delivered the ultimatum: now or never. They saw the black clouds that were starting to fill the sky and knew that once the storm broke they might be there for another week, and whose parched throat could bear that? So while the women stood in indecision the men suddenly grabbed them and bundled them into the boat; Big Neville bent to the oars, and ferried them out.

There wasn't much gear; only suitcases of clothes and enough bedding to make them comfortable in the scrub near the Whitemark pub, so we were soon under way.

I was glad to hear the anchor come up. The boys from the *Sheerwater* had been going to and fro with the loaded dinghy and every time they passed they looked at the *Eden Star* crew and called out, 'Watch'em, Pat. Watch'em.'

The birders sat decorously on deck. Trying, as usual, to preserve their dignity, at least at the beginning of the journey, they appeared not to be too interested in their whereabouts or even in the crew, and sat still on piles of fish nets and gear, whispering quietly to themselves.

I had nothing to do and was enjoying the company of the old man on the wheel. I knew it was going to come in rough as soon as we rounded the tip of Babel and headed across to Flinders, where the birders would be landed. Even now the crew were casually strolling round between the people on deck, lashing down gear and making fast all movable equipment. I looked around for space where the passengers could shelter from the sea. There was precious little of it.

Below the minute wheelhouse were six bunks set against the wall in a small space. I went down to see how useful this space would be, but after a few minutes I thought they'd need to have nerves of steel or be so close to dying it didn't matter to stay down there. I'd never felt like this before. It was like being in a sealed box that had been dropped into the ocean.

I heard a hiss above my head.

'Psst. Pat.'

I shinned up the ladder.

'Pat . . . Paaat!' It was an urgent whisper. 'Is there a dub on board?'

Oh, no! The women wanted a lavatory.

'It's down below, right in the bows,' I told them.

The sea was getting rougher now with mounting waves and occasional clouds of flying spray. I was breathing lovely gulps of cold, nippy air; on my lips I could taste salt. I ran right round them with my tongue and swallowed. It was good.

'Pat! Paaat.' It was a middle-aged woman. 'Paaat. Charlotte's stuck.'

'Stuck?'

'On the dub.'

I raced down. The lavatory was right in the V-shaped bow, and it was such a small closet that it was a miracle that Charlotte, a very large woman, had even managed to get in and close the door. But worse. For some reason the pan was very low, much lower than the average one. There, with her feet apart and knees spread, enthroned in a position of great relaxation and content, sat Charlotte.

'I'm stuck, Paat,' she said, not very much distressed.

Her comfort was such that no one could blame her – it was this very comfort that had trapped her.

I tried to make her put her knees together, but they wouldn't come. She was stuck. I gave her my hand and, propping open the door with one foot, I stood in the space near the bunks and pulled. But she was fast. And then the first big sea hit us. We were round the corner and the roll had begun.

'Paat.' Charlotte's eyes opened wide, and she jammed one hand across her mouth. It was no longer funny. If she were rolled off her unconventional perch in this sea she could be battered unconscious before we could get her off the floor.

A crew member was coming down the companion ladder. He saw me, and guessing that women were there, he apologised and began to ascend. I reached up and grabbed his boot. 'Help me, quick.' He took Charlotte's hands with both his, I squeezed into the V space behind her and, with my feet pressed hard against the wall, pushed. Slowly, majestically, like a great whale rising to the surface, Charlotte stood up.

The deck was bare now. Where the islanders had been sitting, waves rolled across and joined up with the sea on the other side. The little ship was going head on into a mountain range of seas, and every wave that broke over her she took as a joke. She was as sweet a little craft as ever you planted your feet on, and I wished now we could go on for ever charging the seas as they came at us, rearing to the top, and sliding down the other side on our haunches.

I liked her so much I would have chosen to ride out a hurricane in her. But the islanders were uneasy. They were all crowded into the galley, shoulder to shoulder, murmuring. 'Turn back, turn back,' the women urged. The men were more practical. How would they get the women off into the boats in the sea that would be running back at the island now? It had taken the fishermen all they knew that morning to get them safely on board, and the seas were only 'making' then. No, we'd gone so far; we had to go on.

'They must be uncomfortable,' dear old Bill Warne said.

I was standing near the wheel with him, tense with exhilaration. Some women thrill in their deepest sense to the feel of fine fabric, others to the sight of a man's bare arm; many perhaps are moved by nothing except cradling their children. I never felt the majesty of God, whatever or wherever He is, until I stood beside men at the wheel of little battling ships.

A man can weld his living self with this thing of wood and iron, so that as they drive together a marriage takes place, a union. Sometimes he curses the ship. If he never swears he will mutter unconsciously. 'You bitch! You bloody bitch! Come round, damn you.' But when she comes, when she cleaves the sea apart, and when she answers his guiding hand and between them they turn what the sea meant to be disaster into triumph and she rises to take yet another wave, shaking the water off the head of her bow, he says, caressingly, 'You sweetheart. You honey. That's the girl.' And there's no woman who wouldn't envy the ship then.

The sea is so mighty that in small ships when you are going along only a foot or so off the top of it you are ever conscious of its greatness. If you stare into its depths, you feel as though you are being drawn hypnotically down. Even on calm days there is the sense of relentless movement under the surface. And when it is troubled the sea is uncanny in its mobility, in the roll and power of the waves. There is no explaining it; one must look and see for oneself.

Old Bill had built this ship. He had chopped down the trees that supplied its planking. He knew what it could do, what he could make it do. As I stood there, the sound of the motor was drowned by the whine of the wind and the pounding of the sea as it washed over us, completely enveloping the ship at times as it came over the wheelhouse and we instinctively ducked as though there were no stout timbers and thick glass between it and us. There was nothing in the world but this tremendous struggle between ship, man and sea.

But there *was* something else, and I had to go. Through the occasional wails in the galley came the sound of some people being sick. All of them were terrified.

The men stopped muttering when I came up to them, but the women unashamedly hid their faces so that they couldn't see the water, and wept. There were five trying to squash on Skipper Bill's bunk beside the little kerosene stove. As soon as I had mentioned that Bill said they could go below they rushed down where they wouldn't see the sea, and were sick.

It was late in the afternoon when we reached the bay on Flinders where they were to go ashore. We were still rolling badly, the swell coming right into the shallow bay, but the sea was no longer breaking over the ship. Everyone trooped up on deck. The islanders looked at the wild waves between them and the shore, one of the women moaned, and the rest imitated her with alacrity. One old lady sat down beside her daughter on the hatch cover and buried her head in her girl's lap, but the younger woman grabbed her by the hair and yanked her head up so that she, the daughter, could bury her head in her mother's lap.

There were two rowboats on board. The men were first, scrambling over into the smaller of the two the moment it was launched and set off for the shore.

'We'll get things ready to help the womenfolk ashore,' they called as they pushed off. That was the last we saw of them. When they reached the beach they scampered up the sand, over the hummocks, and out of sight, leaving the little boat bobbing out to sea in the choppy waves. Time was lost while the fishermen rowed off in pursuit of that boat, and darkness was approaching.

Now, as well as having to look after the boats, the seamen had to get the luggage and the women off. First they took the luggage. They had to take the bigger boat and consequently couldn't get in close to the shore, so everything had to be carried shoulder-high through the surf and lugged up the beach to the high-tide mark. Boxes, bags, suitcases, bedding rolls – and they didn't get a drop of water on anything.

Getting the women off would have been hilarious but for the worry of the coming dusk. With the boat pitching and bucking at the side of the ship and two men aboard her and two men on the *Eden Star* trying to hold her to prevent her being splintered to matchwood, the women went over.

Old Bill coaxed them, one by one, to sit on the bulwarks, and he and I stood, one each side, holding their arms. As a wave threw the boat below upwards we pushed the woman down, the men in the boat grabbed her and steadied her, and we prepared another. There were no hold-ups except when one wrapped her arms round my head as she was going over. My feet went clean off the deck and for a second it appeared that I would go over too. The fishermen laughed loudly, but I realised it was mostly because it gave them the excuse they'd been waiting for to release the laughter welling inside them.

The people already in the boat were argumentative with fear; it was, without a doubt, survival of the fittest.

Old deaf Minnie was there. She watched what was happening and when her turn came she stepped up without any fuss and went over the side like the veteran she was. I always admired her. I noticed her now as they crouched windblown in the boat, sitting there with the gale howling past her face and her scarf tied peasant-fashion round her head. She was holding a frightened child to her, unafraid, although well aware of the danger. Each time the boat smashed inwards towards the *Eden Star* she put out her hand with the seamen's hands to stave off collision. With her people around her almost unconscious with fear she who had not even been taught conventional sign language kept a clear head.

Big Neville – The Ox they called him because of his strength – took the oars and off they went in the gloaming, now on the crest of a wave, now out of sight in a trough. For a while the sound of their crying came fitfully, then it, too, went.

Through the dusk we watched Neville carry the women ashore one by one, while another fisherman stood waist deep in the water holding the boat out beyond the worst of the breakers, which at times went as high as his head. Big Neville held the women in the air in his two hands, like an offering, and waded in with them, high and dry. Even big deaf Minnie and her sister Beatrice, quite as big, were lifted high and dry and taken ashore with as much decorum as if they were noble ladies.

Rightly was this man called The Ox. And as you watched him in the cold, shadowy end of day, while he ferried these people, his compassion reminded one of another, the man with the staff, the flowing robe, and the small child on his shoulder.

By the time he got his boat back to the *Eden Star* he was spent, but no other man could have rowed through those seas that were fast coming in.

The men on shore reappeared for a moment and beckoned the women over the hillocks to where the smoke from a campfire billowed warmly, and as they went, Minnie and Beatrice turned and waved.

The boat was brought inboard, the anchor hauled up, and we headed into it once more. I was glad. Now I could just stand where I liked to stand most; there would be unbroken hours before I would have to move away. Bill would talk, not too much, and always about the sea; and all the time he would be winding the wheel and the ship would be reeling and plunging and fighting the ocean every inch of the way.

The crew went to bed. You couldn't sit; it was all you

could do to stand. None of us had eaten since morning or even had a cup of tea, but there was nothing you could do about it in sea like this.

Gusts of rain went by us blindly, the appearance of their drops on the wheelhouse windows sometimes surprising us in the blackness. The moon ducked quickly from one black cloud to another, her light lasting only long enough to show us the fierce sea about us, the deep sea which that very moon, so skittish up there tonight, could drag from one side of the earth to the other.

At Babel, too, the weather was bad. I wondered how they would tranship me. The little ships were running for shelter, trailing along behind the *Sheerwater* like chickens after a hen. I'd been looking ahead into the blackness and hadn't seen them until Bill told me to look abeam of us on the port side, and there, in the complete darkness except for the navigation lights, was the *Sheerwater*, so close, that when the moon shone I could see my blancmange and jelly slipping from one side of the wheelhouse roof to the other. The cloth had disappeared. Les pointed to The Cellar and off we all went.

It was small adventure I guess, but the night had thrilled me, and now there was the finale, the grand dash through the black storm clouds that walked on top of the water. Every time the moon ran across an open space her light fell down on the small ships, each on a straight course and each as close to one another as the *Sheerwater* was to us.

Old Bill said, 'Beautiful, isn't it.'

I was wet through and my camera was damaged from the battering it had taken in the storm-tossed *Eden Star*. As I clambered over the side, the boys of the *Sheerwater* said, 'They didn't look after you very well.'

Still the loading wasn't complete, and next morning Les strolled out on deck in the pre-dawn chill while we waited in the galley for his decision, huddled round Old Cold-Bum. Through the open door we could hear the roar of the surf breaking on the beach across at Babel, and nearer at hand there was the slap-slap glug-glug of the sulky sea hitting our sides. The boys didn't want to go inshore. They muttered quietly, uneasily, but when the skipper came back in they were silent. He rubbed his face with the back of his hand, and in the quietness you could hear the rasp of his whiskers.

'We've waited a fortnight,' he said.

That was a long time to keep a ship without cargo, everyone knew. He just stood there, not looking at them and not looking away in his own peculiar way. Like most men of action he had no stance, no gesture.

The boys shuffled round and Alec took off his cap, inspected it, and replaced it.

'Well, what do you say?' Les asked.

'It's for you to say,' Alec said, and the boys nodded agreement.

'I think we'd better get them today.'

While I fried fish the boys got the big dinghy over the side and loaded the long wooden skids onto it.

It was Pete's birthday and I had knitted him a cap. I gave it to him as they went out after breakfast: it was black with white stripes, and a tassel on the top like most of the seamen and fishermen wore, and he seemed very pleased with it.

Alec doubled back from the deck to say. 'The kid's tickled pink with his new cap. Reckon it's the first birthday present he's ever had.'

They were a long time getting the motor started on the loading dinghy. When I went out to empty the washing-up water I happened to look over the side. There they were as usual, wiping the infernal 'maggie' dry. But this morning Pete hadn't borrowed my hanky. He was using his new cap instead. He wiped the oil off the top of the engine with it, then the fuel that had spilled out. By the time they bobbed off into the dawn there were no white stripes left on the cap, but it was jammed proudly on the back of Pete's head.

The *Sheerwater* was moved as close inshore as they dared. The ship couldn't be left unattended in such a sea, but while Les stayed on board he was so fidgety about the boys in the boat that he stood on deck all day watching them through his spyglass. I heard him give them instructions before they left. 'Keep her bow high in the water. Don't load too much in her at any time. And watch those breakers. They're coming in all directions today.'

I made boiling cocoa and put it in empty sauce bottles, and dropped them down to the boys in the dinghy each time they came in with a load. They didn't stop for lunch, so I dropped hot toasted sandwiches down to them.

Alec said, 'You ought to come in and see the fun,' so, as I had finished my work and had the tea simmering on top of the stove, I went. Les Jackson said I'd be sorry, and further, he said not to take my camera. 'The odds are closing in,' he said. 'They can't expect their luck to hold all day.'

But I thought I should get some spectacular shots of the loading, so I went – and I took the camera.

There was a birder, Noel Maynard, on shore. When the boys put the anchor down he came out to the dinghy and carried me ashore on his shoulders. An hour later he came out through the breakers and helped me again, this time because the dinghy was sinking and we were all floundering in the water, swimmers and non-swimmers alike.

The loading had been spectacular enough. Half the time you couldn't see the boys for the waves breaking over them. The dinghy leapt in the air on the end of its anchor rope and plunged down on them as they tried to roll the heavy barrels up the wooden skids. With two men in the water trying to wrestle the barrels on to the skids and the other in the boat rolling the barrel in, they were having a lively time. As the boat got lower in the water with the weight of the barrels, they moved it farther back on to the anchor. Fortunately this load was mostly bags of feathers and there were only a few barrels. The feathers were all humped out on their shoulders and loaded into the bow; the barrels were rolled out and up the skid.

The sea became worse. Great waves were rolling in and breaking all over the place. The boys hauled the boat back on the anchor every time they loaded a weight into it, but still the waves broke over it. Les was shouting something from the deck of the *Sheerwater*, but the wind blew his words away and the crew were too occupied keeping the dinghy afloat to listen to him. Alec carried me out when they were ready to go. I wasn't too willing.

'Don't argue,' he snapped. 'We're flat out keeping the boat afloat without you playing up too.'

So I allowed myself to be dumped in. I'd folded my camera up and put a waterproof cover over it, but the holders containing the pictures I had taken that afternoon I laid on a piece of timbering in the dinghy and that was the last I saw of them.

We were scarcely under way when one big wave then another broke over us. Pete was lying over the engine trying to protect it, but a wave came and swamped slowly and heavily over him and the engine. The motor stopped without a stutter, the dinghy swung broadside on to the sea, and the waves swept it out. The water in the boat was up to the calves of our legs and then it began to flow steadily in like a waterfall filling a basin. The heavy bags of feathers in the bow were pushing the nose down into the water.

Pete began to unload them over the side, but it was too late. 'Grab a bag and hang on,' he shouted, and the boat was gone. I rode upon a bag of feathers like a beach girl on a rubber sea-horse. Noel Maynard had seen us go and now he came out and took my camera and an ear of the bag in his hand. We were close to the shore, but I hung on grimly to his thick black curly hair as he paddled. After a few strokes he told me to straddle his shoulders, and I found he was now walking on the bottom with his head out of water. So I returned to shore. He dumped me down on the hard sand. 'Babel's got her sights on you all right,' he said. 'You watch her, Pat!' I certainly would. The boys got in somehow. They lay on the sand spitting out water. When Alec had recovered his breath he dog-paddled back to the sunken boat. He could scarcely swim enough to keep himself afloat. I wondered what was so valuable that he should risk himself a second time to reach it. He returned dragging only an old leather coat rolled up his arms, flopped exhausted to the sand, and lay there.

We were all beginning to feel cold now, and we were suffering from shock. We began to shiver, then to shake with violent spasms. I didn't notice that the others were doing it too. I just sat on the sand and shook in a little wet world of my own.

Then Alec had me by the shoulder, pinching. 'Come on,' he chattered through his teeth. 'Come on.'

The others were running round the rocks, chasing each other. Dimly I realised I would get my circulation back if I joined in. But they looked so silly! And I felt so tired. I had no option; Alec grabbed me by the hand and pulled me round with him. Round and round we went, then up the beach and back, playing tag when we were close.

Just when we had nearly knocked ourselves out, a little head appeared over the rocks and a child's reedy voice said, 'What are you doing?'

We stopped and laughed. Alec told him. 'Playing silly buggers.'

The child's mother had sent him to tell us that we could come up and dry off in front of her fire.

Alec was very careful to bring the leather coat – still folded – with him. The birder's hut we went to belonged to the mother of young Claude Mansell, and she did everything she could for us. So did her husband, a limbless veteran of World War I. Soon we had our wet clothes off and were dressed in some of Mr Mansell's spares. I, in the man's long flannel vest, Alec in his long cotton underpants and Pete in a nightshirt type of white garment. Billy refused to change and stood in the huge open fireplace with steam rising from him like a man in a sauna bath. And we were warm inside, too, because wrapped in Alec's leather jacket was a large jar of cheap wine.

It is forbidden to bring liquor ashore on the birdin' isles and Alec had been smuggling, but as I drank great china cups full of it so my approval of his misdemeanour increased. In front of the roaring log fire we became a bit tipsy birders, boatmen, everyone; and we were just beginning to sing when the child came in and said the captain was coming for us.

That ended the party.

Les had been alone in the *Sheerwater* watching with the spy-glass when it happened. There was nothing he could do; he had no boat on board, no radio. Later, Ray Friend in the *Fair Venture* came by and lent him their little runabout rowboat. The tide was well out by now and the dinghy was scarcely under water, but because the breakers were so great the little rowboat couldn't get in. Ray Friend brought his fishing boat as close to the shore as he dared, Les took a line from it, Alec dog-paddled out again, brought in the line, tied it to the big dinghy, and so it was hauled up.

I sat on the beach and began to shiver again. My clothes were only half dry and stiff with salt. It was not until hours later when the sea calmed down that they brought the little boat in close and I was carried out. It seemed silly to be carried, because I couldn't be much wetter. Anyway, as Pete was carrying me, it didn't make much difference as he always allowed one part or another of me to get wet.

When the others carried me to the boat they held me the way they hold all women they take to boats, in the arms, so that they can lift you swiftly over any threatening wave. Not Pete. He either carried me over his shoulder like a sack of potatoes, holding me by the ankles, with my head dangling down his back and half the time under water, or he carried me pick-a-back fashion, in which case my bottom drooped into the sea.

The great problem now was taking off the rest of the barrels, and the people too. The dinghy had been refloated and bailed out and was now lashed on to the side of the ship, but it was without an engine and much too big and cumbersome to be rowed.

The boys were so ashamed of themselves for having lost the dinghy that they thought up all sorts of wild schemes, including an almost workable one of tying the barrels to a rope fastened to a long line, which would be taken to the ship, and the whole lot could then be towed out by the winch like a giant string of fire crackers.

The captain quashed that one: 'And won't Japhet, and Reuben, and Morgan, and the rest of them look fine being hauled through the water in the same way.'

Instead, he had Ray Friend send a radio message off to Flinders Island where the *Margaret Twaits* was due, telling her captain to bring her out. By the time she arrived next day, we had all the birds off the island by a little scheme Les kept under his hat until he saw how the day broke.

The day was calm, the sea was flat. The long storm had ended. So he took the *Sheerwater* into the narrow gutway we called Big Gulch. We'd often set the graball net for fish on our way into the gulch in the dinghy and there seemed barely width enough between the rocks and reefs. The boys didn't believe we could get the *Sheerwater* in without disaster.

But Les did it simply and with a minimum of fuss. Every man, woman, and child on the island had come to the cliff-top to watch.

The only exciting thing was to see her lying there, almost landlocked, where no ship her size had lain before. But to hear Honest Tom's description of the manoeuvre is a different matter. Les told him to handle the afterlines on board, while two of the boys stood on the rocks to see that the lines going ashore were handled properly. This would leave only one boy on board, with Les on the wheel.

'But why me?' Tom wailed. 'Why me?' We were sidling in, almost grazing the great rocks, when Les called to him to 'take a turn'. Tom immediately got the line tangled round his legs; Les, who couldn't see him, called out, 'That's fine'.

When he untangled himself he let go the line and Alec on shore suddenly found his taut line going slack and coming home. He bellowed out, and looking over at the ship and seeing it was Honest Tom who had done the deed, he bawled, 'I'll snotter you!'

This upset Tom so much that he hauled suddenly on the line, and Alec who was holding the other end was nearly pulled into the water.

'By the living Harry I'll stir the possums in you if I come aboard,' Alec shouted. 'Grab that thick line beside you!'

'I should never have been asked to do this,' Tom wailed again and again. 'I'm not a sailor.' He raised his voice and called out, 'Wallaby, I'm not a sailor.'

'You're not kidding,' Wallaby replied.

The worst shock Honest Tom received was when Wallaby told him to make his end of the line fast. 'And make a good job of it, or we'll go on the rocks.' That was evident. On either side of the ship the boys were making the lines taut so that she could swing neither one way nor the other.

Tom took up the end of the rope and sighed and looked for somewhere to tie it. But it was so thick it would hardly bend, let alone tie.

Everyone was shouting to him now. The ship was drifting because one line was not yet fast – his.

'This is a most unpleasant business,' he said, standing there with the rope in his hands like a hymn book. 'What do they do with it?' he implored.

'They loop it round the bitts in a figure-of-eight pattern.'

He tried that, but as soon as the boy on shore started to take up the slack it began to slip undone. There were only two ways to lead the line around the bitts, and Tom had chosen the wrong one.

'What do they do now?'

'They stand on it.'

When lunch-time came everyone turned up except Honest Tom. He was still standing on the line on the bollards back aft. Les laughed at him and told him that it was safe to leave it now. Tom stepped off and the line whipped out of the bitts, Les only just catching it as it went over the side.

'That was the most utterly demoralising experience I have known,' Tom said over his lunch. He was so upset that all he could eat was a little mashed potato.

The barrels were becketted on board on ropes and the rest of the operation went without a hitch. The *Margaret Twaits* came up while we were still in the gulch, and the captain thought the message about the dinghy sinking must have been jumbled, and that it was the *Sheerwater* that was wrecked. Expressions of admiration are so rare among sailors in these parts that it must have been very gratifying to Wallaby to hear a thin cheer go up from the *Margaret Twaits* when he sterned his ship out of the rocky gutway that night.

Next day he made a raft by lashing together some empty forty-four-gallon drums and used this to float his father's jeep out to the *Margaret Twaits*. All morning the dinghy we borrowed from the *Margaret Twaits* shuttled backwards and forwards between the island and the two ships, bringing the birders and their gear off.

The day was lovely, the sun was shining, the birdin' was over, everyone was in fine good humour, the cheques had been handed over. On the deck of the *Sheerwater* two birders took out their guitars and began to sing. Honest Tom and I presented a duet.

Beautiful, beautiful Babel,
Beautiful, beautiful Bay-hay-bel,
Beautiful, beautiful Babel,
We'll never see Babel no more,

knowing full well that we would if we could.

I was sad, for my time in the *Sheerwater* must end now that the birdin' was over. The ship would return to ordinary cargo-running and there would be no place for me. I was leaving the Furneaux.

'You'll be back,' old Ucky Mansell predicted. 'You can't help it. Babel will bring you back. If Cabbasheena misses the first time she'll try twice more, three times in all. She's gone after you twice, Pat. She'll bring you back for the last try. You mark my words.'

I did mark Ucky's words, because I wanted to come back. I could believe in such superstitions if it would contribute to the certainty of my return. But when next I sat on the deck of a ship feeling her way down through the Vansittart Shoals and the birdin' was over once again, and the islanders were jubilant because I 'had beaten Babel for the third time', and I looked round for Ucky to tell him that I had believed in his prediction all along, he was dead, and so was Walter Beeton, and old George Maynard, and Minnie my deaf friend, and Beatrice and a dozen others of the old men and women. And the young ones were dispersing.

When first I went to the islands there were a few of the old time skippers still alive – Captain Harry and Captain Jim Burgess, Captain Bill Barrett, and old Captain Leggett. These master mariners became my mentors, taught me the lore, the etiquette, danger, lust and love of the bold waters. At first they must tutor me on the islands. 'A good small-ship's skipper must know the land as well as the water,' dear Harry Burgess told me. While I sailed those seas, Harry himself became a part of the lore. He died on his boat, the *Julie Burgess*, and

Trooper Lew Bailey had to go to the north of the island to bring the boat south. Then came the business of getting the day-dead body of a large man up through the small hatchway from the cabin to be laid out on deck. And he looked as fine in death as he had in life, as we trooped over to pay our last respects.

There was old Bill Riddle, perhaps the best repository of folk lore in the islands. Bill's forebears had provided food for the Aboriginal settlement at Guncarriage in 1826, the account £9 1s 6d, according to documents in the Hobart archives. Frank Jackson was there, a King Islander, who had come over the Straits when he was a lad and settled on the Furneaux. He had known the people whose fathers and mothers had settled these islands and remembered their stories. 'I'll take you to Cabbasheena one day,' he told me, giving Babel Island its now forgotten name.

Old Alec Ross was there, son of the Alex who came here to search the islands for loot stripped off the wreck of the *Cambridgeshire*. On 10 September 1875, this ship struck a rock near Guncarriage while on her way to Sydney from London. While Ross was searching Guncarriage Island, he met Bessie Bates, the first white child born in the Straits, married her and settled on the islands to found a well-known island clan. (Guncarriage is shown on the Admiralty chart as Vansittart Island, but has always been known to the locals from the remains of an old gun carriage from a wreck there.)

There was Beatrice Everett and her sister Minnie Maynard, descendants of black women brought here by sealers in the 1850s. Both the women became my friends; I stayed with this family on Cape Barren Island for three weeks once and for the odd few days at other times when the *Sheerwater* was held up. At that time, living a life similar to that they had known all their lives, I had more in common with these two women than I had with any of my old friends of a past time that now seemed not only remote, but futile and frivolous.

Ucky Mansell was another who taught me much, a little old man, deep shiny mahogany coloured, and very gentlemanly. Cliff Everett taught me the ethnography of the Cape Barren Islanders, as they wished to be called in those days, and George Maynard told me his stories. Walter Beeton, 'the last quarter-caste, Pat' as he introduced himself to me, sat for hours at a time yarning about the islanders. 'Let's talk about things in general, Pat,' he'd say, and we'd sit down wherever we were and tell one another what we thought of the world.

Silas Mansell was another who helped me. A good boatman ('getting a bit long in the tooth', he'd say), he took me to old wrecks and silent, unwalked beaches, and across sand shoals that swirled away and blocked our return along the same route.

It was a wonderful time to be in those islands. Soon it would all go, the times and the people change as must be, but I can feel a pleasure that I knew the islands and the islanders well.

12

Perils of the Deep

I had learnt much about a unique people, about birds, land and water, a whole ecology, from the women and men of the islands. Sailing on the *Sheerwater* had taught me seamanship and the ways of those who go about their lives on deep waters. As well, I now knew a lot about myself. My knowledge and way of life had helped to make me Australia's best known freelance writer of the time because, as well as working my passage on the *Sheerwater*, I was writing 3000-word features for eight major national magazines, averaging one article a week. I had written children's radio serials before 'cutting loose' and going to sea, but the instant I went to sea I began writing differently, stronger, with the confidence that knowledge lends. Publishing under my surname, Adam Smith,

I was thought by readers to be a man, an editor even sent me an invitation to a function including 'and wife'.

Because of the difficulty editors had of persuading professional photographers to accompany me on what one of them had complained of as 'perpetual bloody suicide missions' I decided to cover my own stories. Cyril Pearl of *Australia Magazine* encouraged me, and Otto Olsen of Associated Press advanced me the deposit to buy a Linhof Technica camera using 4 x 5 inch cut sheets of film.

This most beautiful of all cameras, was of course large and heavy, expensive and cumbersome and each sheet of film had to be loaded in total darkness into separate sheaths which then were slotted into holders. I had six holders, each carrying six sheets and even that extra bulk made for more heavy, clumsy carrying. To load this film, with neither glow nor chink of light, was always difficult. I have huddled beneath three grey blankets with seamen holding the edges down to keep light out; engine rooms on ships were great at night with the deck hatch closed – but here I must beware of oil and grease as I loaded. Times without number I have been locked into big wooden refrigerators and here I must work fast to avoid condensation forming on the film or the sheaths. Wardrobes were fine to imprison myself at dead of night when on shore. Once at sea, when I had used up my loaded film and things were still happening, I dived head first with my gear into my oil-proofed sleeping bag and got Pete to do the zipper up. He went off and forgot me and later Mr Hughie Barrett found me more dead than alive in the airless cocoon and released me. Always there was the problem of perspiration getting onto the film sheets as I sweltered in cramped areas. The emulsion of the cut film marked easily and scratched and as I could carry so few I strove to make sure each cut film was without blemish. The camera was a simple and perfect instrument but was not designed to be dragged through spiky tussock grass that could spear holes in the bellows and scratch the precious lenses, or be constantly subjected to salt water spray and sea air. When big seas swamped our motor and sunk the dinghy off Babel Island, the camera went down with me. I had wrapped it in a water-proof coat and when young Maynard got me ashore I took it apart and laid it in the sun with the bellows out at full stretch to dry. The photo I took later that day of the refloating of our craft was taken with it.

With the stories and my photography I was financially secure. I rarely accepted a commission: there was no need, the stories were just all around me waiting to be picked up and editors paid me well over the award rate. The people who travelled or lived as I did were all larger than life. I never have known just when and how I met those peerless companions Dominic Serventy and Russell Drysdale, except that each and all of us were thoroughly immersed in everything and everybody around us. Every day brought new adventures, knowledge and wonder and we would hurry to one another when we could to exchange news.

'I think I'll go expeditioning with Dom and Tas,' I said to Captain Leslie Jackson (alias Wallaby the Shoal jumper). 'They'll work you hard,' he said – as if he didn't! And next time they set off I was with them. Life was just like that.

Thirty years later, when Tas died, Dominic wrote an introduction to a posthumous exhibition of his work. He referred to our days as 'memorable' and recalled 'an unlooked for exciting passage through the Pot Boil Shoals'. There were indeed halcyon times.

But I was not finished with the sea. On the *Sheerwater* I was *persona non grata*, there by grace and favour of the owner/captain, and although I appreciated his chivalry in making a place for me it was not enough. I wanted to be a signed on member of a crew, an articled seaman. I had long left behind me that other world where I figured on the Social Page. Day by day I'd grown to suspect the morality of that existence and the dependence on things outside myself. Like a man who begins to doubt that there is a God, there is no returning to the old undoubting times once the question has been asked.

I was in Hobart doing research at the State Archives, a cold dungeon where water seeped through the convict-built stone walls, when I was contacted by the Public Relations Officer for the Tasmanian Government Transport Commission. Knowing that I wrote for a national magazine he offered me a voyage as a guest of his Commission on the Government vessel *Naracoopa*. I had never seen this ship but through my knowledge of Tasmanian Aboriginal I knew the word meant 'Very good'. I should surely be able to get an interesting story from such a four day voyage. Six years later I left the ship.

Not that that first trip on the *Naracoopa* was the kind of thing that would charm one into joining her rag-tag and bob-tail crew. 'So you've been on the four-day circus,' a friend greeted me on my return. I had thought it was more than four days.

Looking back now, thirty years later, in which time I've been a passenger on some of the most luxurious ships afloat, it seems inconceivable that I should have expected glamour and cruising revelry on such a ship. It also seems incredible that a government department should have advertised such a ship in the way it did. 'Bring your glad rags,' the Public Relations Officer exhorted, as she showed me publicity stills of models and their escorts sipping cocktails at a bar. One photograph caught passengers reclining in deck chairs in sports clothes, in another a girl in a modest négligée was reading in her spacious cabin.

The *Naracoopa* was a 300-tonne cargo tramp. Loosely, a ship qualifies for the term tramp when her route is not laid down before leaving port but is dictated by the demands of cargo. She takes whatever cargo there is wherever it is offered, changing her course and schedule to do so. Within a fixed area, this is more or less what the *Naracoopa* did.

Sixteen passengers and a crew of seven on a 300-tonne tramp live cheek by jowl. There was a middle-aged honeymoon couple in the cabin next to me and I knew it. The doors of the eight two-berth cabins opened into the tiny saloon as did the miniature bar. In conception the whole was compact and workable, but in practice twenty-three people jostled, slept, ate, got drunk and were sick and generally behaved exactly as passengers do on any ship in the world except that here they were too close. On trans-oceanic cargo ships which carry ten or twelve passengers there is an area great enough to keep passengers away from the loading of cargo and out of the wheelhouse. On the *Naracoopa* there was nowhere to sit but the wheelhouse, nowhere to take the air but on the hatches leading to the two cargo holds. When the oil-burning stove in the galley 'blew out' and the wind was in the wrong direction we passengers were speckled with fine black smuts which spread as oil when we brushed them. The ship was non-union, therefore no experienced steward would step on board and a poor clerk had been shipped as steward without training of any kind on this, his first ship.

The lino on the floor was so filthy that my stiletto heels left little round drillings through it. Cockroaches appeared in the food at most meals; the tea which stewed in big enamel pots on the side of the stove was further polluted by glue-blue lumps which plopped from the milk jug. The formula for this rotten chemistry was known only to the steward who at times could be seen adding powdered milk and water to the unwashed jug, crusty dusty rings bearing witness to this. Few of the other fifteen passengers on that ship had been to sea before and they accepted the shortcomings because they had nothing to compare it with.

Because of the publicity the Government's agents had given this ship, I was reluctant to use as comparison the knowledge I had gained on small ships in the Bass Strait islands trade.

None of these ships was licensed to carry passengers, but any one of them could have given cleaner and better service. Before the trip was out I had privately decided that the *Sheerwater*, the most piratical, notorious, rumbustious shoal-jumping, regulation-breaking ketch to sail the wild waters of Bass Strait was a seaman's manual, an antiseptic clinic, in comparison to this hulk.

Mid-morning on the second day out the motors stopped, the aged captain came out of the wheelhouse and began hauling the flag up and down on the little flagpole aft. He was signalling his distress to a fishing boat near the coast. 'What's the trouble, Jack?' 'I don't know. The motor's cut out. I'm an old steam man. Steam never let a man down like these donks.' The fishing boat bobbed up and Jack shouted his message which was to be telephoned to the ship's manager from the nearest village, Swansea, and they bobbed off again. The ship was registered as an AMV (Auxiliary Motor Vessel), the auxiliary being meant to convey that in times of emergency (such as we were now experiencing) the ship could hoist canvas and sail herself to safety. This little ship's inability to do so can't be held against her. I never knew the small ship that could, but all who could possibly do so registered as auxiliary because of the cheaper fee and bought their sails second-hand at the Marine Junk Store on Salamanca Place in Hobart.

Here, off the east coast of Tasmania, old Jack hoisted sail, the passengers hauling on the halyards with the crew, in the hopes that some aeolian aid would be given his inert vessel and waft her into near-by Spring Bay. But no air came, though the old man walked up and down whistling for a wind like Captain Leisk the skipper in David Bone's *Brass Bounder*, and the sails sulked and lay on the boom until he had them hauled down when he dropped anchor until help should come.

It was the most pleasant part of the trip. Anchored in a good depth of water, in complete safety in calm, clear, balmy weather, we waited in a climate of timelessness. There was nothing to do but wait. 'It used to be like this when I was a kid,' old Jack told us, sitting on the hatch smoking his pipe and smelling of salt so you wanted to tattoo it into your olfactory nerve for forever. 'My old Dad – his name was Jedidiah and when someone said to my Granny that was a funny name to give a baby she said, "If it's good enough for the Bible it's good enough for the bush" – he would tie the horse and buggy to the hitching rail here at Swansea and I'd just sit there in the buggy waiting till he was done yarning with his cronies. There'd be the sun, and the peace and the murmur coming from the rubbedy, the pub: it was good. There was nothing to do but wait. I could lie back on that seat and do nothing till he came along and unhitched the horse and headed her for home. There wasn't a clock tickin' in all the world.'

And we heard none either, as the sun corrupted us and we abandoned ourselves like escapees from the tempo of that world we could see across the water and which could see us but do nothing about us. Where one hour before we had been scurrying from one point of land to another landfall, now the drum was stopped, the urging stilled and, foxy in the knowledge that there was an excuse for us, we ceased being alert, intelligent, companionable people doing, seeing, going and being. The crossword puzzles, the knitting and cards and books were put away and we slept in the sun and woke and talked a bit and dozed again.

To borrow from Milne's 'The Old Sailor',

I think it was awful the way we behaved;
We just did nothing until we were saved.

For a short time we experienced a whiff of eternity and slid into the skins of immortals.

When the sun went down we went below and the bar was opened; those who drank got a bit high and someone began to sing and we all joined in. We were at the 'After the Ball' stage (which is after the point where everyone has exhausted their repertoire of modern songs) when an elderly lady suggested we might listen to the nine o'clock news. 'I always listen to the news at home,' she said. The little radio in the saloon was switched on and we kept quiet for a few minutes, then, 'Anyone know "Dark Town Strutters Ball"?' Off we went again. 'I'll be down to get you in a taxi honey, Better be ready by half past eight . . .' A couple were jog-trotting around the tables, others were drumming time with soup spoons on the plates the steward had forgotten after dinner.

Suddenly the old lady said, 'Shhhhh!' and turned the radio up loud. They were talking about us. Us? Us! It was the National News from Sydney.

'A small passenger ship, the *Naracoopa*, is drifting out of control towards the open sea tonight. She has sixteen passengers aboard. The *Naracoopa* which trades from Hobart to the east coast of Tasmania broke down early today and sent a message ashore in a fishing boat that had raced to the aid of the stricken ship.

'Since then no word has been had from the vessel; but watchers ashore report that when last seen she was drifting helplessly towards the open sea. No word has been received about the safety of her passengers.' One man held his soup spoon up in the air over the plate he had been banging for a good ten seconds after the radio announcer had finished. Then he dropped it on to the table. 'Struth!' he said.

The party had ended.

There wasn't a whisper of a breeze to stir the water that night and in the silent ship the snores of the sleepers could be heard.

There were reading lamps over the bunks and I was looking through a magazine when the ship's engineer came round, saw my light, and said if I wanted a cup of tea or coffee the crew were making some in the galley. I joined them. They were a mixed bag. They were so different one from the other it looked as though the captain had gone into a pub and said, 'I'll take you, you, you and you.'

Because she was 300 tonnes the *Naracoopa* was obliged to carry a minimum of two deck officers with Masters' certificates and a qualified engineer. Smaller traders (such as *Sheerwater*) need have one qualified officer only. The mate was a portly, pompous person. Mick the engineer introduced him to me as, 'This is Chum, the mate.' Chum gave a sort of Pooh-Bah-like bow and said, 'Cholmondley Marjoriebanks at your service.'

'Leery Bill' was next. He was sixty and as spry as a thirty-year-old. Of all his teeth, only two yellow fangs were left, one each side of his upper gum. His right eye could, at times, open as wide as his left, but mostly he creased it in a leer as he nodded his head, accentuating a point. He wore the crown of an old felt hat on his head like a fez and put the brim round his neck when it rained. It made him look like a frill-necked lizard but he said it caught the rain and spilled it out six inches from his body like a verandah. He had been at sea since he was eleven years old and had a girl in the two ports the *Naracoopa* called at, as well as a wife in Hobart.

Mick pointed to another man. 'This here is Bright Boy,' he said. 'He's as nutty as a fruit cake.'

Bright Boy banged the galley wall with the palm of his open hand and said, 'Haw Haw. Give the boy the belt.' He gave a repeat performance of this any time anyone said anything he considered smart or when anyone told a tall story.

The other crew member was black, and he had walked out of the galley when I came in. 'I hate bloody passengers,' he remarked. I didn't appreciate his dislike then. I concur heartily with his sentiments now, and sympathise with him. Then there was Bert the chef. 'How are ya, mate?' he said, and pumped my hand. Anyone who wasn't a friend of his had only himself to blame.

Mick the engineer, tall, skinny, and red-headed, played the bagpipes for relaxation. He had them in the galley now and was busy lubricating them with a black syrupy mixture. He was worried about the news item. 'This is a Government-owned ship. We're Aunt Sally for the opposition in local politics. They snipe at us every chance they get. They'll really go to town now! When we get into port we can prove that the news item was a lot of boloney but that's a couple of days away and the damage'll be done by then.'

He guessed rightly how the false story had begun. 'They'd hear we were in trouble when the fishing boat went in to get the manager. Then they'd phone the locals and ask them if they could see us. (There was a break in the rugged coastline here, and we could see farmlands running down to beaches on the shore.) The locals probably looked out when old Jack was manoeuvring her, trying to sail her into Spring Bay. They wouldn't know B from a bull's foot about a ship and would think she was drifting out of control.'

Next morning the early news was the same, except that they added, 'No news has been heard for twelve hours of the disabled passenger ship *Naracoopa* which is drifting helplessly out to sea with a full load of passengers aboard.' The passengers looked at the little mantel model radio. 'It is really rather terrible,' a young woman said. 'God only knows what will become of us.' Some of the others clucked in agreement. What indeed! Talk about the perils of the deep! It was only then that I saw how different I was from the other passengers. My voyages in Bass Strait had made a sailor out of me. I had nothing in common with these fear-full people. I knew that we were in no danger; I also knew that when the day came that danger threatened I would know it as any sailor does.

The fishing boat returned that morning with the manager of the service. He snapped, 'Why haven't you worked your radio?' He meant the two-way radio that sat like a gargantuan museum piece in the wheelhouse.

'I didn't think of it,' said Jack. 'Nothing to report anyway.'

The manager snorted. 'You could at least have reported you were not drifting helplessly out to sea. Work it from now on, three times a day.'

'I can't.'

'Why?'

'I never learnt. I'm too old a dog for these new tricks.'

'Hasn't anyone on board a radio operator's ticket?'

'Chum has, but he can't work it.'

'Why?'

'He's forgotten how.'

The manager was an ill-humoured man; the crew called him the 'Big Fellow'. He pounded off to the wheelhouse, twiddled the knobs of the impressive-looking radio, spoke into it, and a voice answered immediately, 'Hobart to *Naracoopa*. Receiving you loud and clear. Go ahead. Over.'

'It works,' the Big Fellow told Chum. 'See that you do too.'

He left it all set up for him, knobs and dials in their proper positions. He then went below and had a look at the engine and came up wiping his hands on a piece of waste.

'Cracked cylinder head,' he said shortly. 'I'll send a tug. You'll be back in Hobart tomorrow night.'

He asked if any of us would like to come ashore with him in the fishing boat and he would drive us down to Hobart. A young woman, her husband and their little boy decided to go, but the rest wanted to stay on board. It was restful, and the thought of being towed home was novel.

When the fishing boat and the manager had gone, Chum decided to try the radio immediately. 'While it is warm,' as he put it. He stumped importantly up to the wheelhouse. We all followed, Jack, Mick the engineer, the crew, and the passengers. Some sat on the settees, others stood, but we all looked expectantly at Chum. We thought it was very exciting seeing a two-way radio worked. Chum was aware of our interest in him as sole radio expert on board, so he stepped up to the radio, switched it on, turned every knob it had – and it had a great many – and then he spoke into the microphone. 'Are you there, Hobart Radio. This is the *Naracoopa*.'

He switched on to Receive and an orchestral piece came blaring in. He called again. 'Hobart, please answer your radio. *Naracoopa* calling.' Again came the orchestra. Chum turned and smiled flatly at us and twiddled a dial. This time he got the Children's School Broadcast and we listened to a treatise on the benefits of decimal coinage.

'Hobart!' Chum was affronted. 'Hobart! This is *Naracoopa* speaking. Kindly reply!'

Again, the school broadcast.

'Hobart. We are in trouble.' Pleadingly now: 'SOS . . . SOS. Hobart, answer your radio.'

The school session was still on so Chum twiddled the dial and got some jazz. The passengers began twiddling things, knobs, dials, and switches. There was some promising static, but that was all.

Chum tried once again, 'SOS. We are in distress. SOS.'

Then he gave up and went to his cabin. The passengers stayed there twiddling. I even tentatively twiddled myself and a surprising thing happened. The radio spoke our name.

'*Naracoopa, Naracoopa, Naracoopa*. Hobart Radio calling VLQD the MV *Naracoopa*. Are you receiving *Naracoopa*?'

They spelt out their message in case the ship's radio was not receiving 'clearly'; it took about half an hour. 'N Nan, A Abel, R Roger, A Abel, C Charlie, O Oboe, O Oboe, P Peter, A Abel. *Naracoopa*,' And so on. Boiled down, this long message said a tug was on the way.

When the tug arrived it put a man aboard who could work the radio and while we silently slid along the water on the long line from the tug ahead we listened to him talking first to the ship towing us, then to Hobart Radio. It looked and sounded simple now.

But it wasn't all that simple. It relieved us of our

immortality and reminded us of the morrow. We listened to the news that night, below deck on the little mantel radio. Enthusiastically the announcer said: 'We are now in contact with the disabled passenger ship *Naracoopa* and the latest news is that she has been picked up by the tug and is being brought to Hobart. Her passengers and crew are all safe though suffering from an uncomfortable night. Several have been safely taken off in a fishing boat.'

The magical moments of the timeless day had gone. The ship was little and smelt horribly and the passengers were people like me going somewhere, doing something, always doing something, being busy even on their holiday. I escaped up top-side.

The tow rope was very long, its great length weighted down in the water with mighty anchors to prevent its 'whipping'. The tug was so far away from us that it was out of sight and we sailed silently, sail-less, a phantasm on a waveless ocean in a windless world. Flights of silver strings of spray soared back along our timbers as we planed over the smooth sea, and where the water picked up the loom of the lights from the portholes, circular silk-green lustres followed us like luminous jellyfish, wavering and convoluting and keeping pace by our side. There wasn't a wrinkle on the fabric of the water. We glided home over a vast plain of black ice in a sled. Far ahead, a thousand feet above the ocean, the lighthouse sent out its warning. No other light showed. The whole world was water. There was little sound; only the lilting tinkle of tinsel water on the breast of our magic carpet that was made of a tree, the lazy creak of the chain of the gipsy on its way aft to the rudder with the message from the man on the wheel who steered to the occasional glow from the stern light of the invisible tug far ahead.

It is said that there are things about the sea that no man who has felt them can describe and no man who has not known can understand.

As I sat on the tarpaulin-covered hatch coaming and watched the tinsel echelons spray in flight from the deep mystery of the dark element that was our beginning, I badly wanted to go to sea again. Late that night, before the false dawn, the tug returned to us. Since midnight its light had been coming closer and closer as they hauled in the tow line and took up the anchors. Now they made fast to our quarter and we chugged the last miles up the river to port in tandem harness, the tug chuffing and huffing importantly like some small dog trying to give the kiss of life to a St Bernard.

Whenever a bull was winched out to the Sheerwater *Captain Jackson had to slide a strapping beneath the beast to hoist it on board.*

The crew of the Naracoopa. *Clockwise from me are Bill and Wally; the captain, Alastair Maddock; our engineer, Mick; 1st mate 'Chum' Wood, and the cook. The two young men at top left, like many of our seamen, moved from ship to ship.*

Dave Rhodes carries a full spit-load of mutton birds on Great Dog Island.

Huts on the isolated islands were used during the mutton-bird season. Fresh tussocks were laid daily on the earth floor.

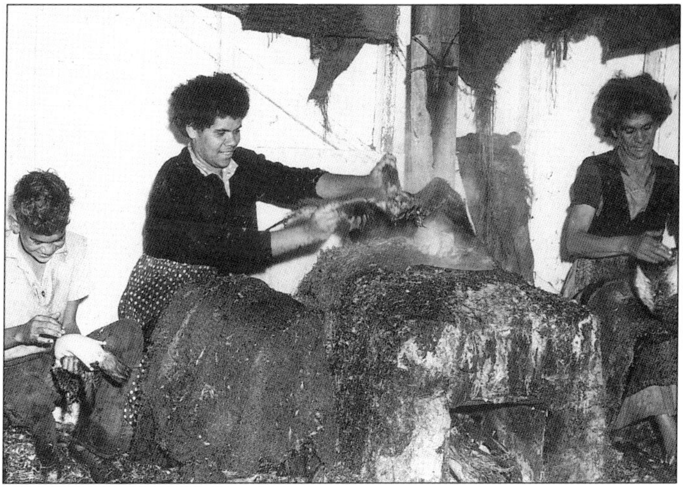

Cape Barren islanders plucking mutton birds on Great Dog Island.

Sometimes passengers helped haul the mainsail on the Naracoopa.

The Naracoopa *took mechanics to the lights around the coast of Tasmania and the Bass Strait islands, including Maatsuyker Island.*

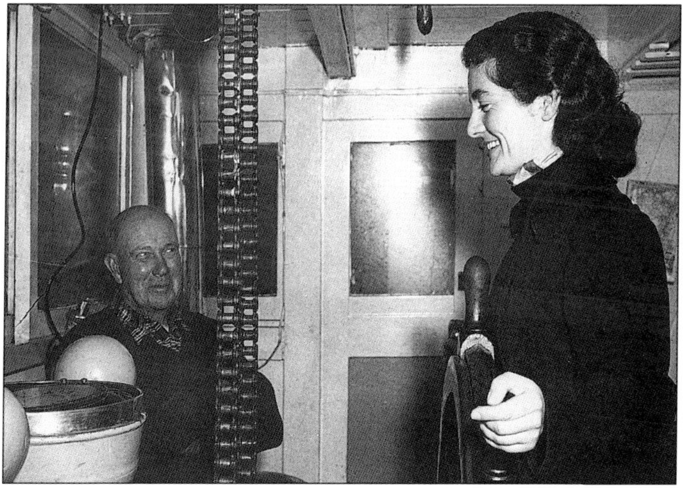

Steering by compass on a very dark night with the company of 1st mate 'Chum' Wood on the Naracoopa.

To get to the top of Tasman Island from the landing, a horse pulled a trolley up a thousand feet. In those days I was pretty fit and ran up the haulage way ahead of the passenger trolley to take this photograph.

The basket that carried all visitors from the rocky shores of Tasman Island to the landing way above the water needed maintenance like any other piece of equipment.

Captain Alastair Maddock (right) loaded cargo as often as did the men. Here he takes the lone wool bale of Mr Robey on the south of Maria Island.

Rolling home.

13

Calavances, Slung-shots and Ship's Biscuits

Why then did I join her? Knowing the worst about her, why would I decide to sail with her?

She was a beautiful little ship, only sixteen years old, not at all old for a wooden vessel, and had been built by a craftsman on the banks of the Tamar River at Launceston. Men would see her in a port and come to her and rub their hands over her timbers and talk about the forest where the trees that became her stem had grown, and how they'd adzed her keel and carved her ribs and fitted her strakes. She had been built for the Holyman empire, the men who took traders out of Tasmanian ports when they were still in short pants and built up a reputation of service and quality and progress that later brought into being the Australian National Airways (later Ansetts). Holymans never built in a great shipyard. The job of building each of their small ships was given to men who used the bank of a river for a cradle and who went themselves into the forests to choose the trees that would become her timbers. *Naracoopa* and her sister ship *Loatta* had been built expressly for the island trade. There's a saying among Straitsmen that the little wooden island trader that hasn't scraped the bottom has never been properly worked. These craftsmen-builders knew this and they built accordingly. In a group such as the Furneaux, where only two out of the forty-two islands had a pier, small ships must go in as close as possible, often lying on the bottom when the tide goes out. In waterways where uncharted sand shoals are a shifting menace, the ship must be able to withstand the occasional shock of striking bars and riding over them.

The *Naracoopa* was built with this in mind. Her frames, hull, bow, and keel were moulded and strengthened to provide for this emergency. That she was built well was proven in the six years that followed the year I joined her. In that time she was worked as I believe no ship in Australian waters was worked. She was kept almost perpetually at sea to build up her trade, and to keep to an economic schedule she took many risks. She was grounded, stranded; she hit a reef; she was left high and dry so often waiting for enough water to float her off that we, her crew, became known as 'the overlanders', yet fault never showed in the ship herself. Whatever men did to her, however she was handled, whatever was said about her, could not alter the basic fact: she was as beautiful a ship as ever took to the water.

I have often been asked, 'But how did you get started? How did you first get on a ship?' More women are interested in going to sea than the numbers who actually do so indicate, and this problem of beginning bewilders a few. But the majority get no further than day-dreaming about it because of a social disapproval peculiar almost to this country alone. The naïvety of laymen imposes a tyrannical fetter against which most have no weapon. From the time the first logs were paddled across rivers seamen have been used to women on vessels (not that there have been many), and they have never objected to a woman sailing if she knew and performed her duties. Ships cost a lot of money to run – even when they are tied up to a wharf – and no owner is going to risk trouble with his crew because of some silly woman who does not know how to avoid tricky situations.

I read once that a well-known deep-sea captain stated he would never sign a girl on his crew. 'Women cause enough trouble on shore without taking them to sea.' I should think few women would want to sail with such a man. A captain must be a man who has control of himself, his ship and his crew. Certainly there have been tales of girls smuggled on board ships for love, companionship or lust, but a miserable time these poor dears must have of it, cooped up in a stuffy hiding place, prohibited the run of the deck, frightened by the sound of the sea they cannot see, eating whatever can be pocketed down to them, seasick, left alone four hours out of eight in their prison. Some girls may go to sea this way but I doubt if any do it twice.

There is little scope on a small ship for dalliance. Lack of privacy is one dissuading factor; another is fatigue. When I read Robert Close's *Love Me Sailor* I laughed and laughed when I came to the chapter where the mate, after many vicissitudes, gets the girl where he wants her, begins to undress, pulls one sea boot off, and falls asleep as he tugs at the other. That hit the nail on the head.

This does not apply on the great passenger liners as any traveller who has witnessed the appraisal and appropriation of talent by ships' officers on the first night out can testify. The great lady liner and the little coastal tramp both travel over water, but there the similarity ends. The sea and those who do business on it are enigmas to landsmen. Many city people have forgotten how much the feel and scent of the seas lapping their doorsteps once dominated their lives. But I was now in Hobart in 1954, and here we were different.

Our city faced the sea; ships cruised right up to within one block of the GPO. Shop girls and messenger boys ate their lunch on the wharves and the talk of the town was around the ships in port, their cargo and the men who sailed in them. In Hobart there have always been women going down to the sea in ships, mostly fishing boats and ferries, although here I once met the only woman – the only person actually – I have ever known who has sailed into every major port in the world. But no woman had been articled on a coastal trader.

I do not know how a woman would go about getting a berth on a ship but I believe that if you are keen enough the sea will meet you halfway, as it met me. Shortly after that deplorable voyage on the *Naracoopa* I travelled to Launceston in a car with the Commissioner for Transport in Tasmania, Charles Bird.

'And how did you enjoy your trip?' he asked me. I had had time to think about the things that were wrong – and told him. Before we reached Launceston on the Tamar, where the little ships on the Bass Strait islands trade tie up, I had been offered a job on the ship, with the same pay as the seamen, which was far more than I could earn onshore, and as I had grave responsibilities this was important. A cabin would be built on deck for me if I would give a guarantee to stay twelve months and study for a radio operator's ticket providing the captain was in agreement. 'Oh he likes me,' I truthfully said. The old man and I had got along well.

As if to assure himself that the offer was to a worthy fellow the Commissioner then began to give me a sort of grilling.

'How would you look on your knees with a scrubbing brush in your hand?'

'It wouldn't be the first time.'

'You'd have to show you were worth your wages.'

'You mean I'd have to work harder than a man?'

'You'd have to fill in your time usefully. Have you a radio operator's licence?'

'I could get one. My mother taught me morse key when she was a bush post mistress.'

'We'd need someone with nursing experience.'

'I've got that. Two-and-a-half years in an army hospital.'

'Might need to cook if the chef's ill.'

'I'm a good cook.'

Formerly, when the Australian Immigration Authorities did not intend to admit a migrant they gave him a language test in Urdu or Biblical Hebrew and I was afraid these questions were meant to be of a somewhat similar nature.

'Our cook can take a turn at the wheel.'

'I can steer four hours at a time.' I felt by now like a migrant who has written an essay in Sanskrit and on demand translated it successfully into Hebrew.

'You're too small to be a help with cargo.'

'Try me.' From being a casual passenger in a car I realised I had now become tense, determined, hauling myself up the gangway on to that little ship hand over hand.

'I'll write to you and confirm it,' he said.

Joining the *Naracoopa* was quite a formal affair. When the preliminaries were over I felt I ought to walk with a rolling gait and smoke a pipe. First I was signed on. It was a most impressive business. With the captain, I marched around the waterfront to the Marine Board offices and lined up outside the Harbour Master's office with the other seamen. When my name was called – just the surname of course, no handles for below decks – I trotted in beside old Jack. When he had recovered from the surprise of seeing a woman in that salty atmosphere, the Harbour Master was pleasant, but he obviously didn't know why I was there.

Old Jack told him it was my name he'd just called out. He looked down and saw the Christian names, Patricia Jean. After turning a few pages and finding nothing to expunge this he rattled off a list of questions. Place and year of birth, name of last ship, whether honourably discharged or not, rank and rate of pay.

When I'd signed on the dotted line he said suspiciously, 'Do you know how big the *Naracoopa* is?'

'Oh yes, I've had one trip on her,' I said.

'Right!' he snapped, and shouted out the name of the next seaman to come forward, as though he'd gone as far as decorum allowed in warning me. Then, as a parting shot: 'You've a right to be shown the Articles.'

'What Articles?'

'The Articles, the contract, between you and the ship.'

I didn't know what the Articles were but if they were to be seen then I felt I ought to see them. When we got back to the ship I followed Jack up to the wheelhouse and there, on the wall, he pointed them out to me, a large sheet of paper, being the agreement between the owners and the crew – the Articles. They gave such titbits of information as SCALE OF PROVISIONS TO BE ALLOWED AND SERVED OUT TO THE CREW DURING THE VOYAGE.

WATER: 4 quarts daily, 28 weekly.

SOFT BREAD: Sunday, 1 lb., Tuesday, 1 lb., Thursday, 1 lb., weekly, 3 lb.

The alternative for the other four days was not so good.

SHIP'S BISCUITS: 1 lb. per day, 4 lb. per week. (There was a ship's biscuit in the Hobart Museum. It was in the section relating to whaling days of last century. It was square, and big, and had large holes drilled through it. The ticket beside it said they had been drilled by weevils.) The ration scale went on to say that on Mondays and Thursdays 1 lb. of pork was issued. Sundays, Tuesdays, and Saturdays there was salt beef.

The scale covered all sorts of things from 1¾ oz. of tea per week to OATMEAL, 4 oz. Tuesdays, 4 oz. Saturdays.

There was syrup or molasses, ½ lb. per week, and ¼ oz. of mustard, curry powder, and pepper also per week.

SUFFICIENT WITHOUT WASTE, was written largely and fulsomely across the page.

There was only one bit of it I liked. The part that said in addition the seamen would be given lime juice and sugar or other anti-scorbutics. I thought that should be both refreshing and good for the health. Then, across the page from the seamen's menus there were printed the REGULATIONS FORMULATED IN 1894 FOR MAINTAINING DISCIPLINE.

WHEREIN, THE SEVERAL PERSONS ENGAGED AS SAILORS AGREE TO CONDUCT THEMSELVES IN AN ORDERLY, FAITHFUL, HONEST, AND SOBER MANNER AND TO BE AT ALL TIMES DILIGENT IN THEIR RESPECTIVE DUTIES AND TO BE OBEDIENT TO THE LAWFUL COMMANDS OF THE SAID MASTER . . . WHETHER ON BOARD, IN BOATS, OR ON SHORE. IN CONSIDERATION OF WHICH SERVICES TO BE DULY PERFORMED THE SAID MASTER HEREBY AGREES TO PAY THE SAID CREW AS WAGES THE SUMS AGAINST THEIR NAMES RESPECTIVELY EXPRESSED AND TO SUPPLY THEM WITH PROVISIONS ACCORDING TO THE SCALE.

AND IT IS FURTHER AGREED THAT IF ANY SEAMAN ENTERS HIMSELF IN A CAPACITY FOR WHICH HE IS INCOMPETENT HE IS LIABLE TO BE DISRATED.

Then there was a list of fines for various offences.

1 5/- FOR STRIKING ANYONE ON BOARD SHIP (I didn't think I was ever likely to strike anyone but I was mistaken. I later hit a man with a teapot).

2 5/- FOR HAVING INTOXICATING LIQUOR ON BOARD.

3 5/- FOR DRUNKENNESS (10/- FOR EACH SUBSEQUENT OFFENCE).

4 5/- FOR TAKING ON BOARD AND HAVING POSSESSION OF ANY FIREARMS, KNUCKLE DUSTERS, LOADED CANE, SLUNG-SHOT, SWORD STICK, BOWIE KNIFE, OR DAGGER, WITHOUT THE CONSENT OF THE MASTER.

5 INSOLENT OR CONTEMPTUOUS LANGUAGE OR BEHAVIOUR TO

THE MASTERS OR DISOBEDIENCE TO LAWFUL COMMAND.

6 2 DAYS PAY FOR EACH DAY ABSENT FROM DUTY WITHOUT LEAVE.

I read each word carefully. There were two foolscap-sized sheets of paper. It took a long time. When I'd finished, I turned to old Jack. 'I agree.'

He was sitting on the settee reading the daily paper and smoking his pipe.

'What?' he asked.

'I agree to the Articles,' I said.

He looked from me to the paper pinned on the wall.

'Oh.' He put down the newspaper, stood up and began to read them himself. When he got to the part that mentioned offences he asked me, 'What's a slung-shot?'

'I don't know,' I admitted.

'I don't either.' He read on.

'Might be a shanghai,' he said later. 'I used to be pretty good with a shanghai when I was a boy. Five bob eh?' he chuckled.

Next he asked what were calavances. I'd wondered that too. 'You're supposed to have ⅓ pint of them per week.' Then he whooped and laughed and slapped his thigh.

'Biscuits! Ship's biscuits! Monday, Wednesday, Friday, and Saturday, 1 lb. per man.'

Bright Boy was out on deck with the rest of the crew, stowing cargo. Old Jack called him up to the wheelhouse.

'You're pretty fond of the tooth, aren't you, Bright Boy? Ever read what you've signed for by way of food?'

I was surprised when Bright Boy said no.

Old Jack read it out to him. Bright Boy looked incredulous for a moment, then he turned and banged the wall with his open palm. 'Give the boy the belt,' he yelled. 'Always out for a joke, that's you, Jack. Ship's biscuits. Haw haw! Wait till I tell the boys!'

He went down and told the boys and they all came up and

read it too. I went away, conscious that I was probably the first crew member who'd ever asked to read the Articles through. I knew old Jack would want me out of the way so he could tell the crew.

14

Ready for Off

Never again will I know weeks of such doleful drudgery. I saw nothing of our route, I didn't see the sea or the shore or the ports we made or the sheltered cove where no man lived and we snugged down for the night. Sometimes I heard the crackle of a command, a scuffle of boots above my head as men ran to heave lines, a confusion of voices and dull thuds as cargo was loaded, the screech of the wood of our ship rubbing on the wood of a wharf, the clang of the engine room telegraph, and sometimes our ship's siren telling other people that we were arriving or departing.

Our coming and going was of no moment to me. I had time for nothing but scrubbing, washing, cleaning, scraping, serving. I slept between midnight and 6 a.m. 'Ready for off?'

the old salt who lives on a boat in Constitution Dock used to greet me as I passed on my way to the ship at dawn at the beginning of each voyage. 'Ready for off?' the waterfront cry that is the tenuous bond between men who work on the water's edge and those who go down to the sea. Ready for off.

The drudge in the waterfront pub had a life as exciting as mine but easier. The floors that had accepted the imprint of my stiletto heels through their deep grime I first scraped with a paint-removing spatula and then scrubbed. Mick the engineer watched the colour come up through the suds on the lino. 'I remember now – it had sort of marble colours when it was put down first,' he told me. 'Pink and green and cream.' He said he never saw it again after that week. He offered me a large tin full of a cleansing powder which he said would 'lift anything', and in my enthusiasm I watched it take the grease from the lino without noticing my hands until the skin had completely gone. The exquisite tenderness in the extremity of my finger-tips and on the heel of my thumb grieved me for months. Once the floors were clean they stayed that way with a mop out or 'soojee' each morning – except when we were on the slip, when the grease from engineers' boots defeated every precaution I took to protect them.

In between my other duties I spent every spare hour the first two trips on this original purge. Muscles I never knew I had ached. Sometimes I felt I had contracted some rare disease and, as with riding a horse after an absence of years, every bone ached including the poll of my skull. It was useless to tell myself that these were joys of strenuous action greater than my friends at university and the conservatorium would ever know. I thought often those days of the quiet of my study. There was no relief from labour here.

There were two high coamings to be negotiated from the galley into the saloon. Up and over, up and over, backwards and forwards until my thigh muscles twitched and I barked my shins on the brass-bound wall of a coaming. If your shins are tender or the blood is running down your leg, you lift your leg high up, up and over.

When I was free I would go to my cabin up on deck and fall into my wooden cot – no thought now of the tinsel tinkle of silver spray and the fabric of the water. I never looked over the rail, just climbed stolidly up the iron companionway along the deck into the cabin and fell on the bunk. The first few nights I was denied rest even there, until it was found that the bunk was twelve centimetres lower at the head than at the foot and I had been lying downhill. (Like any seaman, I refused to sleep any other way but head to the bow of the ship. I did try the other way but was unable to settle. As for a 'skew-wise' bunk, one athwart ships, I can't imagine why they are permitted.)

As well as my misfitted bunk the cabin had another impediment: it was built around the funnel. There were times when it was like being trapped inside a concertina. The whole structure vibrated, walls, bunk, closet. My shoes danced a tarantella on the floor. Rattle, rattle went the door on its hook, shiver, shiver, shiver, shiver undulated the curtain at the door. And at times everything went whoomp, whoomp, whoomp, whoomp for hours on end like the heart-beat of a great animal – with a very tired human being trapped inside for a sounding box.

There was no one I could talk to, no one with whom I felt any kinship. Old Jack the captain was kindly and inclined to conversation, but I had no time yet to accept his invitation to come up to the wheelhouse for a yarn whenever I had a moment to spare. Mick the engineer was kindly too – a spare, scrawny man who spent most of his waking hours in his engine room – but I hadn't yet shared any labours, dangers, or troubles with any of this crew. I was not happy. And the passengers hounded me every day and part of the night. It was not at all like going down to the sea in ships, and I was obliged to stay for twelve months.

When reinforcements to my morale arrived they brought all the carefree camaraderie I had expected on a small ship with them. 'There are three young ... er ... gentlemen wanting to see you,' Chum told me with distaste. We were tied up in Hobart to rickety old Franklin Pier at the end of a voyage.

'To see me?' I knew few people in those days in Hobart.

'I told them there must be some mistake but they insisted you would see them.' He described them. 'One is a pirate with long gold hair, another a thin spiv. and an *enfant terrible* who has a single word vocabulary of "Jeez".'

I hurried to the deck. There, tied up on the other side of the pier, was the *Sheerwater*, as disreputable as ever, and there standing on the pier were Les, her owner-captain, Alec his leading hand, and Pete, the boy. They looked as disreputable as their ship but their grins took the ache from my body. The four of us had shared so many laughs, labours, and dangers we had a bond akin to family ties.

I showed them over the *Naracoopa*, suddenly proud of 'my ship'. When they saw the section aft of the galley door they sucked in their breaths in a whistle of approval. I showed them the passenger cabins, the bunks all nicely made up with clean linen and pink bedspreads. 'Ho!' said Alec, who considered himself a lady-killer but looked like a wet-nosed greyhound, 'they're just like real beds. Very suggestive.' I made them a pot of tea and served cakes. 'Ho, very posh!' Afterwards Les left to visit friends and Alec decided casually that he'd 'go and look up a dame I once knew' (I felt that the sight of those bunks had prompted this urge). Pete stayed to talk. I told him about my duties and when I got to the part where I issued clean sheets, pillow slips, and towels to the crew each week he was incredulous.

'You're having me on,' he said.

Before he left to go back on board the *Sheerwater* he said, 'You'd better get me a job on this tub I reckon.'

Then suddenly he decided that what he had said was an enormity. 'Struth! You don't think I'm serious do you?' he said, guffawing. 'Fancy me! In sheets! Talking to passengers! And the likes! Jeez!'

'I was only "yolking",' he said, using an old *Sheerwater* saying to get back on familiar ground.

'I'll see what I can do,' I called, as he vaulted down onto the wharf.

The seaman who couldn't abide passengers deserted the next day and I mentioned Pete. Old Jack was glad to have him. For someone who was only 'yolking' Pete came over the side mighty fast when Jack told him he could sign on.

Later the same day Alec came down to where I was scrubbing the saloon. 'Hi, shipmate,' he said. He'd joined her too. The *Sheerwater* would be tied up for a time and the crew had been paid off.

The arrival of this outrageous pair lent a buoyancy to my labours and outlook that soared until life took on the contented consistency I had desired. Their very nonsense buoyed me. They were artless, unlearned, uncouth; they called a spade a bloody shovel; their lack of affectation suited well the sea and this small ship. I cannot imagine being as amused onshore as I was at sea by their nonsense. I could go to my bunk weary at night and laugh over the pranks they'd got up to during the day. Once I sat Pete at the passengers' table and after greeting the company, 'I'm so hungry I could eat a horse and chase the rider,' he looked at a dowager opposite, 'Do you ride?' Then he tucked in, slurping noisily at his soup, and dropped great hunks of bread into his bowl. Suddenly he hesitated. He had caught sight of a young girl at the end of the table. She was sipping prettily from her soup spoon, her little finger stuck out genteelly like a skewer. 'Jeez!' said Pete in admiration. The other passengers laughed, but the girl's look would have sent a steel bolt right through a plated deck.

Alec came to me in the pantry later. 'You can't have Pete

going on like that in the saloon,' he said. 'Passengers won't stand for it. The girl will report him, I bet. We should speak to him.' I knew I was no match for that boy but I trotted along beside Alec to look for him. He was hard to find. Alec searched the crew quarters and I looked everywhere else. I thought he must have been hiding through shame. 'Remorse will never catch up with the boy,' Alec said. Alec had worked on plenty of ships and knew all the hiding places. We went to them all. In the end we climbed up on to Monkey Island and looked in one of the canvas-covered lifeboats. There was Pete, but not alone. Snuggled up to his shirtless chest was the girl who sipped soup genteelly.

'Well! that beats the band,' was all Alec could say.

Alec was a great mimic. We once had a passenger who made me very uncomfortable. He said it disturbed him to see a woman working on such a ship. While I scrubbed the floor he sat on a chair, drawing it along the lino, keeping pace as my work took me progressively through the saloon and up the alleyways. 'I don't like to see a lady such as you doing this sort of work.' Alec, until he left the ship years later would only have to see me down on my knees scrubbing to grab a chair and recite his lines, 'You're too good for this sort of thing. This work isn't for the likes of you. I can't bear to watch a woman like you do work like this.' I would try to ignore him but usually I had to threaten him with a wet floor-cloth to make him desist. This simple unsophisticated humour fitted the sea, where subtlety can sometimes seem specious.

15

Rock-hopping, Dog-barking Navigation

As I gradually got the section below decks better organised I began to come up for air and make friends at the out-of-the-way places we serviced. Little ships become figures of fun in large ports precisely because of these funny, off-the-beaten-track landfalls they must make in order to deliver the sugar and flour, the hens and a horse and sheep, pigs, dogs, geese, bacon, vegetables, spirits for Christmas, and everything else people need to turn their isolation into home. The Tasmanian Government bought the *Naracoopa* to provide for the population cut off from other forms of transport provided by the State. Few of the scattered places we visited were accessible by road; for some we were the only link with the world.

To reach the east coast of Tasmania we had the choice of

two routes: 'the long way round', going south past Cape Raoul and round Tasman Island, or 'through the ditch', the canal at Dunalley. This latter was not only shorter but it was through smooth, sheltered waters. The long way round, or, as they sometimes called it, 'round the Raoul', was never smooth and mostly rough to very rough.

'Taking her round the Raoul' was synonymous with 'having the guts rolled out of you' in *Naracoopa* language. But the canal had its moments also.

The first time I went 'through the ditch' I nearly said 'Jeez!' like Pete. The actual cut is through a small piece of land, a narrow isthmus over which the old-timers used to drag their small boats. Near the Hobart-side entrance there is a bridge for road traffic to cross. As the ship neared the canal, old Jack pulled the whistle cord and the mournful hoots went woop-wooping across to the bridgeman who wound the bridge open by hand like a patient beast going round and round the whim. I watched. I thought there must be a mistake. Was that tiny gap all the space we had? The closer it came, the smaller it looked and the larger our ship looked. Old Jack called down from the flying bridge (Monkey Island, the crew called it) 'Full Ahead,' and it was rung through on the telegraph. Speed wouldn't get us through that strongly timbered opening, I was thinking. Then Jack called, 'Half Ahead, then Slow Ahead.' Ah, that's better. He must be going to turn her round and head back to the nice big paddock of sea behind us.

'What's happening?' I asked Alec, who was scurrying by.

'Terrible strong tides come through such a narrow cutting,' he said. 'Big bay on either side. They sweep through like fury.'

I looked over the side. The water was charging along, carrying us with it at a speed faster than our motors could ever have taken us, closer and closer to the shrinking gap. The boys on the fo'c'sle were hanging motor-car tyres tied onto ropes over the bow as fenders and were standing by to adjust them if necessary . . . they'll be needed for sure . . . the mate was standing by to let the anchor go if need be, the wheel behind me in the wheelhouse, now 'ghost driven' by the wheel above on the flying bridge, was swinging first one way then the other as old Jack, alone on the wheel, fought the surging tide.

And then we were into the gap.

'Full Ahead,' Jack yelled, his voice strained and panting. The tide was now running against us from the bay on the other side of the cut and he was countering it.

Even as we slid through the gap I still didn't believe we could make it. Crowds of tourists on their way to and from the ruins of the convict settlement of Port Arthur hung over the gate on either side of the bridge opening, but as we came closer they began to run and were well back as we reached the bridge. Only the bridgeman remained. He smiled through the wheelhouse window at me but I was too startled to return the greeting. Up on the fo'c'sle the boys were hauling the fenders in. We were through. Pete came back to tell me. 'There's almost no clearance when we go through the bridge,' he said. 'Jeez.'

The red mud walls of the canal reared up on either side of us, but the bridge was astern.

When we got into Blackman's Bay we had to follow a narrow channel for eleven kilometres before we reached the open sea, but it was marked with beacons, and Jack left a boy on the wheel for a time and came down to the wheelhouse. He was so exhausted from wrestling the wheel against the tide that he slumped down on the settee and didn't speak for a long while. Sweat was running down his face and the back of his shirt was stained with it. When he took his cap off there was a deep ridge round his forehead where it had cut it. An operator must stand by the telegraph till we reached the open sea as the next eleven kilometres of the channel through the bay were tricky. The mate must stay on the fo'c'sle. When he was rested Jack went back up top ready for the next battle.

This was at the Narrows, the opening of the bay to the sea.

I knew about shoals because of my time in the Furneaux Islands and recognised one on one side of the entrance; on the other side of the narrow-gut way there was a reef.

Pete came in and said, 'Talk about out of the frying pan into the fire!' The sea came hurling in between the reef and shoal and broke over both, but instead of turning out through the opening our ship swung in to a rickety jetty near the reef.

This was Little Chinaman's, where a small sawmill turned out boards for making apple cases. The boards were not stapled together in any way and the whole consignment had to be picked up board by board until an armful could be carried to the ship. A few of the passengers rolled up their shirt sleeves and helped us. It took hours.

When we were ready to sail there was not enough water to float us back out to the channel. One line tied us to an iron stake driven into the shingle beach and another to a tree trunk and there we stayed. When the incoming tide brought enough water to float us, Jack decided to spend the night there instead.

'There won't be a moon tonight,' he told the boys.

'So what?' Pete said.

Old Jack looked him square in the eye. 'You're not suggesting I take the ship up the coast in the dark are you? How do you think a man would find his way without moonlight or stars?'

Pete and Alec showed no sign but I sensed their concern. I waited in the galley. In a few minutes they were there, both talking at once.

'Well! Did you ever! Struth! Well strike me lucky!'

'I never thought I'd sail with a rock-hopping, dog-barking navigator,' Alec said.

A dog-barking, rock-hopping navigator is a man who can't read a chart, hasn't even learnt to use his compass in conjunction with his time piece. It signifies travel from the sound of the dogs barking in one town onshore until you pick up the dogs barking in the next town and so on up the coast. Rock-hopping is similar. You travel onward from one rock until you pick up the next in your sights and so on.

I remembered that Les Jackson would give an order to steer a certain course on the compass for a certain length of time when we were sailing to Launceston. When that time was up he'd come out and change the ship onto another course. I never wondered why. I was as content to steer by the compass as I was to steer to a point of land. The boys reminded me that he'd usually have 'a look round' first, before changing course. 'He took bearings off lighthouses and plotted the course from those bearings on the chart.'

'You can do it by the stars too. You call it celestial navigation then.'

'And that's better than rock-hopping, dog-barking etc.' Pete said. 'Even I know that.'

'That's exactly what old Jack does if it's fine enough. Otherwise he stays put, like tonight.'

'Progress must be slow,' I volunteered.

'That's what's put most little ships out of business. It was all right in the days when wages were a couple of bob a week and a lump of salt junk for food. Mostly they depended on sail and didn't have fuel bills. Now with high wages, the best of food, and expensive fuel . . . the ship-owners just can't stand it.'

I thought the solution was simple. Replace the old-timers with men who could read a chart and could plot a course. Alec explained that it takes the same training to turn a man out as skipper on a little ship as a mate on a big ship. He told me the comfort for officers on the big ships was unbelievable. 'Even got a cabin boy to look after them! Tell me one man you know as young as Wallaby, as well educated and with as much money, who would live the way he has to to make the *Sheerwater* pay? Good small-ships' men are a dying race,' Alec said seriously and truthfully.

Next morning we headed out through the Narrows, and up comfortably in the lee of Maria Island. It was certainly a 'cosy' trip via 'the ditch', sheltered all the way.

Maria Island has had a chequered history. Its old buildings were built by convicts when they were imprisoned here in the early 1800s. Now the whole island was deserted; only a handful of old-stagers hung on, all pensioners except one family trying to make a living from crushing limstone. This day the *Naracoopa* was to load some of the lime and I cut lunches for the passengers so they could go ashore and explore the ruins. I made it sound a cross between Stonehenge, the Colosseum, and George Washington's birthplace to make sure they would go. When they set off with their little cribs under their arms, I set off in the opposite direction. Intending to go to Darlington, the village where the seven or eight settlers lived, I started up an old avenue of English oaks to the derelict barracks square and there I met a little old lame man wheeling a barrow.

He was not as big as me, but his tongue in his wise old head was wittier than most. I told him who I was and where I came from.

'I'm Harry Hunt. Come and meet the Missus,' he said immediately. 'I haven't had a chance to make her jealous since "the works" closed down.' He took hold of the handles of the wheelbarrow again and set off at a fine pace, even though it was dot and carry one because of his crippled leg.

'Did it at the works,' he told me bluntly. 'The Cement Works. It was a huge concern here fifty years ago. Hundreds worked at it. Some mighty fine women here in those days. I was the first man worked there, and the last put off.'

He and 'the Missus' lived in a tiny cottage at the top of a hill.

After we left the avenue there was no road and we walked first along the beach, then up a grassy hillside. As we climbed

I saw the curtains twitch at one of the windows in the tiny cottage above.

'Hee hee hee!' the little old man crowed. 'It's the Missus with the glasses on us. Hee hee hee! I won't half cop it after you leave!'

Harry would be lucky to weigh 45 kilograms. 'The Missus' was 100 kilograms at least.

'Call me Ruby,' she boomed, as I entered the warm, cosy little nook she shared with her wizened spouse.

'I saw you coming so I've got the kettle boiling.' Not only that. She had a snowy white starched cloth on the table, spread with home-made cakes, biscuits, tarts, and scones.

'Just a snack,' she said.

She talked and talked. There was no need to reply, and there was no time. She told me that she worked the two-way radio – which she called 'the blower' – the island had recently acquired.

It wasn't till she moved to the hob to get more water for the teapot that I noticed her legs. They were encased in knee-length, lace-up boots. A spider had bitten her when she was a young woman and she had never been able to walk properly since. Inside the cottage she had the furniture for support, but outside she depended on two sticks and made slow, painful progress.

'I only go outside to care for my hens and my cats and dogs,' she told me. 'But I always watch the *Naracoopa* go by and now that I know you I'll wave a curtain and you can wave back.' I agreed to wave a tea towel from aft near the flagpole.

Harry hadn't got a word in all afternoon, but he looked happy and contented for all that.

'The Missus has taken to you, Pat,' he said, as he walked me back to the ship. 'She'll look after you. I bet she sends you chooks and eggs and all. She'll send you the biggest cockerel every Easter and Christmas. She liked you, the Missus did. I could tell. But I bet she's got the glasses on us all the same.' I'd seen the field glasses on the bench beneath the window. I was tempted to pick the antique little man up and cuddle him to see if the curtains would twitch again.

She had told me she used the glasses to 'keep my eye on the villagers below'. I didn't doubt it at all, neither did I wonder at it. If I lived there unable to move about, year in year out, I would too. She was a remarkable woman doing a remarkable jop to cope, and in time I found her heart as big as her body.

The next port of call was Swansea, a pretty seaside tourist village. There were a few boxes of groceries to put ashore there and the most abominable cargo I ever knew to be loaded – ground wattle bark, on its way to the tanneries in the city. The dust from this was so fine that it penetrated the eyes, nose, and mouth of those loading it till their eyes ran and their mouths became parched. It was so bad Pete had to tear the tail off Alec's shirt to staunch his dripping nose while he sat at the table that night.

We tied up for the night at a near-by fishing village, Triabunna, to pick up a family who leased Schouten Island. Joe Howells, the man from Schouten Island, came down at breakfast time and asked old Jack to wait a while longer because he wanted to load some sheep coming in from another of his farms. So we waited. It was very pleasant. The crew were glad to do nothing for a night and a half-day and still have their pay running up. Old Bert the chef and I saw no appreciable difference in the volume of our work, but as Bert said, 'No one cares nothin' for us.'

Joe arrived after lunch with his wife, three sons, two dogs, and one hundred sheep. He was a likeable old toiler who enjoyed telling us how he started from nothing and now owned three farms, paying £1000 a year for the lease of Schouten Island.

His frisky, friendly dogs lay on deck gnawing away at bones just as if they were on the veranda at home, but within an hour of our leaving for the island they were so seasick they were stretched out flat where they lay, their paws held over their eyes and ears, their bones forgotten beside them.

Getting Mrs Howells ashore was simple. When the ship's boat had been taken as close as possible to the shore, one of her sons jumped overboard and stood with his back to the dinghy. The old lady then straddled his shoulders and was carried ashore so comfortably that as I waded beside her she could even point out to me features of interest with one spare hand.

There was no wharf; each sheep had to be carried, cradled in a man's arms, to the bulwarks and handed down to another seaman in the workboat bobbing alongside. 'Darling,' said Alec, gazing down into the big brown stupid eyes of a sheep as he carried it over to the boat. Cate, my daughter, small and pigtailed, was sitting on a forty-four gallon drum on deck nursing her dolly and watching the fun. Suddenly old Leery Bill gathered her and her dolly up in his arms and carried her over to the bulwarks. When she squealed and laughed he said, 'Oh, it's you, is it, Cathleen mavourneen. Thought you were a sheep.'

Darkness was coming before all the sheep were unloaded so Jack anchored in the snug little cove for the night. Bert put his fishing lines over the side and caught fifty-two flathead before he turned in. As many of the passengers also caught fish I cooked a supper for them all. But at midnight the passengers were insisting that the bar be kept open. It was pleasant for them there in the calm bay, but with my day beginning at 6 a.m. I wasn't happy. As Jack, being captain, was the holder of the licence I went up to his cabin to see if he could insist on it closing at 10 p.m., as the hotels did in Tasmania. He was in his bunk, but when I knocked he put the light on and I was so surprised at what I saw I almost forgot what I had come for. There he was, in between the white sheets, fully dressed. His boots were on the floor and his hat was on the peg on the wall, but apart from that all his clothes appeared to be on him.

He didn't think anything could be done about the bar. 'After all, they are paying passengers,' he reasoned. 'And I don't want to cause trouble.'

They drank on till 2 a.m. I had begun to knit a scarf for my son Mike, at college in Hobart. It was well over a metre long now. Near the end of the evening a passenger lurched up to the bar door and looked at the knitting. 'You know,' he said, 'there's only one thing wrong with it, luv. You've lost the pattern and don't know where to finish off.'

Next day I told Pete what I'd seen in old Jack's cabin. 'In bed, all standing,' I said.

'What did you expect? Birthday suit?'

'Pyjamas, of course.'

'Pyjamas!' He said this an octave higher than he usually spoke.

'Yes, pyjamas. What do the crew usually wear?'

'They turn in all standing too.'

'Between the sheets?'

'Of course. What else? Did you ever see a seaman wearing pyjamas?' He didn't think that was a strange question to ask at all.

I thought for a while. There were two things that came to my mind.

'Pete. Trousers too?'

'Sure.'

'Even the trousers worn yesterday unloading the sheep?'

'Sure. Jeez. I don't know what you're screaming about.'

'And what about when the clothes are wet?'

'Just the same. They dry a lot on you during the night and, anyway, it's not so bad getting out of the blankets in the morning in warm wet things as if you had to put on *cold* wet things.'

On the way back to Hobart we put into Maria Island again to pick up the return mail bag. This trip it wasn't ready, so we sat and waited at the jetty until they finished writing their letters and sealed up the bag. It was Rafferty's Rules and the crew had an easy time. Bert and I commiserated with one another in the galley over hastily snatched cups of tea and wished we were on as good a wicket.

When the mail eventually arrived we steamed off and there, on the hill as we passed, were Ruby and her Harry, waiting to wave. To make sure the ritual got off to a good start they eschewed the curtain waving today and there they were, standing side by side outside their cottage. I was ready, waiting aft with a tea towel. I'd borrowed the glasses from the wheelhouse and I could see them clearly, tiny Harry with his cloth cap jauntily perched on his head, leaning slightly on his single stick; Ruby beside him, immense in her black knee boots and leaning on two sticks. I waved the tea towel and they waved back.

We couldn't go home 'through the ditch' this time because of the tide. It had 'bulled', as the seamen inelegantly put it, gone only part-way out and then come in again. So we had to go 'through the hole in the wall', the gap between Tasman Island and Cape Pillar on the south coast of Tasmania. Etched in outline against the sky, high above us as we hugged down close, the granite-bound heights flared up in tongues of rock or squatted in stolid promontories. A bold coastline with bold deep water to its very base, the Tasman Sea broke in shock upon shock and shattered and fell back from the scarred face of the cliffs. Rocks, tumbled in confusion in the sea where they had fallen, rolled at times into view through the curtain of spume from the hurtling surf. The steady resonant boom of a tortured sea, creaking and straining and escaping from the deep fiords it had itself carved since infinity, sometimes split with a deep whoomph as a delinquent comber broke away and struck deep. One of the passengers said, 'I wouldn't like to be shipwrecked here. A man would never get ashore.'

'You'd be smashed to bits on the rocks.'

'It's only a little ship, you know. The tide could sweep her in clean smack to those cliffs. There's no hope of battling it.'

'It's happened often enough. Ships have been lost, never heard of again.'

'Probably never be able to launch a lifeboat.'

'Has she got lifeboats? Ha ha,' (weakly).

'The *Titanic* couldn't get hers over.'

'Lifeboats would be no good. Look at them cliffs. Just look at them.'

Everyone looked except the man who asked if she had lifeboats; he had gone out on deck. When he returned he said, 'She's got two good lifeboats.'

'Fat lot of use they'd be,' said a young chap. 'Just look at them cliffs.'

'Yeah.' Everyone looked.

We went past the opening to the Narrows and past the Big Hippolyte and Little Hippolyte, two rocks sticking out of the sea over three kilometres offshore where seals sunbaked, and now we came to the gap.

All the passengers and I went into the wheelhouse to watch. Old Chum was on the wheel.

The 'hole in the wall' was nearly as spine chilling as 'the ditch'. On one side was Tasman Island, over 300 metres of sheer cliff. On the other, Cape Pillar, just as big and craggy, and in between a narrow gap. The sea curled up at the base of the cliffs, was sucked back into the channel between, and swirled and fulminated there.

When we were in the centre of this gap, this rip of water between pulverising cliffs, Chum began a little speech to the passengers. 'Ladies and gentlemen,' he said in the grand manner of a European guide, 'on my left is Tasman Island.' He waved his left hand in that direction. 'On my right is Cape Pillar.' He waved his right arm in that direction.

'And on the wheel is bugger-all,' said Alec who had come in unnoticed.

16

M'selle *Naracoopa*

Chum had taken umbrage after his enthusiastic use of the radio when the ship's engines broke down and he was criticised by the owners.

'It wasn't as though I made a habit of it,' he told old Jack. That, according to Jack, was one of the greatest complaints of the owners, that the radio was just an ornament.

'I shall never touch it again,' Chum declared.

Old Jack suggested that I might take it over, so I was given tuition on shore on the understanding that if I passed the necessary examinations I was to work the set.

The radio on the *Naracoopa* was an AT5/AR8 set from an old DC3 aircraft and had as many knobs and switches as the aircraft itself. The types I'd seen on fishing boats were tiny, compact objects with two knobs and one dial and were as easy to work as a household radio. This immense contraption had forty knobs, several sealed switches, and two dials which were marked with numbers that were not applicable to the stations to be worked by ships. It was rather like having a household set on which to get 3AR you tuned to 7ZL and to get 7ZL you tuned to 2UE.

There was a description beneath each knob. The signs read: D/F Traffic Sense; CW/MCW, D/F Reciprocal Sense; Sense Resistance; Beat Frequency; Osc. Tuning; and suchlike.

I learnt that small ships in Australian waters work six megacycles, which I immediately began to speak of intimately as six megs. So that simplicity would be entirely lost, six megs was split up by instructions to SEND on 6280 and RECEIVE on 6405, two different positions on the set, with more knobs to flick. If atmospheric conditions were bad the shore station might tell you to 'go on to two megs'. Then you hurriedly turned more knobs and twiddled the dial around once more. I always imagined the shore station man, ignorant of what faced me and thinking I had the two knobs and one dial of a modern set, tut-tutting as he waited for me to come on the air.

These two bands, six megs and two megs, were not the only ones I must know. Four megs was to be used when working privately-owned shore stations, such as those owned and operated by fishermen's co-operatives. Useful weather information was available from them as we proceeded up the coast.

For ship to ship there was another, rarely used, frequency, mostly employed when one of us wanted to say hello to a friend or acquaintance on another ship.

Sometimes even that four megs was complicated by both ships not having the same 'frequencies'. Then you SENT on the one you had, and RECEIVED on the one they had!

To work any of these frequencies on the *Naracoopa* radio

there were six switches to move, a sensitive dial to twiddle till you got the minute spot that was 'it', a switch to be constantly turned from RECEIVE to SEND as the need arose, a long bar on the microphone to be held clamped IN when SENDING and released when RECEIVING, and a volume control to be turned up when RECEIVING and down when SENDING. And then you had to have enough energy left to send a message, and a pencil ready to take down any telegrams etc. After the mechanics of the operation had been attended to, it was the act of speech that seemed mechanical. To get a Third Class Commercial Operator's Certificate of Proficiency I had to satisfy the PMG examiner that I 'possessed a practical knowledge of the working and adjustment of an AT5/AR8 wireless as well as being able to send and receive messages correctly'. Also I had, so my certificate said, a knowledge of the Radio Communications Regulations Annexed to the Telecommunication Convention relating to the exchange of radio telephone communications. I knew the distress, urgency, alarm, and safety signals. These were so dramatic I'd read them a hundred times in my handbook. If the ship was sinking I must send the call, 'Mayday'. An urgency alarm was preceded by the words 'Pan, Pan, Pan', and a safety signal by the French word, 'Sécurité'.

To get the radio operator's certificate didn't require any excess of intellect, but it did need a lot of courage to get going. The very first time I gave the *Naracoopa* call sign the Melbourne radio operator said, 'I'm imagining things today, chaps. I thought I heard a woman's voice calling then, ha ha.'

It was difficult to call back after that.

In time they all got over the shock of hearing a woman's voice coming from a cargo tramp, and Melbourne Radio even went so far as to greet me as 'M'selle *Naracoopa*'. If several of us came in together when he called, 'Come in, small ships', he'd gallantly announce, 'Ladies first, come in *Naracoopa*'.

Sometimes the shore operator was very formal and when

I'd call, '*Naracoopa* to Hobart Radio, are you receiving, Hobart?' he would aloofly reply, 'Hobart Radio to *Naracoopa*. Come in *Naracoopa*. Over.'

Other times he would unbend enough to tell me it was raining cats and dogs in Hobart and I wasn't missing a thing by being at sea. There were times when conditions were so bad on the air that we could only hear one another with difficulty, particularly during periods of sunspot activity, and then we must repeat our messages in international alphabet, A Abel, B Baker, C Charlie, D Dog, etc. I thought the *Naracoopa* call sign sounded delightfully fey, it was VLQD or Victor Love Queenie Dog.

You could never have anything even approaching a private talk, because apart from being monitored by the PMG every ship could listen in to you as well as everyone who owned a radio with a short wave band, and that included most household sets of that period.

Working the ship's telegraph gave me as much pleasure as working her radio. Unlike some small ships, where the man on the wheel can operate the engine direct from the wheelhouse, the *Naracoopa* was like *real* ships and had a telegraph which indicated to the engineer below which speed was needed.

One day I came on deck as we approached the wharf at Triabunna. Old Jack was up on the flying bridge and he shouted down a voice pipe to the wheelhouse, 'Half Astern!'

After a bit, Bright Boy rang Half Astern on the telegraph and then Mick below in the engine room swung his motor over.

By now the ship was nearly past the end of the wharf and old Jack had to call down, 'Full Astern'.

Bright Boy bent down, looked at the dial on the telegraph, traced the words around with his finger and then rang Full Astern.

After a lot more of this, we finally tied up.

Old Jack came down from the flying bridge. He was never annoyed, but this time he wasn't pleased. 'Does it really take that time to ring an order through on that contraption?' he asked.

Bright Boy explained that you had to find it on the dial first, and as he leant down to demonstrate old Jack tapped his forehead significantly with his finger. Glad to have a third person to put his questions to, he asked me how many keys there were on a typewriter. I thought there were about forty.

'Do you have to look where each is before you hit it?' he asked me.

'No, you learn where each letter or number is and then you can type blindfolded if necessary.'

'There's nine positions marked on this telegraph,' he said. 'Three of them are Ahead . . . slow, half, and full. Three are Astern . . . slow, half, and full. There's Standby when you want to warn the engineer you'll be working the motors presently. Finished with Engines means the voyage is over, it explains itself, and Stop, which also explains itself. You wouldn't think that would be hard to learn.'

Thinking to humour the captain for whom I worked I promptly said, 'No sir, quite easy.'

'Haw! haw!' said Bright Boy. He banged the wall. 'Give the girl the belt.'

Old Jack blew down the whistle pipe to the engine room.

'Ignore the telegraph,' he called. 'I'm testing.'

Then he told me to repeat his orders on it.

Bright Boy was grinning maliciously, so as I took the indicator lever in my hand I faced him and shut my eyes. Smart Alec-style, as he himself would say.

'Full Ahead,' old Jack said.

Full Ahead, I rang. After all, Ahead was one side and Astern the other. You just couldn't go wrong.

'Full Astern.'

Full Astern.

'Stop.'

That was dead centre. Easy.

'Finished with Engines.'

I had to open my eyes for this because I remembered it was close to Slow Astern and I didn't want to ring the wrong one.

'There,' old Jack said to Bright Boy.

'She's been practising,' said Bright Boy.

I told him truthfully that I'd never seen a telegraph before but I didn't tell him it was so simple a child could have worked it.

'I reckon you better go on it in future when we're coming into port and leaving,' Jack told me.

I was delighted. So was Bright Boy. He said it gave him the jim-jams to work it. Old Jack taught me always to repeat his order verbally so there would be no confusion. 'If I call down "Full Ahead", you should repeat "Full Ahead it is",' he said. I added 'sir' to that, and he made no comment.

17

Yo Ho Ho

Some day somebody might write a thesis on the ratio of country men to city men who go to sea, and the factors and social climate involved in their voluntarily embracing the most loathed of all callings. There can be no other job as reviled as this one, and most seamen look forward to going ashore as if they were being reprieved from the galleys of the slaves. And when this thesis is done it will reveal a perplexing state of man that no seaman ever knows exists within him; a fusion of anachronistic primal urge and the herd instinct that has erupted in the twentieth century. A man who desires battle with the elements is different from any man who has never been moved by such forces, and a formal study of this would be worthwhile, for it would be a study of man who has rebelled against evolution.

Small ships' men are almost always drawn from the country. The only figures I have seen for larger ships are those of the French Navy where 'most' of the men of the fleet are drawn from Brittany, a province where seventy per cent of the people are farmers and eighty per cent of the farms are less than forty hectares. The only city-born-and-bred man I ever knew to make a career of the sea in small ships took over the *Naracoopa* while I was on it, but he was atypical; he was a nine-to-five public servant who, after going to sea from Friday night to Monday morning for six months, took out a Master's Certificate and came to show the old hands how to run a ship. To our chagrin he succeeded. True small ships' men are countrymen, as distinct from bushmen, with a heavy infusion of cockies' sons brought up hard, used to bitter slogging, poor pay, no leave – 'my youth was spent in cowsheds pulling flaming teats,' old Jack said. 'I never saw the spud bag that my hands couldn't fill,' Alec said, and he was forty years younger than old Jack and lived, so they say, in another age. 'I lived on salted mutton birds and walked three miles to school,' Pete bragged.

The best mate we ever had, wiry Gordon Archer, was brought up in the orcharding, timber-case making south of Tasmania. 'I was headin' and tailin' out so long as I remember back. I reckon I never went to school,' he said.

The small ship doesn't attract the country grocer boy, the baker, postman, or carpenter. We got school teachers, farm-boys, truck drivers, fishermen, and often we got bums, the riff-raff, the hobos who had been hounded from home and district by parent and police, the most colourless, damned men who ever breathed, with not a decent outrageous crime among them or a horrible habit to set them apart. It is impossible to describe them. There is a theological belief that it is possible to plumb the soul of every man. We had a few that a plumb bob would have failed to determine, men who knew no good but no great bad either. These men drift on and off ships, in and out of gaol, desultorily brawling, drinking, getting maudlin matey with one another only to drift apart and not meet again until gaol or another ship catches them, greeting one another on reunion with no more than a nod or a stare. The bane of the Social Services departments, they have been given every chance and taken none.

Thrown up in relief against these poor things the great men of the small ships are greater still. The wild ones, the toilers, the old men who have pursued their watery working world within sight of the land, are conscious all their days as the shade of the cliffs stabs out to sea that more small ships are wrecked than big ones, more small ships' men drowned than any others who go to sea.

Old Jack was this way. A sailor who had never been out of sight of land, he knew the sea but he knew the land so well from the sea-side, too, that to sit with him when he wanted to talk was an education in the way of the water. Nights when a rough sea drove the passengers to bed, I'd play crib with old Jack or sit in the darkened wheelhouse while we drove beneath the moon and he'd tell the landmarks – the Boy in the Boat, the Lanterns, the big Hippo and the Little Hippo, the Iron Pot, the Cow and the Calf of the Whale, Maria and MacLachlans, the Hole in the Wall and the Bay of Fires, Storm Bay and Orford Roads, Black Jack Reef and Isle des Phoques, Fleurty Point and Wine Glass Bay, the wrecks of the *Guiding Star, Sarah Ann, Venus*, and *Zephyr*; Sappho Spit and Horseshoe Bank, Blackman's Bay and Schouten Passage.

He sang them off like a litany, a rosary of repetition. Alec, who was the only real seaman on board at the time apart from the old man, would sometimes join us, and the two would reel off nautical nonsense and chanties, legends, sea songs, and verse by the hour, a sort of watery wassail.

They both said they did not believe in the Flying Dutchman

or similar tales of spectres of the sea, but any talk of such things would start them off.

'I don't believe in that sort of thing but a funny thing happened to me once . . . I was going up the western passage between Maria and the land one night,' Jack said, 'and it was so clear you could count every star, and when I told the boy on the wheel to steer to a star he said "Which one?", there were so many. We both looked at the sky and I pointed a bright star out to him and he said yes, he had it, and as he spoke the lot blinked out, every one of them, and I looked to starboard and I looked to port and there was no land. A fog I suppose it was, but more like thick milky air blown up from the sea, smothering and crushing us. I couldn't see the fo'c'sle, the mast, anything. "What will I steer to now?" the boy asked me. We were a half a mile off MacLachlans to the eastward – as the Pilot says: Here you continue for two miles, taking care to avoid the shoal ground north of the islet and the shallow water off Maria – and I could see nothing. "What shall I steer to?" the boy cried.

'And then I saw it, directly ahead between where the mast must be and the starboard rigging, a ship's light, a tiny stern light. "Steer to that light," I said. I got out the fog bellows [great leather bellows three feet long] and began to sound. Whoop I pumped, and whoop came the answer from the fog signal on the other ship, and whoop was answered by whoop as we went blindly on. For a full hour we went dead slow ahead, that ship leading us through the murk and then, as suddenly as they'd disappeared, the stars stabbed down again. I looked to port and there was the gap in the land, Spring Bay, and we were dead on course. I went out to the wings to shout my thanks to that skipper, but there was no one there. The sea was empty all around us.'

Alec's spectre was as wild as that lad himself. 'I was alone at the wheel, crossing Bass Strait in the middle of the night in the old Leaping Lena [the *Leprena*] and I was singing I remember, and then I stopped and I never finished that song for there was a bloke, a bloke up aloft, not on the rigging but on the triatic stay. [This stay, or rope, goes from the top of the foremast to the top of the mainmast.] He was coming back aft to amidships, hand over hand, his body dangling fifty feet above the deck, swaying as the slender stay jerked to his movement, hand over hand he came. I daren't call out, I couldn't leave the wheel to go for help; if the ship were to broach to, the roll might put him off balance and he would fall to his death. He was halfway across hand over hand. I couldn't recognise him, he wasn't one of the crew, but I thought I knew him and I felt sick. I felt I knew something terrible about him in advance. Hand over hand he came. I thought, this old tub is so rotten his weight will pull the stick out and I looked up at the foremast and it was whipping, and I looked back at the man and he was gone, the triatic stay was still, there was no movement anywhere. And do you know where I next saw that man? Two years later I saw him in my mind's eye as I went hand over hand along the triatic stay of another ship. I was nearly halfway along it, and when I looked down I could see way below me a shipmate looking up at me from the wheel and I was suddenly sober, the beer I'd been on all day dried up by my fear, and I knew that man I had seen all that time ago had been me, myself.' Alec had made the mainmast safely and had sworn off drink for ever and kept his vow, he said, for three months.

Most tales of a similar nature went out when the Flying Dutchman disappeared with the coming of steam to ships, but like the Flying Dutchman these strange phantasms still occur occasionally to lonely men on watch or wheel, especially in the small ships where the eeriness of the sea is more apparent and the closeness of the elements more real.

All these stories we told in this small company when others were in bed. It was here these two, the old man and young

Alec, told me their thoughts on steering. They were of the belief that if a 'man' couldn't 'feel' the ship naturally there was no way of teaching him to steer. 'It was different in the windjammers. You could learn there all right. The mate stood behind you. "Ship swinging to port, turn wheel to starboard" and then he'd go bang on your right ear lug with his open mitt. "Ship swinging to starboard, turn wheel to port" and then he'd go bang on your other ear lug with his open mitt. "Steady as she goes" and he'd wallop both your ears with both his mitts at the same time.

'Nowadays you can't knock a boy round like that; that's why few good helmsmen are turned out.'

When the talk grew too serious Alec would lighten it with a song, or a chanty:

O! Leave'r Johnny, leave'r like a man,
(An' leave'r Johnny, leave'r!)
Oh! Leave'r, Johnny, leave'r when ya can
(An' it's time for us to leave'r!)

the set chanty for the finish of a voyage:

O! soon we'll hear the old man say,
(Leave'r Johnny, leave'r!)
Ye kin go ashore an' take yer pay,
(An' it's time for us to leave'r)

A favourite of theirs if they felt really playful, this aged man and this possum-faced boy, was:

Should auld acquaintance be forgot
An' never brought to mind
The poor old cook fell overboard
And he's forty miles behind.

Old Jack always set out to amuse me if there was no one about – Alec was counted as no one: 'That wet-nosed Casanova,' old Jack used to say. 'What can any girl see in that greyhound?' This eighty-year-old man would come into the saloon when I was alone, take a short run, and leap up the iron stanchion supporting the deck and spin round and round it without his feet touching the deck while I counted aloud the number of circuits he orbited. And when he was done he would walk on up to the bathroom with not a word to me. We never mentioned this little private joke to anyone else, neither did we mention it to each other.

The infusion of country men into small ships may not bring an arcadian air on board, but certainly a bucolic sense of humour and a rustic peace accompanies them, and old Jack was the symbol of it all.

None of us saw him go. He didn't have much to take off the ship, only his gladstone bag: he'd stuff his change of shirt, his long underpants, and the worn old peaked cap in that. That cap wouldn't carve the ruddy ridge in his forehead again, like it did every time he wrestled the cranky log of wood in which we sailed through the narrow canal. And what would he do with it? Burn it? Keep it in a cupboard? I often wonder what he did with that shabby soft cap with the crown of the merchant marine service on its band.

18

The Overlanders

When old Jack retired the manager of the service joined us as Skipper. He talked a lot. The 'Big Fellow', the boys called him. We missed old Jack and perversely we took our revenge for his absence on the new man. The boys said the Big Fellow not only slept between sheets but wore pyjamas; he owned a tooth brush and put on clean socks every morning. Very squeamish indeed. Not a seaman's bootlace!

They knew very little about him, but they made it their business to find out. God alone knows where seamen get their information – at times I think even He must be stumped. Yet these men can be reticent about inquiring into one another's affairs in a way that is unique in a small community – in all the years I was at sea no man asked me why I had signed on or attempted to pry into my background. Once a passenger asked Alec how I came to exile myself on a ship and I heard the reply. 'She's had some tragedy perhaps, I don't know. It's her own business.' And Alec was a man I had known back in Bass Strait and we had been friends at sea now for five years. Yet given what they considered to be enough incentive they could winkle information from a frog. Within one week of the Big Fellow's joining us they were displaying a carbon copy of his 'time', the time served at sea necessary for a man to sit for a Master's Certificate. They crowed. 'Whaddid I tellya?'

He had been on 26 voyages in a ship, the *John Franklin* (smaller again than the *Naracoopa*), with an average of three days per trip.

This would presumably give a man his 'time' to sit for a Certificate of Competency as Master, Limited Coast Trade, and duly empowered such a candidate, if successful, to take a vessel 'along any part of the southern, eastern and northern coast of Tasmania, commencing at Whale Head and ending at Circular Head but not to the westward of either of these points'. And if a man sat for a further examination – and galley gossip had it that the Big Fellow intended to do this – he could get these limits extended to ' . . . or from any part of those coasts to any of the Furneaux Group of Islands in Bass Strait or between any such Islands'.

'An' yer think I'd risk me skin with him as Skipper up through the Pot Boil?' Pete shouted; of that ship's crew only he, Alec, and I had been through that strangely still maelstrom that Islanders fear, the Pot Boil. 'And what about the Shoals?' The Vansittart Shoals, the eastern entrance to the Furneaux Islands, a maze of channels scored into hard sand where the Admiralty Chart warned, 'LOCAL KNOWLEDGE NEEDED'. 'Feel like going through the Pot Boil and out the Vansittart Shoals with this bloke on the tiller, Pat?'

Yet the time came when we did go through these waters

with this man. He may have been all the boys said he was when he came on board – bellicose, domineering, certainly not masterful, but gaining his way by a confusion of threats and bluster, but he learnt quickly.

'He's only a bloody pen-pusher,' the report came in. 'Started off as a messenger boy after one year at high school, kicked everyone else in the head till he got to be a sort of clerk, and now this year the owners wanted a good clerk to look after the *'Coopa*, and the Big Fellow sees his chance to get out of the office so they give it to him. He's wanted to be a Big Fellow all his life.'

They were very cruel. It was certainly a unique situation, calling for perhaps alarm or even amusement, but the personalities involved made it hateful for a time. The man had the most splendiferous uniform I have seen outside the Royal Navy. On his arms (or, according to Pete, up to his armpits) was gold braid, four gold bars with a loop, senior captain of the fleet – the Transport Commission also ran two ferries, one across the River Derwent, one across to Bruny Island. Old Jack and all the other small-ships' skippers wore the peculiar coasting rig worn by men of little ships all round the world – plain dark trousers and lighter coloured shirts. For hats they wore the black peaked cap of the sea with a loose white cover to slip over the top if passengers were around. Now it seemed like a uniform of competency, no window dressing being needed if the goods had quality.

'Hey! Didya hear? He calls the stays ropes! And the lines too. He says, "What's that rope doing hanging down?"' (Ah, but he made you make it fast and shipshape didn't he? And you said that was because he was a nine-to-five public servant, but the ship began to look better as soon as he came aboard didn't it? And you cursed because he made you clean the brasswork in the wheelhouse every day, but didn't it look better than the days when you used to chip the serpentine verdigris off once a year when you went up on the slip?) I was afraid the Big Fellow wouldn't allow me to continue to work the telegraph but after the first trip through the canal when the seaman he had put on it rang Full Astern instead of Full Ahead just as we went through the opening of the road bridge he had no argument.

He tested me well but old Jack had trained me well. The difference was that whereas old Jack said I was 'greased lightning' the Big Fellow said I 'couldn't be any worse than that other idiot'.

I got plenty of practice because the ship was worked as it was never worked before. Old Jack, with his rock-hopping, dog-barking navigation steered for a point when it was clear enough to see land. When it wasn't he put down the pick. If the night was starlit he steered to a star; if it wasn't he snugged the ship down and slept till morning.

One day not long after he had taken over the Big Fellow came on board with a great roll of charts under his arm. Old Leery Bill came scampering down the companionway to the galley to tell us the news. 'I been at sea round these parts man and boy for fifty-two years,' he said through the gap between his two yellow tusks, 'and I never seen the likes. He, the Big Fellow is gonna mark our course on 'em. Every trip. He doesn't know the way!'

He even expected the mate to take bearings on his nightly watches but old Cholmondeley Marjoriebanks wasn't having any of that. Mostly because he didn't know how to. 'You've got to learn it to get your ticket only,' Chum explained in the galley, where all important things were discussed. 'But nobody expects you to use it afterwards.' But someone did, and for weeks poor old Chum puzzled over laying off courses, four-point bearings, and doing a running fix. At last he gave up. He'd drawn our course overland more often than he'd drawn it over sea. Once he drew a cocked hat near Oatlands in the Tasmanian midlands. Even the new Skipper could see it was no use.

The first trip he made with us he hove to in Fortescue Bay and blew the siren at 2 a.m. to waken the fishermen who lived at the lonely outpost there. Finally, after a lot of blowing on the ship's part, a lantern was lit in the window of the cabin ashore, and in a while their dinghy bobbed up beside us.

'What's the trouble?'

'No trouble,' the Skipper said blandly. 'I thought you had some cargo to be shipped.'

'Sure,' mumbled the fishermen. 'A few boxes of fish.'

'Well, let's have 'em!'

'Now?'

'Now.'

'You're bloody well mad.'

'You'll be bloody well left with the fish on your hands if you don't get a move on.'

The dinghy bobbed away to the station and in ten minutes it was back, the fish were loaded, and we were under way again.

'Old Jack would have waited till daylight,' Pete grizzled. 'Always gave them a chance to have breakfast first. This B's mad.' I reminded him that he had thought old Jack was too slow. 'Yeah, but I got used to him.'

The next night the siren went again. It was 1.30 a.m. and we were in Spring Bay, Triabunna, to pick up old Joe Howells and his sons and take them to Schouten Island. We had got into the habit of waiting for Joe till he was ready. Now we were blowing the siren at some ungodly hour of the night and because they didn't know it was for them Pete was sent skedaddling through the bush to tell them to hurry up.

'By thunder, the Government will hear about this,' Joe mumbled as he came aboard.

The breakfast table was so silent that morning the clatter of knives on plates sounded like rifle shots. Usually you had to shout over the talking to be heard. But the Big Fellow was in Coventry and not only were they not going to talk to him, they weren't going to give him the privilege of hearing their conversation either. They were all such gasbags I knew they couldn't keep it up for long, but it got me jittery for the couple of meals they lasted. The only remarks they made in the Big Fellow's hearing ran on what a good fellow old Jack had been and how he'd once waited two days until Joe was ready to go to the Schoutens.

'Poor bloody old Joe,' they'd keep saying.

You couldn't tell if the Big Fellow had heard or not. So in the end curiosity got the better of them.

'You got a grouch against the world, Skip?' Pete asked him in the wheelhouse. 'No, Pete,' he said. 'Why?' 'You treated old Joe and the fishermen pretty bad.' 'I'm running a business, kid.' Aha! They grabbed that word 'business' as though it were a rope to be pulled over the limb of a tree. Business! So that's where he was going wrong! He looked on the ship as a business! He'd been in an office too long looking at figures. Someone ought to tell him you can't run a ship like a business. Someone did, and all he said was, 'I can.'

We crept into Maria Island the next trip at midnight. The night was so black I couldn't see the forward mast from the wheelhouse where I stood at the telegraph. The Big Fellow was up on the flying bridge. The men were standing by. Pete was on the spring, the line amidships . . . actually he was in the doorway whispering to me. 'He's bushed. That's what's wrong. Betcha.' Maria Island – assuming it was that island we were near – was blacked out. Its ten inhabitants went to bed with the fowls. No man could find the little jetty in this stygian darkness.

The Big Fellow's voice came down the pipe. 'Slow ahead.' I rang the telegraph and the motor slowed. 'Ready with that spring, Pete?'

'She's right, Skip,' Pete replied, looking out into the nothingness beyond. Then he got a bit cheeky. 'What do you want me to do with it, Skip?'

There was a silence for a second, then, 'Put it over the corner pile as we go by.'

'Jeez!' said Pete as he reached out and sat his spring over the usual pile on the Maria Island jetty.

Any remarks we had been going to make about the beautiful landfall dried on our tongue when he came down and told Pete to trot off up to the ghost town and collect the mail bag. 'Tell them I'll have a box made with a key next week,' he said, making a note of it in a book he carried in his pocket. 'We'll leave it on the wharf. They can put the outgoing mail in it and we'll put the incoming in too.'

I saw a light go on in the window at the Hunts' cottage on the hill. Big Ruby and Little Harry would be talking twenty to the dozen wondering what was happening. I was going to miss my wave. I knew just how the boys felt about the new régime.

We crept to the galley for a cup of tea while we waited for Pete, and what we said about the Big Fellow must have made his ears burn because he came down. 'You think I'm a so-and-so, don't you?' he said. We did. 'You don't understand. We're the only link these people have with the outside world. They like to come down and have a chinwag when we come in,' we told him.

'It's like this.' He spoke to us as though we were children in school. What he said was logical and true, but we didn't want to know. The boxes of fish we'd picked up at Fortescue last week were worth only £3 in freight; the fares of Joe and his sons to Schouten Island were £5. The mail bag for Maria Island brought in 30s 0d a week. The ship cost £500 a week to run.

'That's why she lost £16,000 last year,' he concluded. We knew the answer to that. She was a Government ship. She was there to give service, not to make money.

'I intend to give better service, and at the same time show a profit.' The man was mad all right. 'You hate my guts.' Our silence answered him.

'It's the islanders who will feel it most,' I said.

He said, 'In six months they'll be swearing they never had better service. Wouldn't you lot like to see her break even? Make a profit? Not be the joke of Parliament?'

We couldn't care less.

'I couldn't care more,' he said. He went out, and without looking back said, 'And I mean to make you care too, you bastards.' Did you hear what he called us? Bastards! He wasn't half so bad.

By the end of six months we did care about the ship. So did the islanders. Ruby was hanging a lantern in her cottage window at night to guide the ship in and the mail was ready in the box; Joe Howells was waiting on the wharf. The record turn round of the *'Coopa* was the talk of the waterfront. And at the end of the year the Big Fellow's other prophecy had been fulfilled. The £16,000 annual loss had been picked up and we had made a working profit of £2300. The Swansea trip that used to take us a whole week now took us only three days, sometimes only two and a half. We were running regular trips to Flinders Island, my old stamping ground. Sometimes we ran a trip to Flinders Island, leaving Hobart on Monday, and arrived back on Friday morning and sailed again on Friday night for a quick trip to Swansea and back ready to start loading again on Monday morning for Flinders Island. As we were paid by the trip we liked this set-up. Quite often we made £40 a week – those of us who stuck it. The Big Fellow bragged that he had had seventy changes in the first six months of his reign, those who couldn't take it and those he couldn't take. The islanders had never had better service, but they never did like him.

Somewhere in the midst of this organised hustling I found time to do shopping for those who rarely saw a shop. Ruby wouldn't trust her shopping to anyone else and would give me a list of things ranging from 'corn silverside, not too salt, the last piece was just right', to 'overcoat, large, you know, like me'. She wrote to the ship every week. Sometimes twelve pages. We'd read out aloud the important or juicy bits. These were usually underlined and began with capital letters such as, 'I heard Mrs Pat was Sick. I hope it is not her Waterworks. They do say there is a lot of Bladder trouble about these days'. During winter she always sent some suggestions for 'Keeping up Strength'. Once it included, 'Two Large fresh Hen Eggs, shells and all, Dissolved overnight in Juice of Two Dozen Lemons. Add one large jar Best Honey and a bottle Rum, Whisky or Brandy'. That, she said, was called The Old Time Tonic.

Once she got her letters mixed up and included some pages of a letter to someone else. It was evidently to a young girl, because she advised her when Going out into the World to always Put Paper on the seat before she Sat. She was an inveterate letter writer and had a beautiful flowing copperplate hand which was a joy to read. She had, too, the rare knack of writing in a way that kept the reader in close contact with the everyday life she lived. She gave details of her simple uncluttered life that made a letter from her seem like a chat over a cup of tea.

The Big Fellow worked us like galley slaves. Sometimes, stripped to the waist, he sweated it out in the hold with the crew, but mostly he went ashore at the ports to hustle cargo. No cargo was too small or too out-of-the-way to get. He took us regularly to a red granite quarry where we tied up to the massive stones with a reef grazing our stern, and when it was time to get out we warped our way sideways like a crab to escape it.

We took supplies to the lighthouse at Tasman Island. This was most spectacular. The *Naracoopa* steamed about as near to the island as we dared to bring her and from there sent in her boat. The island is 300 metres high and rises straight up from the sea. Thirty metres up the cliff side a platform has been built and from here a cable runs to a rock – Anchor Rock –

in the sea near by. A basket is lowered down this cable until it is above the boat in the water below and into this the boys must load the cargo. The basket is then hauled up onto the platform. Later it would be hauled to the top of the island on a precipitous wooden railway with the tide sweeping round it like a whirlpool, for the seas around Tasman Island are always rough. Sometimes the boat was lifted up on a big wave and threatened to crash into the basket. Other times one of the seamen would be reaching up to put something into the basket and the boat would drop into a trough and he, left suspended as it were in space, had to be grabbed quickly, or, his equilibrium gone, he would topple over.

We visited Swan Island lighthouse in Banks Strait once to pick up some wild cattle but they chased the lightkeepers, they chased the crew, then they chased each other, so we left them. They got one big red bull part way out to the ship but it broke free and charged the man in the boat near it.

We took on a contract to deliver gas cylinders to Forestier Light – The Lemon, as seamen call it – on the east coast. This is an unattended light, so a mechanic from Commonwealth Navigation travelled with us to install the great cylinders. Here, the *Naracoopa* anchored close to the cliffs and sent in the ship's boat with the cylinders, the mechanic and several seamen. There was no landing place, only a small gutway in the rocks. Above this hung a rope, and a man had to grab this rope as the boat see-sawed backwards and forwards, and swing up on to the rocks like Tarzan. The cylinders were hauled up the same way and then partly man-handled, partly hauled up to the top of The Lemon. One of our seamen always stayed ashore with the lighthouse mechanic in case of accidents. As soon as these two men were safely ashore the boat scurried back out of the threatening gutway and waited out at sea till the men signalled they were ready to come down. Few of the places we went to had jetties, and none of them was sound.

Even the one we used in Hobart was condemned and pulled down eventually.

I knew Tasman Light well, as I had done a work tour with the *Cape York*, the old lighthouse supply ship. Before daylight her bosun and a deck hand, a boatman and me set off for the annual greasing of the steel stay on which the basket is hung.

I thought it terrifying until we later went to service Maatsuyker Light. The toughest men on the tough lighthouse supply ships are wary here. A trip which could be done in one day's unloading could take a week, as it did that year. The sea was murderous, and climbing down the ship's side on the rope ladder to the workboat one was almost bashed insensible on the side of the ship as she rolled and righted, rolled and righted. Coming back, at night, wet through, eyes red from sea wrack and wind, the fingers had to be told by the brain, almost by the tongue, to hang on to the rope, to grab it each time one got a foot on another loose rope rung higher up. The reward for such a day's work for me was to be ordered to line up on the deck with the men and officers for an issue of rum.

When this, even for the regular crew, hard tour was over, and the ship on its way back, the captain put in to Port Arthur and twelve of us went ashore in the ship's workboat to what in those days was a little old wooden pub. It was 11 p.m. and we were scarcely inside – the licensee in his pyjamas and dressing gown – when there came a hammering at the door. The police. Well, I thought, for someone who hardly has more than a social drink you're really in trouble now. But the constable had recognised the riding lights of the ship and knowing what a stalwart lot of men these were to have got the supplies to Maatsuyker in such wild weather, he had come down to make sure the publican would open up to give them a drink.

In between the visits of the *Cape York* the *Naracoopa* would take urgent supplies or be sent for other reasons to the lighthouses.

We ran a cargo of superphosphate to a little place called Premaydena a few times, but one morning, just as the last sling load was lowered on to the wharf, the whole structure began to settle in the water and then toppled sideways. Half the crew were on the wharf stacking the super as it came ashore and they came running up as it subsided in the water. The last man up, a boy named Phillip, appeared hat first, then face, shoulders, and lastly body, still running upwards. To get to the tiny jetty at Little Chinaman's when the tide was low a seaman had to swim ashore from the ship, taking a line with him.

Coles Bay, a lovely tourist hideaway, had a jetty with no decking, just beams across piles. Both here and at Swansea there is a fearful surge and tying up the ship was a problem, but I never knew the Big Fellow to bring a stick of cargo home. The first time he went alongside Coles Bay the surge swept him off before the boys mustered courage to jump. But he'd had time to look at it. 'Damned dangerous,' he said.

'Good,' said the crew. They thought he wouldn't be going back in.

'Get ready to jump,' he called, as he headed the old girl in again. 'You, Bright Boy, you take the bow line, Pete the stern.' He'd picked the toughest pair but even they hesitated when he brought the ship in again. 'Jump, blast you!' he barked. They jumped. Pete was like a cat. He ran barefoot along the eight-centimetre-wide parapet six metres above the water and grabbed the stern line. Bright Boy wasn't so sure and in a while he was down on all fours crawling along the woodwork.

For weeks after that we carried a great quantity of timber and nails and when the weather was such that even this man couldn't get the ship into any port to work it, he took the boys ashore and they worked on the wharf, decking it.

At the south end of Maria Island lived Mr and Mrs Robey,

South Africans who had migrated to this isolated end of Maria after World War I. They were twenty-seven kilometres away through trackless bush from the tiny settlement at the north end where we called. Once a month the old man rode his horse through the bush to get his mail, English papers and supplies; larger quantities he got quarterly via the *Naracoopa*. When the Big Fellow took over we'd been carrying the last lot of his supplies for three months in our hold. Even the boys who would do anything to get out of a boating-off job felt pretty bad about this.

On the way home that first trip he anchored in the bay near their cottage and blew the siren. First the old lady and then the old man came down onto the beach. The breakers were roaring and thundering. The Big Fellow sent the boat in first without the cargo. The crew went to see what it was like inshore and were to come back for cargo if it was safe. If not, they were to tell the old man they would try again next week. They had a look, came back, and said they'd give it a go. There were bags of fowl feed, wheat and pollard, and bags of flour and household goods.

On the last trip back to the ship the old man came out. He wanted to see the captain. I was called up to the wheel-house. He had a lump behind his left ear, the skin was broken and it was clearly an old trouble. 'I think it's a cancer,' the old man said. I'd never seen that sort of cancer, but I did know it needed attention. The Skipper arranged to pick him up next trip and take him to hospital in Hobart. I went ashore with him and spoke to the old lady. She was a sweet little dizzy woman, rather like Billie Burke the actress. When the husband told her he'd have to go to hospital she turned to me and said, 'And you've come to stay with me my dear while he's away.' I would have loved to say yes, but apart from any other factor it was likely he would be a long time absent if he had surgery. So she stayed there alone. We took the old man off and she stood on the beach in her tattered English tweeds and English brogues and waved until we disappeared from sight.

Each week for the six weeks he was away we went close inshore when we were passing. She was to come on to the beach if she wanted us, or light a fire. But she managed without help. She had an ordinary household radio and the night after her husband was operated on the police broadcast a message to her immediately before the news to tell her that her man was well. It was really something to see that old couple when we put him ashore. The boys carried him up the beach so he wouldn't get wet, even though he had taken off his shoes and socks ready to wade in, and put him down right at her feet. They stood holding each other's hands, looking into one another's eyes and all the while their heads were bobbing up and down in an old, old intimacy. We all stood and watched them and listened to their endearing words as though we had never known anything like it in our lives. And I don't suppose we had, or we would never have gone to sea. It made all the hard work of the last months worth while to have played a small part in this little drama.

Another time we called in to this end of the island to pick up 'stick bark', wattle bark just as it is peeled from the trees. So many of the crew were sick this trip that we thought we would be excused if we painted a red cross on our funnel. Pete had strained his abdominal muscles trying to start his motor bike, a new acquisition; Alec had 'flu; Bert was 'real crook in the guts'. Two boys were needed to stay ashore and cart the bark to the boat, one boy was needed in the boat, and a man was needed on the winch to haul the big nets full of bark on board. Then there was still the need for a couple of men below to stow it in the hold. The Big Fellow was one man ... I was getting the meals while Bert was 'crook' ... I would be the other.

So down I went, into the bowels of the ship, as I thought dramatically. It wasn't heavy work but it was creepy, because long-legged spiders crept out of the bundles of bark. One actually crawled on my neck. It was only the thought of the hilarity it would afford my fellow workers that stopped me from screaming. When the sling net was lowered we would unhook the full sling, hook on the empty sling and waggle a forefinger in the air as a signal to the man above to hoist away. Then, bundle by prickly bundle, we lifted the bark out and carried it over to the bulkheads and stacked it up. It was too hot to work down in the hold in long sleeves and my bare arms were scratched from wrist to shoulder from the horrid stuff. 'Under below,' the man on deck would bellow as the next sling load was lowered as a warning to cower underneath cover. I took the opportunity of those breaks to examine my arms rapidly for spiders.

The hours were longer, the work harder now, but there seemed to be as much laughter as ever. Often the laughter was of the kind that is touched off by an action being as dangerous as it is funny. Loading cattle off the beach at Schouten Island brought forth this sort of mirth. Sometimes the passengers would be holding their breaths in fear at the same thing that was making the crew double up with great belly-laughs.

A bull lit out one night with the long leading rope tied to his horns and went in and out through the scrub behind the beach in the way a kitten runs around the legs of chairs with a ball of wool. Holding tight to the end of the rope was Pete. 'Hang on, Pete, don't let go for God's sake,' the crew yelled, while the passengers said, 'That poor little boy's going to be killed.' (Pete was adored and pampered by passengers. We could never work out why. One heard me refer to the lad as 'Gargoyle' one day. It was my pet name for him and very apt, but this woman said, 'A gargoyle maybe, but an innocent, sweet gargoyle for all that.')

Of course the bull couldn't be left there to die so the boys had to go into the tangled scrub, free the rope and follow it up to the enraged animal and drag it down to the beach. They led one end of the rope round a strong tree trunk and pulled, but the bull pulled the other way and nothing happened. So they sent Pete into the scrub again and immediately out came the bull, close on the heels of the Gargoyle. 'He thinks you're a cow Pete, look out,' the crew shouted as Pete fled down, leading the bull into the water where the boat waited. But the passengers said it was dangerous and shouldn't be allowed.

We were going out loaded down to our plimsoll every trip now, so we could rarely use the canal on the way out and had to 'punch it round the Raoul'. Whenever there was the faintest hope that we would get through the ditch on the way home, the Big Fellow sent her through the Narrows and dragged her over the bottom all the way up the canal. If we didn't get stuck it cut five hours off our journey home as well as saving us the thrashing we invariably got going the long way round.

But we were often stuck. It was six years since the canal had last been dredged and sand had begun to silt it up again. The channel that had been marked with beacons by the Marine Board had filled up to such an extent that grass was growing on parts of it. We used to come in through the Narrows in real seaman's style, but once in those waters we were on our own, and nothing but the skill of the captain got us through.

One afternoon he took us through the Narrows and anchored near Little Chinaman's, waiting for the tide to take us up the channel. Because there wouldn't be enough water till after dark, and because it would then be impossible to go on since there were no lights to mark the course of the channel, we thought we must mean to anchor till dawn. Not he. The crew were sent ashore to set two big bonfires at points marked for them on a hillside. When the tide was high enough, round about midnight, he sent them off to light them and then off up the channel he went, using the fires in line on our stern as beacons.

He was as superstitious as the best of them and that was saying something. His superstition about the canal at Dunalley was this: if the men shaved their faces before we went through the bridge we'd get stuck. 'It brings us bad luck,' he told new crew members when asking them not to shave till we were in bold water, heading for home. Sometimes, knowing we were only a few hours away from home, they would shave and keep out of sight, thinking to fool him. And as often as not we'd get stuck.

To get through the new drain the tide had cut since our last visit we'd go Slow Ahead after we'd battled in through the Narrows. The slower we went the higher we floated in the water. At full speed the ship was dragged lower down into the water, and seeing we had only fifteen centimetres to spare at the best of times we couldn't afford to lose anything. Also, the slow speed meant that if we rode up on a shoal the ship would not be damaged. We rode up often. Bump, bump, bump we'd go, gently always over the sandy bottom, bump, bump, bump. Sometimes we'd bump on until we got into deep water. Sometimes we'd stick. Then to get her off the Big Fellow would 'wriggle her hips' by winding the wheel first to port and then to starboard as the motor ran alternately ahead, then astern. Apart from swinging the ship round this stirred the sand round and cut a channel for us. 'We ought to send an account to the Marine Board for doing their work for them,' was Mick's comment on this.

There couldn't be many small ships that tried harder than we to make fast turn-rounds and get the most out of the vessel. I've rung seventy-five different orders down on the telegraph on the one trip while we were trying to get her through the canal. She was only taken in on a rising tide, so it was just a matter of wait a while and she would float off, but we couldn't resist trying. After we had been doing this for so long it was almost a habit, we were waiting for the tide to float us off one day when we heard a news item about us on the ABC News. It said, 'The *Naracoopa* is aground on the east coast. We have as yet been unable to learn if it has been possible for her passengers to be taken off or what damage she has sustained.'

The following week we went through the Narrows and up through the ditch without once 'smelling the bottom' only to find there was no water in the canal the other side of the road bridge. As the water wouldn't fill up that side before dark, the bridge-keeper suggested he let us through the bridge right away so that when the tide did flow we'd be all ready to set off for home. We sailed through just far enough to allow him to swing the bridge across for road traffic and we sat waiting for the tide to take us home. We wondered if seamen on the big ships got as impatient waiting for the waters to fill the locks in the Panama Canal as we did, waiting for our canal to fill naturally. While we waited we hit the news again. This time we had been 'stranded, high and dry. The passengers seem in good spirits and unaffected by the accident'.

We were upset, and such was the feeling on the ship now that the passengers joined us in our rage.

The following week we got it again. This time we 'managed to get some of the passengers safely ashore'. They were a man and his wife who lived near the canal and to save them a long drive back from Hobart it had been arranged before ever we left Hobart to put them ashore there if we possibly could. When we cleared the canal we stopped the motors, lowered the dinghy, and the boys took them ashore.

We were so proud of our fast turn-round and the ship itself now, that this unfair publicity enraged us. The Skipper tried to calm us by reminding us (as we had once reminded him) that it was a Government ship and a political football. Also, he said, the newsboys in Hobart just didn't understand the nature of our run.

But we were working too hard not to be upset by it. At that time we were bringing timber from Swansea to be tran-shipped to Melbourne for the village they were building there to house the athletes competing in the Olympic Games in

1956. To get the great quantity needed away in time we worked literally night and day. We'd arrive in Swansea late in the afternoon and begin to load. Load all that night, all next day, and the next night and be finished 'ready for off' soon after daybreak the following day, having seen two sunsets and two sunrises since we last slept.

'Let's have yer,' the mate bellowed and the toil began. My task was to tally the packs on board, noting the numbers painted on the sides of each and marking them off on the consignment note on which was listed the amount of super feet in each individual pack, and finally to add the total. The first night would be okay, and the beginning of the next day, but when the sun was right overhead you got so sleepy you kept nodding and then jerking alert, and worrying lest you had missed a pack. At those times I'd get out my knitting and I found that improved my concentration. This sleepiness wouldn't last long. But worse was to come. About midnight the second night the world ended. You didn't nod, you just dropped dead. When you shook yourself awake everything was unreal. You walked inches off the ground and when you touched things your hands had pins and needles and your mind was a zombie, doing as it was told, nothing more. 'Watch that pack,' I'd tell my mind. 'Don't enter it till it hits the deck. They might decide not to load it. Watch it. There it swings. Write it down. Look at the number twice, three times to make sure. Go for a walk up and down the wheelhouse now till the next pack is ready. Don't sit down. No, you're not . . . (mustn't say the word tired). You're really very bright. Here comes another pack, watch it now . . . ' And then suddenly, it was gone. You'd got your second wind and were right for another day.

The Big Fellow would be in the hold sweating and heaving with the crew, manhandling the heavy packs into every nook and cranny to get the greatest possible load on her. When the hold was full they'd put the hatch covers on and put the deck load on top. By the time we were weighted down to our plimsoll you could step out of the wheelhouse windows on to the deck load and walk clear on to the fo'c'sle head. Then the boys would drag themselves off to their bunks, each foot weighing a ton, and the Skipper and often I would take the wheel alone till we got to Maria Island.

So it was no good telling us not to let it get us down when the only publicity we got was criticism.

19

A Sea Voyage

When passengers came on board, just before we sailed, no one could pick the sheep from the goats by looking at them or listening to them. It is said that a man knowing he is dying can no longer converse as freely as before. He feels cut off, no longer of this world, and the people by his bedside are not part of his world of imminent voyaging. The same can be said of passengers on a ship and the people seeing them off. They are so strained and sometimes so different and unrelated to one another that it is hard to visualise the wife on the wharf sharing a bed with the husband on deck, or the man on deck ever lending a fiver to the friend on shore. There would be long dreadful silences, and now and then an embarrassed meeting of eyes. Then the hardy weekly, 'Brought your seasick tablets?' Usually, 'There's a lifebelt over there. You want to keep your eye on it. There might be a rush for it.' Squeals and jumpings about when the wooden sponson rubbed on the wharf and squeaked. 'Falling apart before she gets away, ha ha.' 'Weather forecast was for rain. Brother, I wouldn't like to be you tonight!' (Unaware that heavy rain would flatten out a rough sea.) 'You don't want to change your mind do you?'

They'd bring small compasses ... both our compasses were regularly swung and adjusted and the amount of deviation was great. I always went to watch when the compass was being adjusted by the Deputy Director of Navigation for the Commonwealth and was fascinated by the work involved in counteracting the pull and push of various elements in the ship.

Once the boys were even made to throw out of the wheelhouse the fruit tins they'd been using as ash trays. Any odd thing would put a compass out of alignment. So when the weekend admirals looked at their pocket compasses and spoke of us heading sou'-west when we should have been heading nor'-east we never panicked. Once I saw the needle of one of these little compasses swinging round and round. The owner was very perplexed. Alec didn't make him any happier when he told him compasses do that at the south and north poles. One passenger looked at his compass and said, 'I do hope the captain knows where he's going.' We hoped so too, but got him out before the captain's wrath came down on him. Of course this didn't apply to real blue-water yachtsmen. The few who came on board were a delight.

There were people who came away with us and, in that one trip, became a part of our lives and left little oases behind in the desert of our social loneliness. Though we knew we would probably never see them again we didn't grieve when they left; we were grateful for those few days and determined not to spoil it by long, embarrassed goodbyes. Old people were the nicest of all passengers, I found, with children a close second.

The most popular couple we had aboard were Max and Thedda Angus, the painter and his gentle, laughter-loving wife. The boys loved them, and I still do because we have remained loving and close friends since they sailed on the *Naracoopa* thirty years ago. Max did a score of pencil sketches on board, one of which was of Bill, my off-sider in the galley, stirring custard.

Premiers and men of rank sailed with us; we got all sorts. There were the drinkers. Three I remember were real soaks. They laboured on board under the burden of four cartons of beer, six bottles of whisky, and six of gin. But they got off at Swansea and travelled back to Hobart by bus because 'poor Reggie has got somethink terrible wrong with his back passage'.

When first they came on board they were disappointed to find we had only two-berth cabins. 'We thought we'd all be together,' Joan said, passing over three tickets, each with different surnames. 'Never mind, you may be able to put us close together, duck; better put Reggie by himself. He's got somethink wrong with his back passage and he likes to read half the night. He's in pain somethink crool.' They hardly had one meal between the three of them the whole trip and drank non-stop, making sporadic sallies up on deck to offer a drink to the boys or to swap a yarn. No one could have frowned on the sharing of the cabin; it was open house, anyone could come and go, night and day. The three of them were obsessed with one thing only: drink, and it bound them so closely together they were like two brothers and a sister. We laughed at them yet we missed them when they left.

I could become angry about many who were sick, because they could have avoided it. They always asked for advice and never took it. They would come down to the tiny saloon, where the white, diagonally planked walls seemed to move in circles in rough seas, and sit down to a meal as though they'd paid for it and were going to make sure they got their money's worth.

The only cure or preventive I ever found for seasickness was to stay up on deck with one's nose into the wind the way a dog travels in a car; or to lie down and keep one's eyes shut, head tucked down and knees drawn up. There is a lot of nonsense written and spoken about seasickness. Many people say it is mind over matter. If so, how do they account for the dogs that were invariably the first to be sick on board, even cattle dogs that regularly travelled with us to the islands, and the babies who were often as sick as adults. Tough men are sick loading the hold while the ship rocks at the wharf, and delicate spoon-fed types weather a gale on the quarter that makes a ship twist like a corkscrew, the worst of all rolls. There's no accounting for it. But with modern medical aids no passenger should be sick. Tablets, taken as directed, half an hour before you get into the rough stuff and repeated if necessary two or three times a day, will prevent any but the most obstinate cases. Until something is invented that does not induce sleep as well as prevent seasickness, a ship's crew cannot benefit, and many's the boy I've seen lying out on the hatch swearing on the tarpaulin beneath him that if ever he reaches port alive the first thing he'll do is sign off. The old saw that says a man was so seasick he spent half the voyage afraid he'd die and the other half afraid he wouldn't is too true to be funny.

20

'Who Called the Cook a ... ?'

I did my share of cooking at sea, in between cooks who were on a bender, cooks who took a swing at the captain, cooks who had unfinished love affairs, and cooks who were so unlike any other group of men that they have earned themselves a well-deserved title the world over. Bert cooked much of the time I was on the *Naracoopa* and he could have been worse, but not much.

In between his appearances scores of other men sailed with us, trying to hoodwink themselves and us that they knew the difference between a pot and a pan. The nice thing about Bert was that he didn't try to kid anybody. He just couldn't cook. He knew it, we knew it, and he knew we knew. It was an admirable arrangement because he didn't mind anyone turning to in the galley and knocking up a decent meal. All the other chefs would down their tin openers and walk off if you as much as put your foot in their galleys, but Bert was a gregarious old soak and ran the galley as an unofficial club. All the crew were members and officers were admitted when members agreed.

There was only one rule, and that was strictly policed – no one was to sit on the preparing bench. This was awkward, because the galley was so narrow you could barely squeeze between the bench and the big stove and the only thing resembling a seat was the bench. In the middle of a quiet natter over a cup of tea Bert would suddenly shout, 'Get your dirty backside off of my table!' Then the club was closed for the night. Bert sank into morbid lethargy and, his hands clutching the edge of the bench, would stand staring moodily at the offended spot, sometimes mumbling to himself, and always 'rumbling down below'. Bert's abdomen was in a state of perpetual internecine warfare and the clash and clang of opposing factors was at all times audible, but in times of stress the battle raged fortissimo. Bert explained this cacophony casually enough. 'That's me stumick,' he would say. If they needed to warn the crew not to go into the galley the boys used to say, 'Bert's rumbling down below.'

One night, after he had been sorely tried by Mick who would often forget and sit on the bench, Bert wrote out a notice on an empty Kellogg's Corn Flakes packet and nailed it to the galley wall. It read, in Bert's own inimitable handwriting:

> 'Any-one pound siting on this bench will be pined one shilling.
>
> By Odder.'

There were many things Bert was not good at apart from cooking; in fact, you could say there was little, if anything, he was good at. He was crazy about the opposite sex. 'Wimmin,' he called them. He spent much time and energy pursuing them. He was never successful. We suffered then because his cooking was even worse at those times.

Once he advertised in a newspaper for: 'Woman, young, attractive, view outings, friendship.' He got four replies. One was a leg-pull, one offered him a night out on the tiles, one was a widow with three children, and the other was the housekeeper of a well-known lady MP in Hobart. Bert wouldn't show us the letter from the leg-puller. 'Crool,' he described it. But he was keen about the second one and showed us excerpts from her reply by covering the letter with his big hand and spreading two fingers wide to exhibit the parts we were to peruse. When Pete came up for air and said, 'Jeez!' a couple of times thoughtfully, Bert decided we'd all had enough and folded it up and put it in his trouser pocket.

'She's hot stuff,' Pete said.

'Unselfish,' Bert said.

'She'll bloody well kill you,' Alec said. She nearly did, but less by her excess of unselfishness than by Bert's unfortunate choice of a trysting place.

He arranged to meet her in the evening after we got into port on Thursday. On Friday he came limping on board, his knees bandaged with handkerchiefs, his trouser legs slashed in a dozen places. He gave us what he called 'Hash' for midday meal, any old thing he found in the fridge stewed in a pan of fat. For the rest of the day he lay down taking swigs of his tonic. Bert's tonic was port wine and brandy and he swore by it for everything, but especially for days when he was 'crook in the guts'.

The crew were doubled up with laughter. All that I eventually learnt was that Bert had parked behind the wharfies' lunch shed. The wharfies used to throw their empty bottles in the space and most of them broke when they fell.

'Bloody dangerous thing to do,' Bert told the boys. 'I was

nearly hamstrung before I noticed the broken glass.' His last mention of the 'unselfish' letter writer was that he 'gave her a bottle of beer, a smack on the backside, and sent her home'.

The widow with three children didn't get past the first interview. 'She expected too much of a man altogether,' was Bert's only comment on her. But the housekeeper of the lady MP made the grade. We knew it when we smelt the meat burning. We hurried to the galley but it was too late – there was nothing but charred bone left on a leg of lamb. Bert was standing there with his fists pushing down on to the bench, his eyes fixed on a pile of soup bones. 'Everything okay, Bert?' I asked, tentatively. 'Beautiful,' said Bert. 'Look at them lovely bones.'

He was no good for weeks. Once he emptied a full packet of tea into the teapot and I didn't know until I went to pour the captain's tea in the saloon and it was solid. Another time he sent the pot in full of boiling water but no tea at all.

He bought her gifts by the score; a pink crinolined china lady statue thing with a light bulb sticking out the back of her neck and a shade supposed to be a parasol wobbling over the top; a cut glass dressing table set; a pair of slippers with pink feathers across the front that made Bert giggle every time he brought them out to show us before he presented them to her; a manicure set in a box with wall paper on it and full of useless things like little tins to put nail polishing powder in.

'She'll like that,' Bert said. 'She's a real lady.'

The real lady broke Bert's heart and almost caused him to suicide. We were halfway to Bass Strait before he told us. 'She never wants to see me again,' he bawled. 'Not so long as I live.'

We couldn't get any sense out of him until by chance I asked him if she'd offered him his presents back. 'I didn't wait for her to offer,' he said. 'I asked her for them.'

'When?'

'When I called for her the night we had the row. You see,

she said she wasn't ready when I called and said to wait. I told her I didn't let my wimmin wear the trousers. I says to her to smarten her up a bit like, ''Now or never or I want me presents back,'' just to let her know I was fair dinkum. Do you know what she said? She said, ''Well here they are,'' and slung them out the door. All me lovely presents. The little slippers and the lovely lady with the light and now the umbrella's broke on the lovely lady. It's made me real crook in the guts I can tell you.'

We hadn't had a decent meal since we sailed but talking about his lost love didn't make Bert any better, and now he tossed the sponge in completely and took the big butchering knife with him and sat up on deck. We were too fascinated watching him to worry about eating. He sat on the deck with his legs spread out and the knife on the deck between them, glaring at the sea, mumbling to himself and rumbling down below.

The Skipper sent the mate round to order him back to work, but the mate came back without speaking to him so the captain went round himself. One look at poor Bert and he decided against reprimanding him and instead, set a seaman as guard on either side of him to prevent him either jumping into the sea or damaging himself.

He was oblivious to everyone around him. His eyes were fixed dead ahead, staring into the sea, his face was working like a man with the DTs. Once he stood up and slowly undid the catches that held the safety line across the opening at the spring bollard. You couldn't tell if he did it to get a better, uninterrupted view of the water or to make it easier if he decided to jump.

It all ended in a dreadful anti-climax. When dusk came, he stood up, pulled his shirt out of his trousers, scratched his tummy, rumbled (but only gently) and said he was going to bed. He made only one more grand gesture in connection with this real lady, and it, like everything else Bert did, was a flop.

He wrote to the lady MP for whom she worked and told her (the MP) to make her housekeeper 'pull up her socks'.

'I expect,' Bert wrote, 'that you will bring her to heel. I am offering her every chance and she is a fool if she knocks me back. She won't get asked by anyone else because she is too long in the tooth. I will wait on the wharf by the ship at 5 o'clock tonight and you send her down to me or come yourself and we will discuss it.' It was a very fine letter, by odder! except for such slight distractions as 'disgust' instead of discuss and 'orfrink' for offering, and 'arst' for asked. We never knew what the lady MP thought of it because although Bert waited half the night no one came. Not long after that the Big Fellow caught Bert straining cockroaches out of the soup and that was the end of him for a while. 'I can't understand that Skipper,' he said when he was leaving. 'He knows every ship's got cocky-roaches. Why blame me?'

In his absence we had a series of chefs but none of them lasted long. There was Jim who used to kick the beautiful new combustion stove when anything went wrong with his cooking, which was often. For a really messed up meal he would kick with both feet at one time, by levering himself up with his hands on the bench behind.

After him was little Snookums (his real name). He was only knee high to a grasshopper. He was very late with the tea one night and when the Skipper came down to ask why, he ran at the Big Fellow and butted him in the middle with his head. So that was the end of him.

The Big Fellow spent a lot of time those days throwing cooks over the side. When each new cook would take over I'd have the galley shining for him, yet every new man walked in, looked round, and then said, 'I'll soon get this place cleaned up.' When each one was signed off back in I'd go to clean, scour, and scrape. It never varied. Our hope of getting a good cook was slender. They went to the big ships for the comfort. We got builders' labourers and the like who had peeled potatoes for an army cook during the war and decided there was nothing to cooking. Sometimes we'd get an old married man who had learnt to cook at home from his wife while practising some other trade. These men were always clean and cooked well enough, but were more cantankerous than most, and that was saying something, for a sea cook is the most unbelievably cantankerous man alive. I was always scared when they'd take on, throwing pots and pans around and hacking at the air with the meat chopper. When Bert was not on board I only went to the galley when I had to.

Once I stood up to a raving cook and came out with flying colours, but it was only once, and by mistake. He had been berserk all morning, racing about with the chopper – he threw it when I was trying to open the big wooden, deck refrigerator and it stuck in the door not fifteen centimetres from my hand. I was nearly distraught. The mate saw my red eyes and I heard him say to the cook, 'What's wrong with Mrs Pat?'

'I don't know at all,' the cook said smoothly. 'You know what women are!' As soon as the mate left I went in and threw the big enamel teapot full of tea at the cook. I was so surprised I stood staring at him afterwards instead of running, while the tea went drip, drip, down off his nose and chin, and the tea leaves lay in big heaps on his hair and shoulders. He walked up to me, edged past me in the narrow space and went to his cabin. I was paralysed with fright. All the enamel had chipped off the teapot and it leaked from under the spout from then on, but I was of giant stature in the crew's estimation. None of them had ever stood up to a cook.

No matter how often he was signed off, old Bert never took umbrage. There he'd be on the wharf when we got in next time, waiting to take our lines and asking if there was a vacancy on board.

At first I didn't know how he could work out to the very minute what time we'd be in. Then I learnt about the Signal

Station belonging to the Port of Hobart. Here ships were still watched for as they had been since the whaling fleets used to return last century. When our ship was first sighted its house flag was run up to the masthead at the station in the heart of the city, then, when it entered the river, the flag was lowered halfway down the mast. Anyone knowing the house flag of the ship he was awaiting could estimate its time of arrival accurately.

Bert's tenacity paid off, because time and again he'd be waiting there just when a cook had been paid off and the captain would take him on in desperation.

I always liked to see him come back. The ship never seemed the same without his long white woollen underpants and grey 'flannels' hanging up to dry on a rope stretched across the galley. His return meant I could come and go as I pleased, keep the galley clean, boil the tea towels, and cook my own meals without subterfuge. And his return also meant more laughter as he freely discussed his amorous adventures with us. Once after his return he didn't discuss 'wimmin' all the trip. On the way home he asked me to send a message over the radio and then I understood and I was deeply moved. It was the anniversary of his wife's death and Bert was sending a memorial notice to the paper. 'Never forgotten, always remembered,' he wrote.

That night, tied up at the wharf at Hobart, the ship was swinging on her mooring lines and I was about to go ashore when suddenly Bert began to talk in his cabin.

'Darling,' he was saying. 'Darling.' Talking in his sleep, remembering his wife. I couldn't help but hear, he was speaking quite loudly. He was remembering the nights he had spent with her, in her arms, and all the intimate words they had spoken. I nearly wept when I thought of his funny, ugly old face and lumpy body . . . always remembering, never forgetting. 'Darling,' he said. And then a woman's voice replied, 'Give us another drink.' It was the unselfish letter writer.

Bert, I felt like going in and throwing a bucket of cold water over you for that!

In between new appointments I would cook. I liked it, and didn't find the work too hard, but it was very awkward both to cook and work the radio and telegraph because these were very often worked just at meal-times, so I rarely stayed as cook for more than a few months at a time.

My first job each time was to paint the concrete floor and all the woodwork, scrape the accumulation of months off the stove, and declare war on the cockroaches. Every ship has cockroaches and if they cannot be eradicated at least they can be controlled.

Contrary to the ration scale laid down in the wheelhouse, the provisioning for the ship was not at all miserly. It was generous to the degree that no order for good food was ever queried. Tea or coffee was available first thing in the morning. For breakfast we had porridge or rolled oats, or corn flakes and hot milk; eggs and bacon or steak, sausages, chops, lamb's fry, kidneys, or tomatoes; toast and marmalade and one other jam. For morning tea there were scones or tea-cakes. Midday dinner was the main meal of the day, soup, roast joint, baked and mashed potatoes, two veg. and sauces and gravies etc.; followed by sweets with fresh cream.

For afternoon tea I made biscuits or cakes, sometimes getting very fancy and turning on cream buns, lamingtons, and jelly cakes. Tea was one meat course, steak and kidney pie, fish and chips or the like; cold meats and salad and as much bread, butter, jams, and cheeses as you could eat.

The galley was always unlocked and the fire kept going twenty-four hours a day so the crew could make tea or coffee whenever they were free and the men on night watch could cook a grill for themselves.

As the Big Fellow got the service running at a profit, so did the cook take a greater thrashing because then the ship ploughed through all 'reasonable' seas (reasonable to a good seaman is plain homicidal to a landlubber) to keep on schedule. The first time I was chef on the *Naracoopa* it was so rough for three trips running that everything on top of the stove had to be lashed down. The first morning out she was rolling gently, but with the top of the stove packed with pots and pans for breakfast nothing slid around. There was a twelve centimetre high 'fiddle' or iron rail around the edge of the stove and smaller fids to fit across.

With sixteen passengers and ten crew to feed I put on the usual three-course midday meal early, and as if by pre-arrangement the ship stood on its beam ends in a prelude of things to come just as I got the big soup boiler bubbling. It took off at a fair rate of knots and sailed clear over to the other side of the stove, taking two smaller saucepans with it. When it hit the iron fiddle it pulled up so short that half its contents leapt over the side. The mate was going by and I asked him, 'This likely to keep up?' He said no, it was only a bit of a blow. That bit of a blow turned a three-course meal into a matted, foul-looking, churned-up, lumped togetherness that later prompted Pete to make a rude remark.

Thinking that conditions would ease any minute I added more pots and dishes to the stove. No matter what the conditions you must always cook a complete meal at sea because likely as not, though the ship has been standing on her beam ends all day, she will reach calm waters just at meal-time and everybody will sit down for the usual meal just as though nothing had happened. By midday all the dripping from the roast leg of pork had run out the oven door on to the floor. I opened another door and a baked potato shot out at me as though it was fired from a rifle. Its companions were bounding round the bottom of the oven, not half a dozen of them remaining in the baking dish. I looked in the hottest oven where my apple sponge was cooking. The sugary apple was burning into sticky caramel where it had run out of the pie-dish and the feather-light sponge was like plastic leather from the kneading it had taken as it rolled first one way, then another. As a compromise to its various positions, what was left of it finished up setting towards the front of the dish at a seven centimetre depth while the rest sloped off gradually till it reached the thickness of paper down the other end.

I'd criss-crossed iron fiddles on the top of the stove and the pots there were held fast, but the ship pitched and tossed so much that everything slopped into everything else. Custard, mint sauce, brown gravy, boiled potatoes, pumpkin, green peas, and soup were each in the other.

I hadn't put on morning tea, hoping no one would want it, but someone did – old Chum – and he stood grizzling at the door about it. I took a fiddle out to make a space for the kettle of water and as I lurched to the tap I saw from the corner of my eye something coming at me and jumped over the coaming and out into the wings and drew my tummy in as the soup came by in a boiling slick. Before I could grab anything, bedlam broke loose. Every pot on the stove went over, the potato pot jumped clear over the fiddles without touching them and from a standing start the custard pot leapt at the gravy. I caught the pumpkin pot by the handle as it went by and, turning, flung it into the sink. By now I was standing halfway up my shins in salt water that was flowing over the deck and slapping over the coaming and then into the wings and then again over the coaming into the galley and along the alley leading to the saloon.

A bag of coke fell from the top of a bin where Pete had carelessly put it and as it fell it split and the black nuggets floated round on top of the water on the floor. Shortly, they were joined by potatoes from a wooden case that gave up the struggle after it had been pounded from one wall of the galley to the other once too often. From the pantry came a funny sound like . . . plonk-splash . . . plonk-splash. I waded in and leapt aside as a large bottle of tomato sauce went by, falling from a high storage cupboard. Plonk-splash it went and joined its fellows in the sea swishing round the pantry floor. I pushed a wet tea towel between the door and its frame to hold it and while I was recovering the bottles of sauce a door behind me sprang open and a thirty-five kilo bag of sugar rolled slowly over and spilled out into the water. Mick came by and said, 'Having fun, kid?'

'Well, at least there's nothing left to go wrong,' I replied.

Immediately the ship reared up on a sneaker, lifted her stern high in the air then smacked it down like a dowager slipping on a ballroom floor. There was a small bang, and then a new sound, this time from the saloon. The fire extinguisher had torn adrift from its lashings, fallen on its side, and with a small hissing sound was steadily filling the whole saloon with its airy spray foam. I ran towards it, stepped on the slippery liquid and went skidding under the table on my backside. Mick laughed, ran in to help me, slipped, and before he could grab anything fell on his back and followed me under the table. The ship plunged and rolled and water poured in over the coaming and washed over us as we crawled out on our hands and knees. Coke and potatoes floated in and bobbed around us. 'Look out!' Mick shouted, and as we ducked, the little mantel radio tore out of its moorings and crashed down, wires trailing brokenly after it. Chairs not fastened to the floor rolled round and became stuck cross-wise in the alleyway and stacked up under the tables.

The passengers had got into their bunks early on, and all the crew not on watch had turned in too, because nobody could be expected to work in these seas – no one except the cook, seemingly.

As suddenly as it had started, the pitching and diving stopped; we were under the lee of Maria Island. Out walked the sixteen passengers, down came the crew. They were ready for their midday dinner. The Big Fellow came down to see why I hadn't rung the bell. 'I haven't got anything ready,' I stuttered. I showed him the mixture in the sink where I'd thrown all the things that had rolled over and that's when Pete came by and said, 'Pooh! Who did that?'

The Skipper was quite pleasant. He said, 'If you're finding the work too much let me know. But we must have meals on time.' He looked around and then was a little less pleasant. 'And we must have cleanliness! Look at this place!' I put the starched cloths on the tables and sprinkled water on them so the crockery wouldn't slip off, and hoped and prayed the rough stuff would start again so the passengers would go back to bed. But it continued real Sunday-river-cruise-stuff, so I had to grill chops and tomatoes, and chip potates, make soup from tinned tomatoes and cream, chop fresh fruit into fruit salad, and swab the saloon dry after the boys had got the worst of it out by bucket brigade and swept up the potatoes and coke. Through all this I had to keep my temper while the passengers called out and banged their cutlery on their plates. With all that time and energy to spare they could have cleaned up the mess they had made in their cabins, I was thinking. I was still stewardess as well as chef, the owners acting on the assumption that it was all woman's work anyway, not to mention my time on the wheel, the radio, telegraph and cargo.

For all that there was a lot of satisfaction to be gained from cooking. Particularly when hard-working crews would come out with their plates wiped clean and say, 'I'd like to wrap my laughing gear round a bit more of that!'

21

AMV Fetch and Carry

Our captain made many errors. How could it be otherwise? But if he endangered our lives and that of the ship in the early days when he was gaining his sea-legs, were we in any more danger than if we had sailed with an experienced man? During the six years I sailed with the small ships in Bass Strait no less than six small ships were wrecked – total losses – in that very strait (this included the *Sheerwater*, the first ship on which I sailed) and these ships were all skippered by experienced, trained seamen.

The loss of each was the result of an Act of God, not lack of experience. Anyway it didn't take long to gain experience on our type of run – either you learnt or you left, master or man, it was no different. You couldn't last the distance if you couldn't match the pace.

We were the fetch-and-carry service for the port of Hobart. We went to all the places that big ships couldn't get near and brought their cargo down to them where they waited at their safe deep-water piers in the city. But we never envied them their safety because we heard from them of the boredom of such a life.

We were never bored. From the time the Big Fellow came on board five hours was the longest rest we could have, and this only under special circumstances. On many trips we snatched only three hours between working ports.

Hanging down from the mountains and over the port as though it might topple into the water, Hobart runs right into the River Derwent. The GPO squatted only one block away from our rickety regular berth and its four-sided clock tolled us away from the city as punctually as the Big Fellow had forewarned us. If he said we sail at midnight then dead on midnight as the clock began to strike we cried, 'All gone forrard, all gone aft,' aboard our scruffy little tub and as the last stroke died away we were easing out into the stream, past the gleaming ocean-going ships that were thirty and more times our size – why, we declared, it takes us half an hour to steam their length as we pass them at the wharf. And then we were off down the river past Long Point, John Garrow Light, and the Iron Pot where the sea came to meet us as we set off to those places where *we* were the big ship, the ship that was waited for everywhere.

Sometimes the whole population of a place we visited crowded down to meet us. Once we left Hobart we were on our own. There was no authority to guide us because we were now the authority on this route, we alone plied it, we alone knew it. If we got to know it by rolling off every reef and getting stuck on every sand-bar, as we were accused of doing, then let it be said to our credit that we never hit the same place twice!

And our pathfinding pioneered the way for others who might follow – although it was doubtful if many would follow in our wake: the days of the small ship were ending.

As the last of the chimes on the GPO clock faded away we'd move off Slow Ahead, Half and then Full, the boys on deck lashing the cargo down as we went. When all was fast they'd turn to, polish brass, swab the wheelhouse, clean the windows, and attend to the maintenance of gear while the mate was splicing and rigging and testing equipment. Before we got into each port the cargo would be unlashed ready for unloading as soon as we tied up, the gear and rigging ready too. If the tide was right for us to go through the canal we had only three hours' sailing before the order came to Stand By. I'd go up to take the telegraph, the mate went to the fo'c'sle head, two seamen ranged along the side of the ship with rubber tyres for fenders to hang on ropes over the side and two seamen went up to the flying bridge with the Skipper to stand by in case he needed a hand to swing her in the fierce rip tide. He always took the wheel here.

If we were too deep to go through the canal (loaded down to almost four metres [or twelve feet, as it was in those days] we risked the canal only if the weather was so bad as to stop us going the long way round) then we went down through 'the hole in the wall', between Tasman Island and the island State of Tasmania. Sometimes we'd leave Hobart at 10 p.m. and by 3 a.m. we'd be through the Tasman Passage and hooting our siren in Fortescue Bay for the fishermen isolated there to come and collect their fuel or bring their fish for transport to the city.

Within eighteen hours of leaving Hobart we could be tied up in Swansea after working as many as four places *en route*. On the Hobart to Swansea and return trip we never slept in port from the time we left Hobart until our return. If we were tied up in Swansea *we worked*, for we could take it in turns to sleep on the way home down the coast – and a sleep of utter exhaustion that was. I found it bad enough in my nice deck cabin aft, but one day I saw the conditions under which the boys slept, and marvelled.

A young seaman was ill and the mate took me forward to take his temperature and pulse as he lay tossing in his bunk. As I bent over the boy the sound of the sea, assaulting the bow of the ship that was the wall of the room in which he lay with three other seamen, was so huge that it was like an artillery barrage. Whroompp, whroompp, whroompp, ceaselessly it thundered and smacked in tumult as it attacked the wooden-walled ship.

The boy was feverish. I sent for a bowl and towels from the chef and while I waited I looked around what was known as 'the crew's quarters', which comprised four bunks built into the sloping side of the ship and a separate room, 'saloon', with a table and four chairs. The whole had the atmosphere of a place where refugees have been suddenly incarcerated rather than the living quarters of hard-working men. The floor and part of the walls were wet when water seeped through the ventilator and down the hawse pipes to the anchor chain locker which was in their section. Table and chairs, boots and suitcases slid backwards and forwards over the wet slippery linoleum; the walls were festooned with clothing – oilskins, hip boots, sou'-westers, wet woollens, and hats – the accumulation of years. A sour musty smell from the sea-damp clothes filled the triangle in which these boys lived and to this sourness was added the dull aggression of mouldy damp boards under the lino. Over all sounded the gross onslaught of the sea. The movement of the ship here was totally different from that at any other place on her. Here she took the whole spite of the sea. She trembled, shook, wobbled, dived, twisted, reared, fell into a void, smacked down on a hard sea, and rolled in a corkscrew motion, and yet from this limbo these boys must come after two, three, or four hours' rest fit for toil the like of which they would never know on shore. I never hunted a boy from the galley after I had seen these quarters.

My cabin, though attractive and well appointed, had, of course, the funnel through it, but it was better than the boys' quarters – except for the times the funnel caught fire. One night, well after midnight, I turned in, dog-weary with the fatigue that penetrated into the heart and the head when the body could absorb no more. I fell on the bunk with all my clothes on, even my shoes, and was in a heavy sleep when I heard the boys calling. I tried not to hear and then I pretended I didn't hear. They banged on the door and knocked on my porthole and flashed lights in but I wouldn't listen. It was not fair, I thought, always being roused out. And then I felt it and smelt it and heard it. The cabin was stupefyingly hot, the paintwork on my wardrobe was burning and the steam hissed out into my cabin from the water the boys were pouring on to the funnel and under my door. We were on fire.

As I unlocked the cabin door the mate and a seaman rushed in. They tore the plywood lining from the back of my wardrobe and threw it and the smouldering lagging out on the deck, where other seamen hosed the flames from it. They were now able to direct water on to the funnel from inside the cabin. Every man was calm and busy. While the mate and a man worked in my cabin the Big Fellow and another seaman cut down the mainsail, part burnt, part charred, and stowed it safely back aft.

When I joined the group, silhouetted black shapes in a red-ruby haze on deck, I saw the beam of the lighthouse on Tasman Island. It was on our starboard quarter when it should have been to port as we had been heading *up* the coast, not *down*, and we were in so close to the massive rock that is the island that the glow from our fire lit up the basalt.

Then the Big Fellow went to the wheel to take her in closer under Tasman. It was now clear to me: we had turned back down the coast, putting our bow into the wind because the fire was aft, and we were creeping as close as we dared under the lee of the island in the hope that the lightkeeper would not see us and report a ship on fire at sea. How they missed us we never knew, but miss us they did. None but we knew of the fire, yet a holocaust of sparks and flames vomited fifteen metres into the air and spread into a fiery glow, lighting us up in a way that must have been visible from the horizon. We had had other fires but this was the first at night, and a wonderful spectacle it was. When it was all over and we edged out of the shelter of the island my cabin was a shambles, but I lay on the bunk in my greatcoat for the few hours' sleep before the alarm bell would ring for all hands to stand by to work South Maria Island.

While the flurry and excitement of the fire was on I had heard no obscenities, no blasphemy at all, yet all had had their hair singed by falling fiery soot and several had burnt their hands and eyebrows. I use this occurrence as an example when pious people ask me about 'language' on board. This usually takes the form of 'I suppose you had to put up with a lot of filthy language from the seamen.' My reply invariably is, 'Only the passengers used filthy language.' In six years of mixing with small ships' men obscene language was never used in my presence. I've even known them to come and close the galley porthole if someone was playing up on the wharf and cursing. There may have been some of it around, but I never listened for it so I never heard it.

If I walked up to a group of boys and there was sudden silence I moved off as soon as I could naturally do so and let them get on with it. I liked to whistle tunes and this was handy to attract attention over the noise of the motors and to warn of my approach. (The so-called superstition of seamen against whistling is – on small ships, anyway – just a writer's fancy. If men wanted to whistle, they whistled.) Passengers were not so careful. Sometimes one had the impression that they felt obliged to demonstrate their manliness, toughness, and crudity and could only do it by parading obscenities, even dirty stories, in an effort to match the vigour of these tough men of the small ships. In doing so they demonstrated the degree by which they fell short of this standard of courage, initiative, and endurance.

In contrast to this manliness (or is it an integral part of true manliness?) was the compassion the crew showed sometimes in situations that left landsmen quite indifferent. We once witnessed the mass suicide of a herd of whales, and while our passengers rushed from one side of the ship to the other to take pictures the seamen stood staring, horrified, so distressed they hardly spoke. The herd had gone in on the shoals at the Narrows, the entrance to the bay which led to the canal.

There, stranded, gasping, dying on the sands that so often threatened us, were a hundred whales. Some were high and dry, others partly out of the water, while others were in the shallows driving relentlessly on to destruction, the urge that man has not yet fathomed so insistent in them that they didn't falter until they grounded and the weight of their massive bodies, devoid now of the buoyancy of water, crushed their lungs. We had little fairway here and to deviate would almost certainly lead to our destruction as surely as to that of the whales, but when one doomed mammal crossed our bow the Big Fellow eased the helm to avoid it and stopped the motor until the poor thing cleared us and heaved its way to the nearest shoal.

'Oh the stupid bastard,' Pete cried. All about the ship the men were gathered, their eyes riveted on some palpitating creature: a little eye peered out, a huge body sighed and pulsated.

'Oh God!' Alec cried. Some of the great beasts were already dead, their inert bodies undulating as our steady wake purled past them; others rolled an eye as we went by, vibrating a little in distress and lurched in a desperate spasm to get relief; a few were in deep water between the shoals moving with the grace that only leviathans can achieve. I counted ten creatures still uncompromised by the land that would kill them and as I watched one came up and blew and another followed and then a third, great eructations as they ventilated their massive bulks. The animals already stranded were sobbing and soughing in their death throes, but these still free whales exhaled and dived in beautiful health, the water which was their element and playground easing their internal organs of the weight of their bulk.

But we couldn't tarry. We had to move steadily through the Narrows or strand as the whales themselves had done. When we came back out through the Narrows the next trip a few were still alive. By our next voyage they were all dead. It took many weeks for them to decompose and disappear entirely, and by this time the stench of their corruption wafted to us half an hour before we reached the Narrows and as long after clearing land.

The crew were very good to my children and had a sympathetic understanding of the difficulties of a parent bringing up children singlehanded. My Cate was with me much of the time I was on the *Naracoopa*. She was not yet of an age where neglect of formal schooling could affect her. She was a good sailor and was never seasick. On really rough trips I would be alarmed if she were out of my sight because she so loved playing on the open deck where she could watch the wild sea that I was afraid she might tumble over as the ship lurched, and be injured before she could be rescued. I had less work to do for her than I would have had on shore. There were always four or five men on watch and they seemed to enjoy her company. They taught her many things, including poker – about which I did not know until we visited my parents on Cate's sixth birthday, and she suggested we play it instead of Donkey or Old Maid.

The only time anyone complained about her presence on

the ship was when a relieving captain, who was very prone to sea-sickness, saw her playing with her doll on the forward hatch while we rolled around the Raoul. He, in jealous chagrin at the laughing child, cupped his hand to his mouth as he disappeared into his cabin saying, 'A ship is no place for a child.'

For her birthday one year the mate took up a collection and gave her the money to buy a new doll. When she arrived back at the ship with a black 'mammy' doll they were all surprised and for some time I would hear them discussing her choice. They taught her to fish and when we were at anchor she would climb on to the railing and let down a line. She often caught flathead, once a shark, and another time a crab which frightened her until Alec pretended to be a crab and made ludicrous sallies across the deck towards her. Whenever the boat crew went ashore they took her if it was safe, and she played on the sands until they carried her back through the surf to the boat to return to the ship. I think she must have made more sand castles on more isolated beaches than any other Australian child.

Mike, my son, was at college in Hobart and could come with me only on long weekends and during school holidays. He, too, was a fisherman and caught many a meal for us, including a big conger eel that he fetched up one night.

Cate had simple tasks on board, such as laying the cutlery for meals and tidying her bunk, but Mike helped in the hold and was sometimes quite valuable in simple tasks such as unhooking the cargo slings down below, thus freeing a man for stowing. One trip he worked so hard for such long hours that the crew threw in 5s 0d each to pay him, and he had the problem of working out how he could take so much money back to college because it was in excess of the amount allowed to eight-year-olds for pocket money!

The canal was the scene of more disasters than triumphs for us; not for nothing were we known as the Overlanders.

One trip we were stuck for several days with a herd of wild cattle on board, ravenous for food and us with nothing but bread to feed them. We'd come down from Flinders Island in a gale; it had taken us six days to get as far as the Hippolytes and all the fodder we had brought on board for what we thought would be a four-day voyage was now gone.

We were deep laden, just over three and a half metres aft, but we had to try the canal; the gale was such we would never get around Tasman Island and with the hungry cattle on board we could not afford to shelter. Some of the bulls corralled on deck had not seen men in their lives; cattle from outlying islands, they had been rounded up only days before we drove them on board. The boys built high corrals on deck with timber we'd brought along for the purpose, but some of the animals were so fiery they broke this down like match sticks. Finally, all had to be tied with a very short lead from the head and the tops of the corrals timbered over also. Feeding and watering them the first few days was a problem, for they charged anything that moved and went berserk when we loosened their halters, but the boys persisted. By the time we reached the canal they were eating hay from our hands and drinking from hand-held buckets. Then we got stuck in the canal. A night passed and then a day. The tide perversely refused to 'make' sufficient to float us off.

On the second day we took stale bread to our poor beasts but they cared little for it. They were still in prime condition but a few days without food would alter that. Then one of the crew members remarked hesitantly that he had once worked on a property near by and that they always put by much hay for the winter. So off went the seaman, the Big Fellow and the engineer, ashore in our rowing boat, and by midday we could see them returning down the canal like a floating haystack, the three of them clambering over the biggest load of hay a little rowboat could ever have carried.

Our sea-going herd smelt their coming and lifted up their heads and roared their approval.

The following week we watched the papers and were proud to see 'Island stock' topped the market prices for prime beef. The press made no mention of us, only that we had 'gone aground'. Our sole amusement at such reports was our own secret knowledge of the headlines they could have had, had they known of the scrapes we really landed in. With an inexperienced Skipper trying to make a ship pay, an indifferent crew, and a coast that overseas masters have at times called 'the worst lit in the world' we had, on occasions, an exciting time.

There was the night the Skipper was awakened from a catnap by the mate asking if it was the lights of Scamander we could see. The Big Fellow stared to port, we all stared to port, but none of us in the furry gloom of interrupted sleep could recognise the lights, and then the Big Fellow let out with a roar like one of our enraged bulls. 'Town lights be buggered! It's an ocean-going passenger ship and we are so far off our course we are *outside* of it!' These ships sometimes stood out to sea twenty-five kilometres and we were so much further out to sea that the lights of this ship were barely visible. We turned and sailed due west and nearly three hours went by before we picked up the coast of Tasmania. 'Thank God that liner came along. Another hour on his original course and Chum would have hit New Zealand,' the crew declared.

Another night a seaman, alarmed, woke the Skipper, 'I think we're inside the red sector,' he whispered. The Big Fellow ran out and there loomed the red light of Eddystone, the light you see only when it is too late. (This was in fact true and because of it the red light has today been removed from this lighthouse.) But then we were within the orbit covered by this light. The *Australian Pilot*, published by the Admiralty, said this of the red light of Eddystone: 'Victoria Rocks which lie off Eddystone Point comprise the following:

. . . Norgate Rock with a depth of fourteen feet, one and a quarter miles eastward; Greyhound Rock with a depth of five feet three-quarters of a mile eastward; a one and a half fathoms rock, three-quarters of a mile east-south-eastward; and Eddystone Rock, nineteen feet high, half a mile south-eastward of the outer end of a shallow spit extending from Eddystone Point and having on it two rocks, which dry about three feet and some rocks awash, between Eddystone Rock and the point. The Victoria Rocks are covered by the red fixed light exhibited from the lighthouse on Eddystone Point.' And we were drawing over 3.5 metres and travelling Full Speed Ahead.

I do not know how we reached bold water. I know the motor was stopped, we drifted a little as the Big Fellow got his bearings and then he started Slow Ahead with a seaman standing out on the bulwarks near the ratlines swinging the lead, calling out the marks because he didn't know what they signified, 'Piece of leather with three ends.' That would be three fathoms. 'Bit of rag' could be white calico which would give us five fathoms or red bunting which gave seven. Either was safe for us. Then, 'Nothing.' The motor stopped. It could be a 'deep,' it could be four fathoms, six fathoms, eight or nine fathoms but it could be one fathom, almost two metres right beside the ship, or a rock. 'Again,' called the captain. 'Three bits of leather again.' Three fathoms – eighteen feet in imperial measure. The motor purred and the next call came, 'One bit of leather – it's got a hole in it.' Ten fathoms. Next, 'Bit of rag.' The boy lit a match and in the second the flame held he saw the colour, 'Blue rag.' Thirteen fathoms. 'Nothing.' 'Deep!' Alec called in anger and relief from where he waited with the mate to let go the anchor if need be. We were in bold water. The mate was relieved of his watch. 'For God's sake go to bed,' was all the Big Fellow said, so dissipated was his nervous energy. The rest of us were too excited to sleep and sat around a pot of tea talking for hours.

Lead lines are curious things with marks that are inexplicable until their origin is explained. These marks were first used by the old Dutch seamen in crossing the narrow strips of shoals which abound off the coast of Holland. Soundings only were marked on the shoals, safe depths were unmarked and were called 'dieps'. The English later corrupted this to 'deeps'. The line is marked with different types of material so that the mark may be distinguished by touch at night-time when the colour cannot be seen.

To weight the line a piece of lead weighing about four and a half kilos is used. This has a hollow which I've seen fishermen fill with a soft mixture to enable them to identify 'the bottom', the sea floor. (Cray-pots are usually 'shot' over a rocky bottom only.) When examined, this 'arming', sometimes butter, will show grains of sand or the indentations of rock.

Old Chum was for ever enlivening our lives with his jokes, or 'yolks', as the crew cornily called his errors. He was supposed to call the captain before going through 'the hole in the wall', the narrow passage between Tasman Island and the Tasmanian mainland, but he rarely took orders to heart. One day, a fine sunny day on a calm smooth sea, I went into the wheelhouse as usual to watch the spectacle of our passage between the canyons of rock nearly three hundred metres high on either side. Chum was alone. We turned and went in; the cliffs darkened the glassy limpid water of the sea around us. We were half-way through. Then, apparently from nowhere, the sea rose up and rolled towards us, and as it came it gathered height until it was higher than our deck housing, and from where we stood we were looking up at it. It hit us slightly on the quarter, we bucked, pitched, then dropped down the crevasse left by its passing. I heard the crashing of china down below. But when I looked back there was nothing to be seen but a slight swell left by its passing.

'What in hell was that?' the Skipper was out.

'What?' said Chum. He was not an observant man.

Two years later the captain came to me. 'I know now what made your face go white in the "hole in the wall",' he told me. Going through one night he had experienced a similar phenomenon himself. 'It came from nowhere and disappeared into the same place.'

Another time, Chum rolled us on to Black Jack, a reef near Schouten Island (most reefs are 'Black Jack' to seamen). While the crew ran to lift the hatches and clamber down into the hold to see if we'd been holed, old Chum sang away on the wheel. Apart from being quite charming to passengers (he made up for the lack of charm in the rest of us) Chum was not of much use. So useless was he that when our whole deck crew were ill one trip we did not call on him for assistance but berthed and cleared the tricky wharf at Coles Bay with Mick below on the motor, me on the wheel, and the Big Fellow on deck and on the wharf and back on the deck making lines fast.

We put off our small cargo and sailed across the bay to Swansea, tied up at the wharf there and woke the boys to help us load, and they swore we had never worked Coles Bay. 'Ha! Gave it the go-by,' Pete crowed, until he saw the space where the Coles Bay parcels had stood. The boys were so ill this particular trip that when we reached Hobart two of them could not make the deck to help unload. We had our deck stacked high with timber for the ship waiting opposite our berth to take to Melbourne. Chum worked the winch, one sick seaman the guy rope, one in the hold with the Big Fellow hooked the straps on the packs, and on the wharf Mick drove our fork truck and I ran beside him with dunnage all night long, and before morning broke and daylight sent me into hiding we'd all earned eight hours' overtime. (In Hobart at the *end* of a trip we got overtime working cargo after 5 p.m.)

We had little illness and few accidents and it was as well. A ship is a terrible place in which to be ill. Jack London summed it up for all time in *Sea Wolf* when he wrote of Wolf

Larsen suffering from the headaches that presaged his blindness. 'He suffered as wild animals suffer. As it seemed the way on ship to suffer, without plaint, without sympathy, utterly alone.'

Of the many stories we told and retold about Chum the one I liked best was about Hell Fire, a prominent bluff on the east coast of Tasmania. A passenger one day asked Chum for the name of this landmark on our port side. 'Hell Fire,' said Chum. 'A very distinctive and aptly named prominence.' Half an hour later the passenger came up on deck again and spoke to Chum on the wheel. 'What's that remarkable bluff on our starboard side?' he asked the old mate. 'That,' said Chum with the best guide accent, 'that is Hell Fire, a very distinctive and aptly named prominence.' He had quite unconsciously turned the ship around and was heading back the way we had come.

The long periods at sea had turned Pete into quite a little gentleman. He now owned two pairs of trousers, three shirts and a pair of shoes. Because of the quick turn-round of the ship he was unable to spend all he earned, no matter how hard he tried. 'It seems such a waste,' he used to say. I suggested he open a bank account. After much cajoling he yielded. He would come with me to the bank and see what he thought about it when he got there, he said. So next time we were in port, in Hobart, I gave him two hours' notice before I was ready to go up town. When I met him on deck he was still in his dungarees, boots, working coat, no shirt, and old woollen cap. 'It's me money I'm putting in the bank, not meself,' he said.

The Commonwealth Bank in Hobart is a fine building, faced with red granite we had brought down from Coles Bay and decorated with murals and sculptured figures and peopled by uniformed attendants. The floor is polished stone, and as we went past a great bloc of people lined up at Withdrawals, and went round a corner to the empty section marked 'New

Accounts', Pete's hob-nailed boots slipped on the stone and over he went.

'Jeez!' he said, at his loudest. 'Fair on me arse!' I tried to help him to his feet but he had big iron plates on his heels and he slipped again, nearly taking me with him, so I let go. I couldn't look as though I'd never seen him before because he kept talking at me and no one else. Finally he got on to his hands and knees and pushed himself up that way to a standing position.

When we got his money entered in the book he said to the teller, 'I hope you're honest. I'd better have a look.' He looked at the figures entered in the book and said they looked okay. 'Thanks, Cock,' he said in a matey fashion to the teller and walked out over the polished floor holding on to the counter all the way like a child learning to skate.

22

A Bird of Ill-Omen

The literature of the sea is vast and wonderful and there can scarcely be a man alive who has not at some time been under the spell of the beautiful words that writers of the sea have employed through the ages. There is much music in things of the sea – man, mate, master, it sings. In the craft of the mariner alliteration, romance, mystique and valour have combined to excite the imagination of the writer.

Psalm 107, verses 23 and 24 – ' . . . they which go down to the sea in ships, and occupy by the great waters, they see the works of the Lord, and His wonders in the deep . . . ' – leads the imagery, but Coleridge's *The Ancient Mariner*, that marathon verse of the 'damned accursed albatross', has bitten deeper into readers of English literature.

We sailed in the albatross latitudes. The wandering albatross, the largest of all surviving birds, ranges from roughly 60° to 40° south and sometimes almost to 30°, along the three currents that sweep up the west coast of South America, Africa, and Australia.

I have said that I found no superstition at sea about a woman whistling, although much talk on shore that sailors cannot abide it, but, like many another well-read landsman turned seaman I was amazed when I found the seamen had no compunction about killing an albatross. In fact I never met the seaman who had heard that the albatross was an omen of any kind – ocean-going ships today being of such a size, and the work no longer involving long hours on deck, that the creatures of the sea and birds of the oceanic air currents are literally unknown to the seaman or casual traveller. I believe the men of the small ships observe such life more closely than any others, yet I have questioned men who travel as widely as the Antarctic, along the South American coast, and the old sub-Antarctic whaling stations as well as round the Australian coast, in fact men almost within the whole ambit of the wandering albatross's orbit, and I have never met a man who considered this to be a bird of any supernatural significance. Admiral Sir William Jameson of HMS *Ark Royal*, whose book *The Wandering Albatross* contains the finest writing about this great bird, set himself the task of tracking down the origin of the fable 'upon which Coleridge had presumably based his Rime'; but was forced finally to admit that it was the poet's fine imagination, not the seaman's superstition, that created the myth.

But if the fable of the bird is false, what is too real to the seaman is the fit that comes on the ancient mariner, the urge to talk, to tell of the sea. Few men who have been to sea have escaped this plague – they may not delay the wedding guest or even give tongue to their desire but every seaman knows the longing of that 'grey-beard loon' to tell the tale.

'There was a ship,' quoth he. 'There was a ship.' What landsman can match that?

Ruby Hunt provided us with our own bird of ill-omen, a bird that to the men on the *Naracoopa* rivalled Coleridge's albatross as a harbinger of misfortune. It was springtime. We knew it because there were no curtains at the windows of the Hunts' cottage on the hill at Maria Island when Ruby waved to me on our way up the coast. As I stood on deck near the flag back aft waving a tea towel I could see her curtains flapping away on the clotheslines out on the green hill together with cushion covers, bedspreads, and floor mats. She was spring-cleaning.

Ordinarily the seasons made little difference to us on the *Naracoopa*. Summer, autumn, winter, and spring – it was all the same, the routine never altered. The only difference we noticed was that it was warmer at sea in winter than it was on land. When we sailed back up the river on our way home to the port of Hobart you would see layers of woollens being dragged on where shirts alone had sufficed on the water.

When we passed Ruby's cottage next trip she waved as usual and I noticed her curtains were back up on the windows. This week she had got around to blankets and the paddock was grey with them. 'Still hard at it,' her note in the box on the wharf read. 'I've gone through everything including the hen-house. Hence two cockerels you will find enclosed in box as gift to you.' There, bearing a tag, 'Mrs Pat, *Naracoopa*,' was a crate with two prize cockerels crowing lustily.

I put them on the after deck outside my cabin and fed them with scraps from the galley. We were bound for Flinders Island, always my favourite place, and the boys said that by the look of the 'glass' we would have an armchair ride each way. The boys were quite happy about my cockerels at this stage. Alec even went so far as to make jokes about them. He said he would teach them to whistle a tune before we got back to Hobart, and if he were in the vicinity when I went to my cabin he would squat in front of their crate and whistle to them over and over the first four bars of 'Westering Home', the song that was a sort of theme song of our trips to Bass Strait, while the birds crowed and cackled and scratched in the straw Ruby had provided. Yet less than a week later, when one of them made a sound Alec was to lead a group who threatened to throw them overboard.

Had we gone 'outside' immediately we left Maria Island we might not have gone on. We would have gone past Isle des Phoques, our White Rock, even as far as the Hen and Chickens and Schouten Island perhaps, but then we would have known what the seaway was like and have turned into the shelter still offering. Instead, we stayed inside the shelter of the islands because we had a little cargo for Coles Bay and night was nearly on us when we turned to go out Geographe Strait, Schouten Passage, the narrow race of water between Schouten Island and Freycinet Peninsula leading to the open sea. And as we turned and steamed to go through, night fell and there was no light. 'It's as black as the inside of a dog,' Pete said. We were all in the wheelhouse.

The passage through is quite beautiful, bound on either side with red granite heights and down below off shore in the water the Cow and the Calf, the two rocks washed over by seas, seem to rise and fall like the whales they are named after, the large Cow and the small Calf. Tonight there was nothing to be seen. We could not make out the opening. When darkness fell we had steamed almost to where the gap in the land ought to have opened up and as we ploughed on in the darkness the Big Fellow watched the compass and the clock. Then he went out on deck away from the faint glow of the binnacle light and stared into the night. In a while he called the change of course, then, steady as she goes; we steamed on and no one spoke, then another change, another and it seemed a long time later, 'Okay. Bring her round into it.'

We were heading north up the coast. We were through the

passage, we could now see The Lemon, the lighthouse on the seaward side of the peninsula. Before we could feel relief the sea hit us. Its turbulence was offensive after the calm afforded us by the shelter of the islands. We steamed on for half an hour but it neither eased nor grew worse. But no one left the wheelhouse. It was as though we all knew we would be needed.

'There's something brewing,' the Skipper said. For a while he thought of turning back. He was talking aloud, but to himself rather than to us. 'If a man goes on he might get caught. If he turns back he might lose a day holed up and nothing happen out here anyway.' We switched on the ship's radio and listened in to two ships 'working' one another eighty kilometres up the coast. They said nothing about bad conditions; it seemed as though we were going through an isolated patch. We should soon sail out of it. The decision to go on was easier to make because we had no passengers aboard. We were pitching so unevenly I went below to see that the supplies were well secured. I closed the damper on the stove and made everything fast in the galley. 'She's having it on,' Mick said as he passed on his way down to take his watch in the engine room. Ten hours were to pass before he was able to come up.

The further we went the worse the sea became. We were now past the point that the boys called the point of no return, where to go back or to go on was the same equally hazardous course; this was the stretch of coast where there was no shelter or harbour for us in a day's sailing.

I was on my way to my cabin up on the exposed deck when a sea came over the side and drenched me. I hung on to the shrouds as it went over me and when at last I opened my eyes they were of no use to me; the darkness was so intense and I had lost my bearings. For a while I was very frightened. I couldn't tell where I was and when I calmed down and realised that if I clung to the railing I could go hand over hand the few steps necessary to make the position opposite my cabin, I remembered the rusted railing that made us so nervous when passengers leaned upon it.

The ship lurched again and I fell face down on to the shrouds. If I fell like that on to the railing not my fear but my common sense told me I could well follow the rail into the sea. So I got down on my hands and knees and when the deck lifted again crawled quickly to my cabin, terrified now of something more horrible than the sea, that of being seen by the boys crawling so fearfully. I should have had no fear. Before morning scarcely a man on board had not been down on his hands and knees.

The door of my cabin opened outwards, so I put on my light before I attempted to chase it as it swung backwards and forwards across the deck with the roll of the ship. The light streamed out on to the water that was rolling across the deck and, as the ship reeled over on her side again, I saw the crate containing my two Maria Island cockerels go skating by. Then as the ship rolled the other way it reversed its movements and skied back. My head went from side to side watching it.

As soon as a sea washed the cockerels near my door I reached out and juggled the crate inside my cabin. There was little space left once the cockerels were there. The two once proud birds were squatting dejected and deflated on the floor of their crate, their tails drooping wetly.

The moment I put the light off and lay down I knew this was no ordinary storm. Until now I had been actively employed, and its strangeness had not been impressed on me. But there had never been anything like this in the time I had been at sea. It was not its violence that was unique – I had been rolled out of my bunk before this – but the formless assaults of the sea were so unpredictable that the ship itself was bewildered. We rose on a great wave and began to fall into a deep trough but half-way down a sea from the port side hit us and rolled us over, then when we were recovering another wave lifted us and while we were scarcely over the crest, just beginning the headlong dive into the abyss scooped out by the first wave, a second and bigger sea hit us and we leapt back, shuddering, and canted over so far that the cockerels now were lying on the wire netting front of their crate.

The wind and the sea came down on us. Sometimes the two fused together, trying with their unity to pin us down beneath the water; sometimes the sea hit us in one place while the wind attacked from the flank to prevent our escaping. Once as I lay on my bunk there was a noise of silence and suspense and I believe the whole ship was engulfed for a time, the sea covering her completely. My small cabin squeaked, a different sound from the creakings and groanings of a ship 'working' – this was an uneasy sound, a sound made by wood twisting on nails. I dressed again, crouching on hands and knees on the bunk and opened the door. As I stepped out on deck I looked up to where, six metres above our stern, a wall of water was about to fall on us. I sprang back into the cabin and closed the door and leant on it and waited. But the fall of this wall seemed no more than the other constant onslaughts. I went out again, the ship lurched to starboard, and before I could get a hold on anything I fell across the steep slope of the deck and onto the winch, crawled from there to the mast, and stood with both arms up around the derrick, bruised and sore. While I waited sleet stung my face and tore at my clothes. When the chance came and the ship was momentarily about to be rolled to port I fled around the starboard wing and into the wheelhouse. The men hardly noticed my coming though I brought with me wind and sea before I could drag the door around to shut it.

Above the hoarse roar of the water and the moans of the ship taking the shock and onset of these relentless seas was another sound, and the men were hanging out the wheelhouse windows, staring. 'The fork truck's walking,' the Skipper said. The cargo in our holds was superphosphate for the islands; on deck we had a truck, eighty forty-four gallon drums of petrol, and in a space near the deck housing our own fork-lift had been lashed fore and aft with a 'handy Billy' block and tackle and made fast with chains from either side. These had snapped with the violent lurching of the ship and now the five tonne machine was loose on the deck.

I stood close to the old man we had taken as mate for this trip as he directed the searchlight onto the deck. Four of the boys were down there trying to capture and lash it down. 'Watch it below,' the old man cried as the heavy escapee began to move with the roll of the ship and then gain momentum and crash into the wooden bulwarks. The sea swivelled us around and lifted us up again, rolled us a little one way and back with a hurting lurch the other way, and the fork-lift seemed to be a battering ram rolling back only a short way to gain power for another assault.

'Watch it below!' Another sea was coming and two boys scarcely had time to leap up on to the forward hatch and to flatten themselves against the deck housing as the monster lurched past again. In the darkness, with the lights flickering as the spray came over them, it was frightening and confusing. The difficulty was to lasso the fork truck, but once this was done they quickly made it fast. Their swiftness and efficiency in an emergency always surprised me.

When it was done, two climbed up to the wheelhouse and two crawled on hands and knees over the drums to the fo'c'sle. They had scarcely closed the fo'c'sle door behind them when the ship reared up, faltered in her swing, staggered as a mountain of water arrested her lurching roll, and then was thrown off and dropped so hard into a sea below that we scarcely felt the cruel jarring to the ship for the concussion it caused within our heads. While the pain was still on us the fo'c'sle door opened and the two deckhands came scuttling out, across the drums on hands and knees and up to the wheelhouse. 'Oh Jeez,' said Pete. 'Oh Jeez! I thought we'd opened up.'

The uneven jerking continued for a time, then round about midnight the motion altered. It seemed to us up in the wheelhouse that the ship was slipping around underneath us, as though the wheelhouse were suspended from above on a string and the ship below swinging from side to side oilily, sickeningly. We all complained of headache. The deckhands went back to the fo'c'sle to lie down.

They had scarcely gone when Mick blew up the whistle from the engine room. 'Tell Skip the bilge pump's packed it in. We can't keep the water down.' When the Skipper returned to the wheelhouse he said there was two metres of water in the ship. The violent motion of the ship had disturbed some residue of oakum and waste left since our last slipping and every time the bilge pump began to pick up, this teased-out hempen rope blocked the mechanism.

For Flinders Island trips we had to carry a second engineer and this man was sitting on the floor awash with water taking the pump to pieces. They had taken it to pieces twice before this. The Skipper was pressing both buzzers on the wall as he spoke. These alerted the crew and the whole ship. 'Man the deck pump,' the Big Fellow called as the crew tumbled out of the fo'c'sle. In the darkness they fell over one another, everyone shouting and asking questions. They were looking for the lever that operated the pump. Then they directed the searchlight accurately and saw it.

'Hey Skip! what would you say if we couldn't man the pump?'

'My prayers,' he replied with spleen. 'We're filling up.'

'If you want a dry burying,' he said so calmly that it was ominous, 'you'd better get that pump working. There's more than two metres of water below.' The lever, the handle for the pump, had been smashed by the fork-lift truck during its walk but now they found a bar and began to pump, two men at a time.

I was in the galley making cocoa. A boy on his first trip with us came in from the deck. 'I don't feel so bad if I can't see it,' he said honestly.

'Is it bad?' I asked. He said we were so low in the sea the water was lapping the deck.

When I took hot cocoa up top the Skipper was poring over the chart. By the lines he had drawn I could tell we were on course. Speaking aloud he said, 'If I can get her that far I'll put her up there.' He pointed to a small beach.

'Shelter?' I asked, puzzled.

'There's no shelter for us. I'm going to run her aground.' He felt that that way he might save our lives, but if he kept going he would lose the ship, and in such a sea there would be no chance for us. There can be no job so lonely as that of a ship's master at times like this.

The whistle from the engine room went. The second engineer had been thrown off his feet and fallen, his trouser leg had caught in a fly wheel and before he could be released his leg had been dragged into the machinery and pinioned there while a revolving shaft bore through into his shin bone. 'Send down some stuff,' was all he wanted. He refused to be 'mollycoddled', as he called it, slapped a piece of lint on his leg and went on working. From his ankle to just below his knee the skin had been burnt through and fifteen centimetres of the skin had been cut into and the bone exposed. But he sat down in the water with his leg raised on a box and went on reassembling the bilge pump.

The frightened boy came into the galley after his turn on the deck pump to report that twenty centimetres of water was rolling over the deck now. 'I wish they wouldn't shine their torches on it,' he said.

I crept up to see if we were near the place where we were to be beached, then turned on the radio. A ship up the track ahead of us was 'having it on' also. But she was 2000 tonnes and had radar and gyro compass and echo sounder; we were 306 tonnes and had no aids. Still the sea lusted on. The noise was tremendous and the shouts of the men in the darkness lent fear.

'We're holding our own,' the Skipper said when next I took cocoa to him. And then the crew began to make headway with the deck pump.

We came east-about to the islands, up the outside and through between Vansittart and Rabbit Island rather than risk our waterlogged ship in the strait. 'Ha,' said the fishermen, 'been having it on, eh?' Mac came to take our lines, his own ship already tied up at the jetty. He looked at our hull. 'There's more water in you than under you.' And all our island friends came down to wonder at us, the biggest ship that visited this port and now through such a storm! In Hobart we might be a stock joke, here we were in our element.

We all had friends here and, as each trip we were forced to stay for at least two days unloading and loading, there was time for a little social life. We often had a party on board, captain, crew, fishermen, the local policemen and wives, and anyone else who cared to come. Mick brought out his bagpipes and after tea he walked up and down the wharf and skirled till the little fishing port of Lady Barron reeled to his music. We opened all our portholes to let in the music, and men from the fishing boats tied up along the wharf came up on their decks to listen and then trooped up to join us. All made some little concession to the trappings of civilised living we represented to them. Many wore ties; those who had no tie buttoned their shirts to the neck. All wore socks. A fisherman from the Scottish Isles sang 'Westering Home', Mick came down to the saloon and the bulkheads bulged with the melancholy call of the islands. We all joined in:

And it's westering home with a song in the air,
Light in the eye and it's goodbye to care
Laughter and love and a welcome is there
Isle of my heart, my Islay –

'Westering Home.' Our theme song . . . Laughter and love and a welcome is there, Isle of my heart, my Islay.

This spring we sang: 'There will I bide me and there will I rest, back home with my ain folk in Islay', and next day we sailed out into the strait, Bass Strait, where the seas towered above our bow and rolled over our fo'c'sle and across our great deck load and then into Banks Strait, where the confusion of tides threw us around until we feared we would lose control of the ship. But the wind was with us and we went through.

'Just as well too,' Mick complained. 'I didn't want any more of that. I had no wind left after last night's effort.' He had played the bagpipes for six hours.

Down the cost we went, the ordinarily rough sea a balm to our sore bodies after the thrashing we'd had coming up. I carried my two Maria Island cockerels out to enjoy the air; they picked at the scraps I gave them and one lifted his head and crowed as a breeze rippled through the crate. 'Shut up! you Jonah!' said the old mate. 'You're lucky we don't put you over the side,' said Alec. I thought they were joking.

We took on a full load of timber at Swansea – 'Let's have yer!' called the mate – filled both holds, put on the hatch covers and loaded the deck till the stacks reached our wheel-house windows. We climbed over it to come aboard when we cast off. We were going straight home, calling at no other port, because a ship was waiting impatiently at the wharf in Hobart for the timber to take to Melbourne. 'We'll sleep all the way,' the weary crew said as they climbed over the packs to their quarters. 'She'll be having it on by the time we get to the Corner,' the mate said. He looked at the sky as he spoke. 'There's a wind up there would blow the horns off of a bull.'

By the time the storm hit us we had all had at least four hours' sleep and were ready for it. All except the new boy. 'What hit us?' he said, when he ran to the wheelhouse. We were all there before him. No one spoke. The night had fallen on us with the storm that thundered down the wind. 'Will it be like before?' We sailed in a black bag struggling for vision, for air in a torrent of air. Surely nowhere can the sea 'make' as quickly as it does here. 'Where are we going?' asked the new boy. The spume sprayed back green and pink from where the port and starboard lights were forced in upon us by the encircling quilt of blackness. 'We're heading for hell,' the Skipper said and the new boy laughed, but we didn't. We call it heading for hell when we can't get 'round the corner', when the sea is such that to turn a ship our size would be to capsize it. There is nothing for it then but to keep charging southwards. 'Is there anything between us and the Antarctic?' the boy asked.

The storm bore us along, the noise of our going adding to the sense of increased speed; there was a sense of being in league with the wind, as though some secret of the sea would be unlocked by our fusing together in this way.

We saw out to starboard the light on top of Tasman Island, winking like a dim star, the squalls blotting it out and exposing it, at times making it appear to waver about. And then we were past it and there was nothing. We drove on for an hour. The wind invaded every corner of the ship searching for loot. We rolled and rolled and rolled and rolled. 'It's not going to break,' the Skipper spoke.

'Eight, nine hours I give it,' the old mate said. 'Daylight maybe.'

'We'll have a go,' the Big Fellow replied.

I went to the telegraph. 'Stand By.' The engine room telegraph rang. 'You there, Mick?' He blew down the engine room voice tube. When Mick replied from his tomb beneath the water he was told, 'I'd like to give it a go. Everything okay?'

'Yep.' Mick's motors were beautifully kept. 'She's sweet.'

Alec went to one side of the wheel, Pete to the other. The Big Fellow had the ship. I stood to the telegraph, the old mate was ready to go out on deck if need be.

For a while we stood thus, none moving except the Skipper as he lay on the wheel weighting it with his strength this way, paying off that, his eyes peering out through the blackness, conning the ship, awaiting his chance, his lips silently counting the great rolling seas as they came. Twice he started again, one, two, three, then, 'Okay, ready.' We were ready. Alec and Pete put their hands to the wheel to get the feel of her but they wouldn't take the weight until ordered by the Skipper, who was silently counting and peering and feeling the sea through the soles of his boots.

Then, 'Give it to her!' I chopped the telegraph lever once, Full Ahead, and snap! down again, the unmarked command, 'All she's got!' The bells shrilled through the wind. 'Now!' Alec dragged the spokes up from the floor, the Big Fellow forced them over the top, and Pete dragged them down to the deck on the other side. Again, up, over, down, a spoke at a time. Again. The ship didn't answer. 'You clapped out old bitch.' There is less than one and one-half minutes to get her round or she will broach on the next big sea. 'Ring for more.' Again the shrill clang once, twice, answered from the bell buried below. Mick opened her to the end. She could last a hundred seconds on this and then her motors would be finished. Again up from the deck, over and down. We worked in silence while we waited and then we felt her start to spin, pitting her wooden stem against the ocean. Silence. Then, 'Come on, you bitch. Faster.' He wanted her round. 'The daddy of them all's coming. Keep her open!' he shouted down the voice pipe.

'Yep.' Mick knew it wouldn't be asked for if it wasn't needed but the fumes and the heat and the thud in the cylinder heads must have been telling him what it was doing to his motor. We were almost round when it hit us. It picked up with all unspeakable power our 306 tonnes, rolled us sideways, hit us amidships then bowled us down a valley. The jitter of our propeller sounded above the wind as it bit air, clean out of the water. We fell.

It seemed we would hit the floor of the ocean. All that sea was up above us. If someone threaded a line about the crest of the waves and pulled it tight they would have us in an air bag inside the sea. 'Single,' said the captain, and I swung the lever, the bells rang out and the engine was relieved. We were on course, due north into the wind and Hobart our home.

The wave followed us down into the trough, we rode to the top of it, it pushed us sideways out of its way and disappeared into the wasteland of heaving ocean. We recovered slowly, rolling sluggishly, groaning, creaking.

'I bet that shifted something,' Pete said.

We didn't have long to wait. Out on the deck the mate was shouting. 'The load's walking. Look out!' The derrick had left its cradle and swung free, swinging its tree-trunk length of heavy timber from side to side as the ship rolled. The chains securing the timber packs had been made fast to the derrick. Now, snapped like string, they had parted. Again the derrick swung and we in the shelter of the wheelhouse ducked with the old mate on deck as though this murderous swinging pole menaced us. Again it swung and this time it jerked as the ship rolled and once more. 'Get that light on!' The wind blew the mate's words around.

Again the ship jerked as the derrick swung.

The searchlight bored a tunnel in the black void and we crowded round the window to see the damage as the ship rolled. And we saw it. The timber now undisciplined by chains was moving its great packs and with every roll of the ship lurched further to starboard. Already we were listing. Pete said, 'We're going to turn turtle.'

'The stick'll be dragged out first,' the captain said as the stay whipped and snapped taut at the masthead each time the derrick lurched. In the light of the big lamp we peered up to the top of the mast where the stay was foul of the mainhead block. 'We'll have to clear that block.' The captain gave the wheel to Pete. 'Rather you than me,' Pete said. 'Jeez! You wouldn't catch me up there!'

The Big Fellow climbed out the window on to the drunken timber packs where Alec was helping the mate. 'I can't do it,' the old man said. 'I haven't got the strength.' He pushed the crowbar into the captain's hand. 'I'll go aloft,' and he climbed over the reeling packs and out on to the bulwarks and round to the rigging where the ratlines swayed and twitched away from his grasp and the sea rolled right over him before he got clear and began to climb. He knew every third or fourth rung on the ratlines was broken and had been tied by string to present a shipshape appearance, but there was no way of telling which rungs were damaged until he put his weight on them. Up he went, one foot firmly after the other, waiting between the dizzy swings of the ship when he clung with his legs around the stays. Twice he slipped. Then he started up again.

Down on deck Alec retrieved the chains and climbed on his hands and knees on top of the timber to bring them to the captain who with a crowbar was trying to lever the unwieldy packs back into place. As the sea in a sullen slick rolled over them in the darkness they couldn't find a second crowbar. Alec grabbed the broken deck pump handle and took it as a bar. He climbed up beside the captain and thrust with him. 'Heave . . . ' they levered a pack across a few centimetres, twenty centimetres. 'Again, ugh, ugh, ugh,' they heaved together. At times they used one another's bodies for leverage. 'Heave, ugh, ugh, ugh.'

From up at the masthead came the voice of the mate. For

a time we couldn't pluck his words from the music that came down from the shrilling of the stays and the contrapuntal thrumming of the sea on her timbers. Then, 'he wants a marlinspike'. The captain couldn't leave the timber now; crowbarred high in the stack but still unbound, the danger on deck was worse.

'I'll take it,' Pete called. 'The boy can have the wheel.' The new boy. 'Keep her head up into it,' Pete said and climbed out on to the timber. 'Watch it!' the captain shouted. 'You'll be jake.' Pete was so frightened he climbed stiffly, hardly able to bend his knees to rise to the next rung. He went up to the old man who was waiting for the spike and then he began to come down.

He felt with his foot the missing bar but misjudged the distance down to the next and slipped a little, holding on by his arms and legs which were tightly knotted round the rigging in fear. It was this that saved him when up in the wheelhouse the new boy let go of the wheel and walked across to shut the window. In the same moment as the ship reeled to the sea and broached and the timber screeched as it began to roll against the two men and their bars and the captain screamed like a horse as he slipped and his arm fell between two packs, the sea silenced for a moment and in that silence a clear hard voice carried out over the storm, a woman spoke to the new boy in a way and with such words that caused him to spring back to the wheel and wrench it round until the ship answered.

The timber lurched again as the ship was brought back on course and the captain, off balance with his arm pinned, fell between the packs as they opened. Quick as a flash Alec leapt down in the gap with him and straining back with his buttocks and forwards with his knees he held the vice apart while the man climbed out and the vice began to close on the seaman. The Big Fellow leant down and thrust the short handle of the deck pump between the packs and hauled him out. Then they stood up and together began to lever back the timber. 'Heave, heave, heave. Ugh, ugh, ugh.' And we were on our way home.

'I suppose I'll get the bullet when they come up,' the young boy said. Instead they laughed. 'I thought you wouldn't say damn for sixpence,' Pete shouted at me. 'What a recitation,' the Big Fellow said as I bandaged his injured hand.

In a few hours we were in the river, the lovely Derwent. The rain had gone, the sky was clear and the sea no longer had the menace of the night. The yachts were out for the Saturday events and their pretty white and yellow and red sails speckled the water. A big yacht with a striped spinnaker bellying out crossed our course and we had to change to avoid her (the rule of the road dictates that steam gives way to sail). The men in their white suits and yachting caps waved a thank you to us and we waved back, scruffy, unwashed, our men unshaven. And then a tiny boat with a sail and another, and a third crossed our path, all eager to try the rule of the road. We zigzagged and avoided them, so weary that anger could not get a toehold in us. 'Green to green or red to red, Perfect Safety, go ahead,' we told the new boy of Thomas Grey's rhymes to aid the mariner.

Both in safety and in doubt
I always keep a good lookout.
In danger with no room to turn
I ease her! – Stop her! – Go astern!

But our training was wasted on the boy. This one trip was enough and he never came again.

The bad weather was widespread and many small ships in southern Australian waters had been caught in it out at sea. The crew of a yacht that was in the centre of the disturbance in Bass Strait arrived in Hobart with the amazing story that the yacht had completely capsized. Its mast had gone down beneath the waves and its hull had looked up at the sky. Then it righted itself. So the crew said. Some of the waterfront believed the story, others didn't. We didn't say anything. We unloaded our timber and crawled into our bunks and slept the clock around.

23

Death of a Small Ship

The following dawn the big seas and the gale that had nearly driven us ashore were still lashing the straits. We thought no one would be out in it, but when I switched on the radio to warm it up I head a voice we all knew. The *Willwatch* was battling across that part of Bass Strait between Tasmania and King Island, her old ninety-three tonnes taking the full brunt of the wind as it swept through the gap between the islands. And Mac, George McCarthy, Master Mariner, was calling for help.

It was 7.10 a.m. and I took notes of his call. 'Fo'c'sle full of water,' he called. 'Deck cargo has to be shifted. Am down by the head. Collision bulkhead holed; plugging holes with blankets. Forward bilge pump blocked, aft bilge can't pick up because of angle of ship. Don't worry too much. I think I'll be able to save her.'

It wasn't the first time the sixty-four-year-old ship had been involved in a similar situation. Several times in the past the King Island Marine Board had lent their pumps to pump *Willwatch*'s fo'c'sle free of water when she had reached Currie after a battle with wind and sea.

Once, Mac had dragged the water-heavy ship home to Tasmania across the strait with the fo'c'sle completely flooded, held only by the collision bulkhead. (This bulkhead separates the fo'c'sle or the forepeak from the rest of the ship.) That time, several of the planks had sprung in *Willwatch*.

Now he thought he could save her again. In any case, he probably decided there would be plenty of time for explanations of causes and effects when he got *Willwatch* safely home.

When the official short-wave shore radio stations, VIM (Melbourne) and VIH (Hobart), operated by Overseas Telecommunications, first heard from *Willwatch* it was 8.15 a.m. As on the *Naracoopa*, the radio on *Willwatch* could be worked on several frequencies and in sending the earlier messages to Currie Mac's radio had been on four megacycles.

At 8.15 a.m. he switched to six megacycles and that is when *Willwatch*'s plight became known to the listeners, official and otherwise, who tune in on that wave-length at that time. In these set-time calls precedence is given to any ship calling for help.

On the morning of 17 December, when *Willwatch* called up, Bill Watson at VIH Hobart heard him and so did Don Clayton at Melbourne's VIM Clayton's voice came on: 'Stand by please, all small ships. Stand by.' We stood by our radios. 'Go ahead *Willwatch*.'

'I'm shipping water,' Mac told him. 'Cannot control the vessel. Request a ship to stand by.'

Immediately, Clayton called all ships in the vicinity to report their position, course and speed. Only the captain of a distressed vessel can requisition a ship to come to his aid.

McCarthy's call provided the authority for that, but he gave neither of the two distress signals laid down by international code: 'Mayday', the spoken word for SOS, or 'Pan Pan Pan', the lesser distress signal.

At 8.25 a.m. his call was 'Ship lower in water.'

Next, all ships were asked to report their positions. Few replies came in. Most ships were sheltering. Usually a dozen or more small ships can be contacted around these waters. I had alerted our captain and he and the crew crowded into my little radio shack.

The only ships who reported being anywhere near the spot were *Rhonda H*, from Table Cape; *Pandora* and *Tuna* at Port Davey, about 300 kilometres away but hearing *Willwatch* perfectly; *Peter H*; and *Olympic* at Three Hummock Island; *VSP* was also at Three Hummock Island, but didn't have her radio switched on at that time as the crew were too busy battling the heavy seas to reach the shelter of the island. Though *Peter H* was closest to *Willwatch*, various factors made it more practical for the much larger, sea-going *Olympic* to go, as it could cover the distance in less time and more surely.

Owner-skipper 'Dugger' Warren was ready immediately, but estimated it would take him at least three hours to reach *Willwatch*. As he sailed from the shelter of Three Hummock Warren reported gale-force winds, huge seas, and poor visibility. Neither he nor *Willwatch* had radar; none of us did in those days.

At 8.45 a.m. McCarthy reported that though she was hard to control, *Willwatch* was under way again, heading NNE at three knots. To laymen this may seem strange, as that meant he was heading out to open sea, away from land; but to us seamen grouped around short-wave radios it was clear.

The rough weather was coming from SSW, and if McCarthy had turned about and headed back to Tasmania (presuming it would have been possible for him to turn a hard-to-control ship in such a big sea without rolling it over) the little vessel would have been taking the heavy seas on her bow, the place where she was already damaged.

The same would have applied had an attempt been made to run to King Island. Mac's only hope was to run before the wind and sea. He did not say at this stage what had happened (and even at the end he didn't), but we who listened and who had worked on small wooden ships thought *Willwatch* had either sprung a plank – old ships sometimes become 'nail-sick' and the *Willwatch* was built in 1895 – or 'spewed her caulking', the inelegant but accurate phrase used to describe the ejection of caulking from between the planks when a vessel is 'working' in a heavy sea.

At 8.50 a.m. Mac called again. 'Conditions not improving. Seas worsening, wind freshening. May use distress call.' By 9 o'clock *Olympic* was well under way with a twenty-five to thirty knot wind howling over her stern. *Willwatch* contacted her on the four megacycle band. 'Position has deteriorated. Men standing by in life jackets. She is well down by the head.' Mac's hopes fluctuated as the weather worsened and then abated briefly when at 9.30 he told VIM: 'Position not desperate. Might be able to make port.'

A little later rising seas and stronger winds caused him to say, 'I don't think we will be able to make it now.' He said the deck cargo was being shifted aft in the hope it would bring *Willwatch*'s head out of the water. Hanson, his old engineer, was below, battling to keep the motor going, and this left one man and three boys to move fifty big petrol drums and three horse boxes on the rolling, plunging deck.

At 10 o'clock Vic Hardy on *VSP* switched on his radio to send a message home reporting that he was sheltering at Rape Bay on Three Hummock Island, but when he heard that *Willwatch* was in trouble and *Olympic* was going to her aid he called up the distressed ship.

'Can I do anything, Mac?' Hardy asked.

'I won't say no at a time like this,' McCarthy replied. 'I've got my crew to think of.'

Hardy pulled up his anchor and in his own words 'gave her all she had' as he, too, headed north in the strait.

But it was too late. The end came shortly after. At 10.09 McCarthy said to *Olympic* and *VSP*: 'Position very bad. I'm going to fire a red rocket. It may guide you to me.' Soon after he called again. '*Willwatch* to *Olympic*. First rocket gone. Did you see anything of it?' But the ships coming to his rescue were still too far away to sight it.

Then came another call from *Willwatch*: 'Bulwarks awash. Won't last long.' *Olympic* asked if it was possible to launch the lifeboat in that sea, with the ship down by the head as she was. McCarthy replied: 'We can't free the dinghy.' A little later he said, 'We've freed the dinghy, but can't launch it'. *Olympic* suggested it might float off and McCarthy answered that he and the crew were depending on that.

The next call came at 10.19: 'Decks awash. Don't know how long we will last.' A minute later: 'Position deteriorated even more. Fifty drums have washed over the side.'

Hardy in *VSP* said 'We're coming fast, Mac'. McCarthy told them he was sending up another rocket. Warren in *Olympic* and Hardy strained their eyes ahead, trying to pierce the spray for the rocket's glow, but they saw nothing.

At 10.30 McCarthy said, 'I've ordered the crew over the side in their life jackets.'

At many points along Tasmania's northern coast and on the mainland word had been passed around, and in dozens of private homes dual-wave radios were switched to short wave and tuned to the wave-lengths on which the fight for the life of a little ship and its crew was going on.

And we in little ships . . . we could hear the noise of that other little ship dying around that lonely figure, the horses screaming as their boxes rolled across the deck, the lashings snapping like bootlaces as the crippled *Willwatch* leapt and plunged at the mercy of the deep sea waiting to engulf her. Each of us had our own memories of Mac.

It is said that a wooden ship should be able to 'work' like a breadbasket, but the creakings and groanings of *Willwatch*, strained beyond all bearing, were like screams in the ears of us listening, though no sound of it came from our radios. As the minutes ticked by the boys shouted at our radio. 'Oh God! Where are the boats . . . the planes? Where are the planes?' The RAAF had been asked for a plane.

We knew they were all going full speed, but we knew, and they knew, that they wouldn't be in time.

At 10.35 Mac's voice came through. 'I'm still here, but I can't hold her now. The sea has her.' He had kept a rocket for the very end. 'I'm going to let it go now,' he said.

Hardy said later: 'When ''Dugger'' and I told him we hadn't seen his last rocket, he remained as he had been all the time, perfectly calm.'

Finally, at 10.37 there was a lot of static and noise, then Mac spoke through it: 'It looks as if this is it . . . see you later . . . cheerio.' There was nothing more.

Then, again and again, Melbourne called. 'VIM to *Willwatch*. VIM to *Willwatch*. Come in *Willwatch*. Come in *Willwatch*.' But I never heard his voice again.

24

The Writ on our Masthead

As have seamen from time immemorial, small ships' men hold in contempt the pronouncements given out by courts of inquiry. We faced two courts of marine inquiry and the results, we thought, were what could be expected. What man who knew and had worked ships was competent, articulate, and had such training as to fit him to sit as an assessor in such a court?

We had a writ nailed to our masthead – at least they could *nail* it to our wooden mast, they didn't have to use Scotch tape as they did on steel-masted ships – which said we were under arrest, that our ship did not satisfy the requirements of the Marine Board as to seaworthiness. It was charged that strain on the hull had caused structural damage to the vessel.

We certainly had a great crack in a deck stanchion. A relieving captain who had run up on a sand-bar in the canal gave evidence that he had heard it snap when the soundings gave but a metre of water. The Big Fellow believed *he* had caused the fracture by loading gross weights of timber on the deck and called as witness a professor of mathematics to give evidence of the effect the stress and strain of timber stacked in such a way would have. We were tied up for two weeks while the case dragged on. Then we were released, freed. We were scarcely over that excitement when we brought upon ourselves a terrible trial. On a night of bitter sleet and driving rain we ran aground on the spit of Low Island, a few hundred metres from the canal. Because of this we were subjected to an inquiry that wasted our time, tried our patience, and brought out much of the hatred to which small ships' crews are prone.

We had come in through the Narrows in rain, and followed the beacons up in rain; it was cold and wet but still clear. The tide was right but the wind was shrieking through our rigging, blowing the orders back from the flying bridge. The windows had to be left open to enable me to hear the orders clearly. I was nearly as wet as the boys and just as numb. It was raining so hard the mate and the men up forward were soaked, the water running from the bottom of their trouser legs. Up on the flying bridge the Skipper and the two boys with him were stripped to shirt and trousers because of the exertion of manning the wheel.

We went through the bridge and out the Hobart side of the canal and within a few seconds the sky blacked out in a rain squall. We could not see the bow, and suddenly the noise beneath us was like a million marbles rolling as we rode on to the spit of the island.

As quickly as the blackness had come the moon now sprang out, and the rest of the night continued so clear we could see the lights in the windows of the cottages of the little canal-side town. The Big Fellow and Mick worked non-stop on her but we were stuck fast. At 2 a.m. they told me I could leave the telegraph and turn in, but at six I was called and we went at it again. Full Ahead, Full Astern, Half Ahead, Half Astern, Slow Ahead, Slow Astern.

It was no use. We waited for the tide; it didn't come. Tides are nowhere near as regularly high and low as they taught us at school. We waited for the next one that night but still it didn't come. We were riding on a shoal amidships. There was deep water all round us.

We shifted the cargo of 500 bags of ground bark further forward in the hope that it would make her slide off that way, but it didn't. So we lifted the 500 bags out of the forward hold, and put them down the after hold to try to topple her off that way. The boys lifted the heavy bags out of the forward hold on to the forward deck, and the Big Fellow lifted them on to the poop deck. Mick was down in the after hold ready to stow them alone, so I had to trundle the 500 bags, all morning and part of the afternoon. They weighed ten bags to the tonne and didn't get any lighter as the day wore on. The almost healed scars of some salt-water boils on the back of my neck opened up, and the sweat was stinging them unbelievably. We had radioed for a tug and it arrived while we were still moving the cargo. We knew the tugmen. 'We'll give you a job any day,' they called to me.

Still the ship didn't come free. We radioed for a second tug. Next day, just as it arrived, a high tide lifted us up and over and we nearly ran down a tug as we sailed off. If we had thought the publicity before was bad, now it was terrible. My mother wired, 'All at home praying for your safety.' She and the rest of the family had been listening to the radio accounts of our 'danger' for two days.

All this hullabaloo caused such a sensation that a Court of Marine Inquiry was set up with three men to sit on the bench. It was Gilbert and Sullivan at their best and lasted for two weeks. As it didn't sit until a year after the incident no one could remember anything much but that didn't worry anyone. The court president remarked that the captain had not had the assistance of a trained crew; apart from Mick and me he said the rest of the crew were not co-operative. As none of the former crew now worked for us their assistance to the court was negligible and their antipathy of the ship great. The Skipper was fined £50 for 'going to the north of the channel instead of to the south' (seeing he didn't know just where he was going at the time we thought that was neatly put). He said he wouldn't pay the fine and he didn't, so that was that. Chum resigned, and our passenger trade ended, because now the owners decided we should not use the canal because of adverse publicity. It took only a couple of rough trips 'round the Raoul' to finish our passenger trade off for good, and none of us were sorry about that.

25

Finished with Engines

He who hath known the bitterness of the ocean
shall have its taste for ever in his mouth.

—CONRAD

There had been so many changes of crew since the Big Fellow came aboard that often I hadn't learnt a boy's name before he had left the ship. I was never sure if a face appearing on deck was a crew member or a visitor. For the first six months of his reign the Big Fellow had had seventy crew changes. Some of these he signed off, 'Pick up your time' being a common remark to be heard on the ship in those days. Sometimes men would bluster and say, 'See how you'll go without me!' but, as Mick said, 'The graveyard is full of men who couldn't be done without.'

Apart from those men who were told to 'pick up their time' there were the others who didn't turn up when we were due to leave port. 'Snatching their time.' Very few gave notice or said they wouldn't be back.

Leery Bill and Bright Boy left in this manner. Alec and Pete did too. Alec had found it harder and harder to part from his wife after each brief stay in port, now he had a baby named Maria after the island and the wistfulness in his wet-nosed, dog-eyed face was eloquent each trip as we set off. Then one day he just snatched his time and we never heard of him again. I hoped he would be happy. We had been friends for a long time.

In Alec's place came Paul Cook, an English boy working his way round the world. Paul was small and skinny, blue-eyed, fair-haired; his accent was Oxford-side according to the boys. He was so puny and unimpressive and colourless looking that he was immediately dubbed 'another Pommy bastard'. But Paul Cook was a lot more than that. He was such a big man inside his frail-looking body and such a tough worker in the sweat of the hold that within a week he was so well thought of by the crew that they could call him a 'Pommy bastard' to his face.

Down in the hold the men usually paired off for loading, each pair taking it in turns to unload the pallets as they came below. There was always great competition between them, even when they were tired, to see who unloaded the best and most quickly. 'Beat that, you Pommy bastard,' they'd yell to Paul. He'd set to work and beat them. 'That Pommy bastard's always there when the whips are cracking,' Mick said admiringly. I later had reason to thank my lucky stars for the day that brought that same little Pommy bastard to our ship.

When Pete left I was surprised at the detachment with which I viewed his going. He had been on board the *Sheerwater* when I made my first sea trip and had gambled ten shillings with the captain that I would be seasick. I'd knitted him a cap for his seventeenth birthday and now he was twenty-one. But when he had gone it was hard to believe we'd lived almost as a family for so long. Now, as always, when a man left the ship his going was not noticed. Another took his place completely. The trip after Pete had 'snatched his time' I mentioned his name to Mick. 'Pete?' he said, 'Pete who?'

The ship and its never-ending labour possessed all of the mind of each of us.

Of the few of us who stuck it for any length of time each of us had different reasons for staying. Mick stayed because of a loyalty to the ship, a loyalty I thought had died with old shellbacks. Old Chum had stayed until the grounding on Low Island because it was a good berth for him even though the killing hours and unending labour must have been torture to such an old man. I stayed because the money was good, or so I told myself, £40 a week sometimes for weeks at a stretch. In time I knew I stayed for a different reason. As the months went by, and I saw men who had been used to manual labour giving in because they said, 'the work isn't fit for a nigger', I developed a sort of stubborn pride that I was still hanging on. I knew Mick had this feeling too. Often we'd grin at each other when we saw a seaman climbing over the side with his bag and say, loud enough for him to hear, 'Couldn't take it, eh?'

But there came the time when I must ring Finished with Engines to my own motors, cry all fast forward, all fast aft, step over the side for the last time, and swallow the anchor. I debated long and alone.

O! leave'r Johnny, leave'r like a man,
(Leav'r John-ny, leave'r!)
Oh! leave'r, John-ny, leav'r when ye can,
(An' its time for us t'leave'r!)

I had saved the money to make a home ashore for my small family. For myself, I knew I was not heading towards any goal. I must make a break now before I got to the point of no return, no ambition, no future. I knew there would be times when I would long more than a landsman could imagine, or more than any of the poets who haven't been to sea have described, to feel the deck rolling beneath my feet and to hear the creak and groan of the ship's timbers as she was 'having it on', but leave I must. My last trip would be to the islands, to the Furneaux, and out to Babel Island to load the season's mutton birds in their casks and take the birders off the islands and return them to Lady Barron. It was school holidays, so my children would be with me; when I left the ship this life that would then end would be a bond between us, not a barrier.

It was the first and the last time a ship as big as the *Naracoopa* had worked Babel Island, and because the Big Fellow had not worked this island he wrote to Les Jackson who had captained the *Sheerwater* and asked him to sign on as mate and pilot us out over the Pot Boil and through the Vansittart Shoals to Babel.

As the clock on the GPO began to toll the twelve strokes of midnight and the city of Hobart slept, we silently slipped our lines and drifted down the stream with the motors ticking over quietly.

And where do you go? the ladies ask when you say you sail in a ship on the sea. To San Francisco or Kamchatka or round the Horn or across the ocean? Oh, they pout when they learn that we're off to the islands, hugging the coast, heading for Babel, for though they've never been there Babel can't be far away because it's only up in Bass Strait, and it can't be very exciting because it isn't marked on the atlas that you get by saving the coupons from the breakfast cereal. And while they're sitting there wondering how any woman could bear this life I'm standing with the bitter salt of the sea on my lips wondering how I can live without it. Babel. Twice I've been rescued from drowning off beautiful, beautiful Babel. She'll come again, the islanders say. Watch Babel, Pat. If she misses twice she'll try again, always the third time. But would I miss it?

It is my last trip. The sky is dark and there are no stars but the lights of the pretty little city fuzzy with sleep stretched around the sides of the river divide the sea from the shore and the shore from the sky. In the darkness the loom of our navigation lights throws green mist to starboard and ruby to port as spray spumes over the bow. It is darkly beautiful standing here in the wheelhouse with the windows open, the Big Fellow and the captain from the islands talking quietly in a corner, the man on the wheel silently winding, steadying, then winding again. When he gives the wheel a spoke the chain rattles in the gypsy on its way aft with the message to the rudder.

Am I really going to leave all this? The ship and the men who sail her, the good and the bad?

'Okay if Mrs Pat takes her while I go below for a cuppa?' the helmsman asks the Skipper. Take her? I wish I could take her for ever. I cut inside John Garrow Light. 'You'll frighten the pants off the bathers!' 'This hour of night they wouldn't have pants on.' No, the humour isn't subtle but the laughter is spontaneous. The two captains follow the helmsman down to the galley and I am alone. You feel a ship right through the soles of your feet when you stand at the big wheel like this. She is steering so easily she needs no more than a spoke either way.

By daylight we were 'round the Raoul' and through 'the hole in the wall' between Tasman Island and Cape Pillar and turning and heading north-east past the Hippos, the Hippolyte Rocks, and the Narrows where we'd held our breath so often.

We were at Maria Island by midday and I stood on deck waiting to exchange the last regular tea towel wave with Ruby at her cottage. I'd sent word the week before that it would be my last trip, so she walked outside to enable me to see her clearly and waved something so big it could only be a sheet or a tablecloth. Looking at her through the glasses I could see her boots buttoned up to the knee, her big black straw hat, and her dogs and cats and roosters and hens clustered round her. She stood like that the first day I saw her but then small Harry was by her side to trundle the wheelbarrow down the hill to the beach with his hop and carry one. Harry was dead now and Ruby stayed on alone. The remaining few islanders fetched and carried for her. On the wharf was a crate she had sent down with a hen and eight chickens to start a poultry run 'in your retirement' as the note said. The crew roared when they saw them. 'Batten down the hatches, secure the lifelines. Mrs Pat's got poultry again!'

We had three Greeks aboard who had been sponge divers on the island of Leros. They had recently migrated to Australia and joined the crew of the *Naracoopa*. None of the three had more than a smattering of English and it took Paul quite a time in his polyglot mixture of half a dozen languages to explain. Finally they caught on. 'Omen,' they said. 'It was an omen.' They hurriedly blessed themselves and stared balefully at my poor old hen and chicks.

At Lady Barron we took Honest Tom aboard and two island men to add to our already augmented crew. Altogether we had nine seamen on board, three deck officers, two engineers, Bert the cook and me. It was the biggest crew we had ever carried and we would need it: this was the toughest job we had attempted.

At that time four islands were made available by the Fauna Board for commercial birding; three of these were in sheltered Franklin Sound close to Lady Barron port. The great casks containing up to 550 salted birds could be brought in regularly from these islands. Babel, out to the east of Flinders Island, surrounded by shoal waters and reefs, was so difficult to access that the whole six weeks' catch was taken off in one ship at the close of the season.

To aid us we had hired a big, flat-bottomed barge. We could tow this close inshore, load up to forty barrels on it, and then tow it back out to the ship with the motorised dinghy lashed to the side. We tried this out in the Sound and it worked well. In addition to the barge we hired a fibre-glass dinghy, and Honest Tom lent us his *Mutton-Duck*, a six-metre, double-ended, flat-bottomed punt that had a decided tendency to drive her bow under in a calm sea. I had once had a hair-raising trip from Big Dog Island to Lady Barron on her and the whole way the boy in charge of her bailed water and moved cargo trying to keep her afloat. Now, years later, when they hoisted her on board *Naracoopa* I remembered his words, 'She's a floating coffin,' he had said. At Babel we were to rendezvous with a fishing boat owned by Les Jackson. Manned by a skilled crew, this boat and men would work with us. We were well organised.

Out on the oily Pot Boil we sailed and into the Vansittart Shoals where the *Pilot* warned: 'Local Knowledge needed here', and up to the twin-peaked island, Babel, shrouded in sleet and rain and squalls. A sixty-five kilometre an hour wind whistled down on us, the sea whipped up in an instant, and we rocked as though we would capsize.

'So this is the beautiful Babel!' Four of us had been here before – Les Jackson, the two islanders, and I. The others were dismayed as we pointed out the gulches and rocky shores from which we would load our cargo. There are few beaches on Babel. The birders when the time comes to ship their casks tap the hoops on firmly, secure the bung, and roll them down the rocks over a carpet of tussock grass cut and spread for the purpose. Once the casks hit the water the birders' responsibility ends. It is for the seamen to get them loaded.

Standing in the wild water – and Babel is invariably wild – they must roll the barrels up a set of wooden skids and manhandle them into the boat, which is all the while bucking and pitching and stamping down on them as they wrestle, shoulder deep in the sea, with the casks that weighed up to five hundred weight in imperial measure. This I had seen done many times but never under the ferocious conditions of that year. Gales raged the whole time, the end of April gales that blew the birds away on their migration to the north

Pacific. The winds roared from one direction then another. If the men could work one of the sheds on the southern side of the island before midday they could not work it after. We were constantly having to move the ship, round up our various barges and boats, get them on board, and steam off somewhere else leaving a job unfinished, and all this with a notch in our belts.

Old Bert was in love again, worse then ever before; it was so bad that he forgot to get supplies in. Some of the crew swore he did it on purpose in the hope that he could get back more quickly to his new love. But he reckoned without the tenacity of the crew of the *Naracoopa*. He broke the news to us one day after we'd got to Babel.

'No bread, sugar, flour, butter, tea, coffee, cocoa, biscuits, cheese, jam, potatoes, vegetables, milk, or meat.'

'Have you got any skewers?' Mick asked.

'What for?'

'To punch the extra holes we're going to need in our belts.' After he'd got over the shock Bert came to me. 'Strike me lucky,' he said. 'They're willing to starve to death.' I wouldn't have put it past the boys if that had been the only way to get the job done. Their hackles were up. The locals at Lady Barron had done it. They were taking odds against our getting the birds off. They thought the crew wouldn't stand up to the rough, tough, wet, hard work involved. Our boys had had more experience at rough and ready loading-off than any crews who ever worked these ports, but few knew of it because of the comparative isolation of the places to which we sailed. The crew were determined to lift the birds.

They would have stood all day in the water at Babel anyhow, but because of the baiting they stood there in conditions that have never been equalled for ferocity. By the fourth day they were doing it with the extra notch in their belts as predicted. Les Jackson broached a barrel of salted birds for us and he got us some crayfish, but without bread or potatoes this was poor nourishment for men who worked as these did.

I had left my hen and chickens at Lady Barron, afraid that their presence if we met with stormy weather might incite the crew to cause them some harm. Now I wished they were with us. That old hen would eat well.

There is always chicanery involving the ownership of barrels on the islands so I was sent down to the hold to tally the casks on board. Crouched under the deck in the rolling ship the smell of the oily birds leaking out and mixing with diesel fumes had a nauseating effect on my empty stomach. My head swam and I had constantly to climb out on deck to save myself from seasickness.

The fishing boat was now with us and the two crew – Eric Maynard, a Cape Barren Islander and Jimmy Sholto Douglas, a fisherman, two old island friends of ours – ate with us adding to our numbers.

The sea was angry, treacherous. A mighty crest picked up the fibre-glass dinghy on its way to shore and flung it clean off the top of the water and dropped it on to the bow of our ship's boat that had been towing it with such force that a hole as big as a fist was punched through the fibre-glass. Another sea looted us of another vessel. Running for shelter around the island we were towing the big barge from our stern and the tow line parted and the barge came adrift. The Greeks had secured it carelessly.

We chased it for two hours. Les Jackson, who was brought up on these islands, took the ship's wheel and skirted reefs and rocks by a knowledgeable whisker. Several times the barge was right beside us but the sea was so capricious that there was always the danger of it ramming us. For a while it stayed afloat, then a wave rolled it, the hatch swung open and it filled and quickly sank.

The Greeks were embarrassed because one of their number had been blamed for this. That night after tea (one mutton bird per man, woman, and child) they came to where the Big Fellow, Mick and Les were having a round table conference and put forward a plan they had developed. It would be dangerous and hard, but, said Angelo the leader, 'We lose the barge we must get the birds.' Their plan was this. The *Mutton-Duck* was to be towed into shallow water by the fishing boat. The three Greeks would be in her, and when in shallow water they would pick up a line attached to a sea anchor and haul her ashore. As each barrel was loaded she was to be hauled out a little to keep her afloat until she had ten barrels aboard. They would then haul her out to the big anchor and pick up the tow line again from the powerful fishing boat and so be towed out to the ship. This manoeuvre repeated many times would eventually lift all the birds.

After this was agreed, we had a party. 'Tomorrow will be danger,' said Angelo the Greek. 'This may be the last night for some among us. Let us laugh then and sing, and let us dance.'

So the Greeks laced their arms round one another's shoulders and danced their traditional folk-dances up and down the saloon. Mick played the bagpipes, Honest Tom hopped up on a chair and sang his evergreen, 'Now all you men have been to sea, I know of course you have.'

'Come on, Mrs Pat,' Angelo called. 'Dance modern with my brother Sid.'

Angelo's brother Sid took my arm . . .

Angelo's brother Sid had hold of my arm. 'Hold on, Mrs Pat,' he said. 'Hold on, Mrs Pat.'

There was a woman screaming near me, 'The children, the children, the children.'

The voice screamed on and on, 'The children, the children.'

Sid said, 'Don't worry Mrs Pat. Sid holds you.'

Again the woman screamed, 'The children,' and suddenly I knew it was me screaming. I was in the water and Sid was holding me up and somehere in the blackness beyond were the children. 'Oh God, Siddy,' I cried. 'Where are my children?' He said nothing.

I had been put on shore by the fishing boat earlier in the day to take lunch to the men working in the water at the beach loading the *Mutton-Duck* each time it came in. Eric Maynard, who was in charge of the fishing boat, suggested my taking the kids with me so they could have an hour or two playing on the lovely beach further round. He lifted us all ashore, dry as a bone on rocks jutting out into the deep water. 'I'll pick you up there later,' he said.

I delivered the lunches of mutton bird and crayfish and for the rest of the afternoon sat on the beach where the kids made sand castles and carried water up from the sea in tins to fill the moats they dug around them.

Boat load after boat load was taken back to the ship but still they didn't signal for us. They were keen to finish that day. Not till long after dark did they come, saying it was the last load. Two seamen carried the children shoulder high and put them on top of the load. The big searchlight from the ship was playing on to the boat. I ran down the sand after them. 'It's the coffin,' I said involuntarily. The crew had painted on one side of her the words 'NOT SAFE', on the other side they had painted, 'HALF SAFE'. The light was stabbing across the heaving water on to the ugly square thing, silhouetting the great load the boys had put on her to finish off. There were drums of beak oil, forty bags of feathers, islanders' cooking gear, a barrel, the long wooden loading skids, eight men, and on top of everything else the two children, and then me. I was standing on the bulwarks, there was nowhere else to stand, trying to get a grip of the cargo to hang on to. She was being hauled out to the sea anchor.

The fishing boat hadn't begun to tow us, yet the water was slopping over my feet that were higher than the six-metre boat itself. I tried to get off and grabbed at the children's feet to pull them off but they were sitting on top of the load in a hollow amid the bags of feathers, and I couldn't budge them so I had to climb back up on to the bulwarks again to be with them.

Now they took up the tow line, we were past the sea anchor. There was a splash and the *Mutton-Duck* rocked. Someone had decided to get off before it was too late. As the ship's searchlight picked us up outside the breakers it shone on the water running clear over the top of the boat beneath our feet. Nothing but the speed and strength of the motor on Eric's boat pulling us on a long line through the water was keeping us afloat but of course he knew nothing of this. When he let the line go as we came alongside the ship we would sink. I told the children to take their boots off and their overcoats. 'Don't be silly, Mrs Pat,' Paul the Pommy B. said. He was standing next to me. 'They'll get cold.' I hadn't realised till then that the others didn't yet know. I had come out warm and dry to the boat while they were cold, wet and weary. They had felt the cold wetness of the sea all day on their bodies and did not now notice it.

'Can you swim, Paul?' I asked.

'Sort of.'

'I can't swim at all. Neither can the children. When we go would you take Cate for me.'

The children were quiet and good when I told them the boat was going to sink. I told them to hang on to bags of feathers and someone would come and get us soon. I wanted to hold their hands but I couldn't reach. 'Mike, hold Cate's hand,' I said. 'Yes,' he said quietly. Then we went on top of another wave and the ship's light flooded us again and the crew who hadn't noticed till now saw the water washing over their feet as they stood on the bulwarks. Some thought it would be best to cut the tow line and yelled for a knife. Others screamed that it was the tow line that was holding us up. They began to call and shout and scream for help, hoping they could be heard on the ship. But from that distance all the

Big Fellow and Mick could hear was an odd shout. First they thought it was the Greeks celebrating the end of the season, then they thought the searchlight was annoying the men and they wanted it off. As the searchlight went off someone cut the tow line on the *Mutton-Duck*. In the last glow of light I looked up to speak to the children and instead of them I saw the wooden skid sticking upright, then beginning to fall.

In the water with Sid holding me up I could feel the place where it had hit on the very top of my head. Now I was thoroughly alert and wouldn't scream again. Instead, I called out loudly but as calmly as I could, 'Has anyone got the children?' There was no answer. Something warm with long hair brushed past my face and I grabbed at it and panic swamped me. But it was Smokey, the children's cocker spaniel. I held on to his collar for a while but then he tried to climb on to my face so I pushed him away and let go.

I called for the children again and this time Dave Rhodes answered me. 'They're all right, Pat.' I'd known Dave ever since I first went to the islands. He was Les Jackson's brother-in-law. He had called out just to comfort me. I knew. He was scarcely able to keep himself afloat and grabbed at the skids but as soon as he touched them they settled a foot or two beneath the water. When next I called we had all been swept so far apart neither he nor anyone else could hear.

Although I'd got my overcoat off before the boat sank I hadn't been able to get my fur-lined boots off and with their weight and that of a pair of old heavy velvet slacks and two pullovers I was getting too heavy for Sid so when a bag of feathers came sweeping by on the current he grabbed it and tried to get me to hold it. All I managed to do was somehow get underneath it with it resting on my chest and me with my arms coming up and around it. There on my chest it remained. Sid had hold of the back of my neck and my face was out of the water. I stared hard into the blackness. I could see nothing. There was no way of knowing where we were being swept.

When Eric picked us up we were scattered far and wide. 'A sea of feathers and cooees from a dozen directions,' he described it. He threw a line to us but I couldn't take it. 'For God's sake, Eric, get the kids,' I sobbed. He hadn't known they were on board. He'd thought we'd come back to the ship earlier in the afternoon when another seaman had had charge of the fishing boat.

When he came back he had Mike with him and four or five seamen including Dave Rhodes and Angelo the Greek. I couldn't climb up the side of the fishing boat and fell from the rope they threw into the water so Eric flung himself down and lifted me on board. I sat on the cockpit floor and Mike came to me. 'I let go of Cate's hand,' he said. 'It just went. It was pulled away.' The blackness came inside my head. But then Eric leant down and put a sodden bundle into my lap and Cate said, 'Oh Patsy, I'm glad they got you out.' The searchlight from the ship shone over the three of us together again, our arms all round each other as we huddled on the floor.

We were all there except Honest Tom. It was he who had gone ashore just as we left the sea anchor. 'It's an old dog for a hard road,' as the men said. Many of them had thigh boots on, the so-called anchor of men who fall overboard, some had heavy waterproof clothing. All except the children and myself had been able to swim but some admitted to only a dog paddle. When the boat went, Paul had taken Cate. 'Hang on tight, Cate,' he told her, and set off to do the dog paddle he'd not tried since one summer in Brighton, England, when he was eleven years old. Cate wrapped her arms round his head. Each time he tried to ask her to release him a little she said, 'I'm hanging on tight, aren't I Paul.' Paul said he didn't have the heart to ask her to let go after that. They were the last to be picked up because in the darkness Paul had gone on paddling round a point towards the open sea. Mike had merely put a bag of feathers under each arm and kicked off like a penguin. A seaman who was a good swimmer was guiding him towards the shore when they heard the boat coming and turned back to it.

We huddled round the stove in the galley and sipped boiling water when the quakes of shock began to attack. Two of the men dozed sitting on the bench – my word, you'll be pined by odder – and some took off their wet outer clothes. Paul stood in his underpants, an immaturely developed Pommy bastard, and Siddy with shoulders like a wrestler, and they both shook. The two children were less affected than any of us except that they were worried about Smokey, their dog. I didn't tell them of his having come to me in the water; when I told the mate he said this was typical of dogs in such mishaps – they try to climb on to anything to save themselves, even a head as I found out, and the mate knew too that they always swim for shore. 'He'd see the lights in the huts and swim to them.' And so he had. The Big Fellow and Mick got a lifeboat over and handled it through the surf to ensure that Honest Tom had made it safely ashore and when they returned they brought a wet and excited Smokey with them. 'Sitting up to a fire with Honest Tom he was.' And he went to sleep wrapped in a blanket on the end of the bunk where the childen were asleep in oven-warmed blankets.

Next day we began at daybreak boating out the islanders, using the fishing boat and our lifeboat, and before midday beautiful Babel was sinking down in the sea as we sailed through the Shoals and the Pot Boil heading for home. And weren't we heroes! Kings for a day. Gods. We'd got the birds off better and more quickly than ever before and as for the *Mutton-Duck* incident – we were walking wonders to be stared at. It unnerved us all to see these people who spend their lives in a slurry of boating accidents taking our deliverance as little short of a miracle.

'There were screams for help, screams that the *Duck* was sinking . . . then there was nothing for a long while until Patsy began to call her children.' And the children! was there ever such a pair? Not a squeak out of them. 'We said no man would get out of that sea alive yet even the children did.' Our clothes and boots were hanging on the rigging to dry and each article was felt for wet weight and gasped over. My goodness! And Pat! To think Babel had a go for her three times and she beat it every time!

I was to stay on the islands with Barbara, the wife of Honest Tom, while I got my land legs back, so next morning I stood on the Lady Barron wharf at dawn watching the ship leave, my luggage beside me, no more than I had brought with me, my shin bones gashed and scabbed, scars from old brushes with the coaming pieces; on my neck the salt water boils that wouldn't heal and my hands, ingrained with dirt that no detergent could leach out, wrinkled and old for ever from the work and grime of ship things. Behind me were hard years when I could have been studying and taking degrees and building a career. I had learnt nothing at sea that would be useful to me on shore. On the contary, these years would be a hindrance to my becoming an ordinary convention-bound woman again. To be accepted, and to prevent causing distrust and discomfort by having embraced a life outside the ken of those unable to understand either the life or the desire to lead such a life, I must speak of these years as having been just an amusing episode in my life. And it was not so hard to do. For I who had known bitter loneliness could now truly say with men like Nelson, 'Such a band of brothers'.

They were feeling their way out between the Dogs. Paul the Pom beside the Big Fellow at the wheel on Monkey Island where wet-nosed Alec used to take his position.

O leave'r Johnny, leave'r like a man

and Sid the Greek at Pete's position on deck.

An' it's time for us to leave'r.

They hooted the ship's siren as they slid behind Little Dog Island, a long plaintive farewell.

Leave'r like a man.

Then walk along the wharf, between the two lines of fishing boats tied up either side of the jetty, with the men turning away so they wouldn't have to greet me because I was not a man and my tears showed it and my hands were not free to search for a handkerchief and the fishing boat that was with us at Babel would be there and dark-skinned Eric would be winking and laughing goodbye to the kids and Jimmy Sholto Douglas with his lovely voice and wicked ways – I wish I'd said goodbye to you Jimmy before you sailed out into the strait in your own boat and were never seen again – and up past the crayfish caufs and the barrels of birds and scraps of cargo to the road and up the hard dirt track away from the smells that thrilled my senses, up to the grass and trees and houses and lounge suites and pianos and people the likes of which I hadn't known for six years.

Epilogue

There is little more to say. What can one say looking back on six of the best years? I was going through life at an enormous speed. My song was 'My candle burns at both ends/ it will not last the night/ But ah my foes, and oh my friends/ it gives a lovely light'. And the memory of those days and those bawdy, brave, bad, heroic men has stood me in good stead no matter how often the light has flickered and threatened to go out.

It used to be said: 'Send the lad out into the world and make a man of him.' Well, I thank those outcasts of the small ships and the six captains I sailed with for making a woman out of me; not the cakes-and-chiffon woman of my day (I had enough of that and have never returned to it) but a woman who is at ease with herself – and with men. On small ships it is the quick and the dead. If you were to survive you swiftly found the hidden being inside you, recognised your strengths and boldly presented your invincible persona to the world. I know many do this in other ways; all I say is that for me it took the little wooden ships to make a real woman out of me.

My marvellous mother backed me all along the way as she did all my life. 'If I was growing up in your generation I should live just as you do,' she told me. 'I'd shut my eyes and jump into life and see if I could swim to the top.'

She came on a trip on the *Naracoopa* and sewed on buttons and patched trousers and shirts and knitted no end of caps for the boys, all day sitting out in the sun on the hatch cover with the off-watch crew gathered round yarning with her. She and my Dad, the dear old sailor-bushman, helped me with the children by holidaying them on their farm, on the odd times my work schedule or the anticipated danger of a trip prevented their being with me. And together they prayed for the souls of my friends who died at sea.

I fell in love with a small-ship's captain but the sea took him. No, I never sailed on his ship nor he on mine. Through listening carefully on our radios on Small Ships' Schedule, we always had a fair idea where each other's ships were at any time and the ETA at any port. And if absolutely necessary, or urgent, we would manage to get the odd cryptic message across.

I recall once we were both to be in the port of Currie, King Island, and it did seem that we would be able to see one another for a few hours and, with the captain of my ship, walk up to the old hotel on the island and share a beer and a still-hot-cooked-fresh crayfish with our island friends. But on the evening radio schedule, when he called up VIM, Melbourne radio, he was humming a few bars of a song as he came on air; quickly he apologised for it, and gave the weather and barometric reading as we always did from our various stations at sea, but I couldn't fathom what I knew must be some message to me. When we tied up at King Island along the jetty from his ship, I was surprised to see his crew letting go his lines. He was sailing. 'But I got a message over to you,' he called. He had been singing 'Meet Me Tonight In Dreamland', and I'd read no message into it. 'Sweet dreamy dreamland/ There let my dreams come true.' So he said: 'Right-o. Shut up, give me a kiss and wave me goodbye.' And I would have said the same to him if the boot had been on the other foot and it had been us who had been ordered to sail early.

Life and death, laughter and tears, good and evil blurred at sea. Only the absolutes remained.

We were all rovers, the sea our only master, our only mistress.

There are no small, wooden, island traders left now. The *Naracoopa* blew up and disappeared off Port Lincoln in South Australia, and the pretty little *Sheerwater* hit a reef near the mouth of the Tamar River and was lost. The rare times – four, I think – that I have seen an old shipmate, their sense of place has impressed me. Once, on a Hobart street, walking with a friend, a passer-by brushed my hand as he went by. Pete. We had sailed together for four years. I didn't call out, I made no sign. Rolling stones have no past. In Melbourne one night at old Romano's restaurant, a waiter served my soup then, almost imperceptibly, fluttered his fingers like a fish's fins when swimming. I looked up into the face of Sid, the Greek, who had held my head above water when eleven of us faced drowning that dark night in bold water.

'I hope everything is satisfactory, Madam,' he said. (Did he almost say 'Mrs Pat'? I wondered.) 'Yes thank you. All is very well.' 'I'm so happy,' he said. We have our own ways, we people who have tasted bitter salt sea.

This year I met again with Captain Les Jackson, Wallaby, and his wife, and the talk of ships we had known sent a whole flotilla of cheeky, tough, admirable little tubs back into the outpost ports and across the wild waters of Bass Strait to the islands as we went 'westering home' once more.

I have been back to the islands often, but only once to Lady Barron jetty. I walked along to the end, where we used to tie up after our sometimes tumultuous voyages up the coast, and lay down on my abdomen and peered over. Here, on the timber facing the water, seen only by those on board ship, the small-ships' men had painted their names, one by one over the years. There were boys from the *Leederry, Leprena, Loatta, Willwatch, Jabiru, Prion, Margaret Twaits, Lady Jean, Sheerwater, Naracoopa*, and many others. And one day, when we sailed in with more water in us than under us, Frank Henwood had taken a paint brush and handed it to me as I came down from working the telegraph. 'Time you put your moniker along with the others,' he said. So I carefully painted, 'Mrs Pat.'

But now, there were no names. There was nothing. 'It's a new jetty Patsy.' Bill Riddle had followed me, knowing what I was seeking. 'It's all gone.' And it has. Except when that tune clutches my heart.